Every Day's a Saturday:

Road Trips, Recipes and an Empty Nest

Happy reading!

Shelley

Every Day's a Saturday:

Road Trips, Recipes and an Empty Nest

SHELLEY CAMPBELL BOGAERT

Friday Island Press, LLC
Friday Harbor, WA

EVERY DAY'S A SATURDAY:

Road Trips, Recipes and an Empty Nest

Shelley Campbell Bogaert

ISBN-13 978-0-9845938-0-4
ISBN-10 0-9845938-0-2

COVER ILLUSTRATION

Shelley Campbell Bogaert
Editorial Credit for Cover Van Image:
Anton Novik, Shutterstock

PERMISSIONS

Adair Inn Recipes: Provided courtesy of Judy Whitman

Lou's Cruller French Toast Recipe: Provided courtesy of Toby Fried, Lou's Restaurant

Jam Recipes: Provided courtesy of Kraft Foods

Brown Sugar Baked Salmon Recipe: Provided courtesy of Chicago Review Press

California Avocado Halibut Ceviche and George's at the Cove Black Bean Soup Recipes: Provided courtesy of George's at the Cove

King Crab Stack Recipe: Provided courtesy of Guy and Linda Colbert, the Oyster Bar on Chuckanut Drive

Wild Ginger Sichuan Green Beans, and Wild Ginger Seabass with Peanuts and Herbs Recipes: Provided courtesy of Rick Yoder, Wild Ginger

Grandma's Ocean Crest Clam Chowder Recipe: Provided courtesy of Jess Owen, Ocean Crest Resort

Chocolate Stout Cake Recipe: Provided courtesy of Gary Happ, Barrington Brewery and Restaurant

Published by Friday Island Press, LLC
Book designed by Nina Kannon
Printed in the United States of America

FIRST PRINTING

Dedication

For John and Kelly, without whom this book, or life as I know it, would not be possible.

Acknowledgements

I would sincerely like to thank Hensley Peterson,
for taking a first perusal at the book,
Alice B. Acheson, for her valuable literary insights,
and Gavin Caruthers, editor extraordinaire.

The Recipes

SEPTEMBER

September 2

I nestled into seat 6B on the flight from Denver across the country to Boston. Kelly sat next to me at the window, while my husband John reclined in first class (having been upgraded, he was remorseless about leaving us in coach, based on his recent revelation that he was far too old at age seventy to sit in the back of the "bus"). John and I were escorting Kelly to college. Even though we knew that someday this moment would arrive, we still didn't fully comprehend the reality that our only child, a close-to-perfect eighteen-year-old raised in the warm embrace of a small Colorado ski town, was now leaving home to attend college.

After years of talking about colleges, touring colleges, writing essays for colleges, getting the grades and test scores to get into college, the moment was close at hand. Sitting on the plane, I finally understood that it all came down to some simple, yet universal parental concerns:

Would my daughter survive playing beer pong in the basement of the Animal House fraternity?

Would she remember how to separate the whites from the colored clothes in the dorm laundry room or would all of her clothes turn a paler shade of the fabled Dartmouth green?

Would she be able to successfully navigate calculus with her painstakingly acquired study habits?

And would she email me every day so I could vicariously revel in the ultimate college experience?

We arrived in Boston on a sultry East Coast night and meandered through the narrow, cobblestoned streets of the city's North End looking for the Italian restaurant recommended by the hotel concierge. After finding it in a back alley, two hostesses cornered us at the entry, inviting us to peruse the menu's photographs of meals such as Spaghetti a la Bunker Hill and step inside. Not what we had in mind for real Boston Italian food on our first visit, so we walked to Hanover Street (an auspicious sign, since Dartmouth College, Kelly's home for the next four years, was nestled in the heart of Hanover, New Hampshire). The street was still congested with diners at nine o'clock at night, but a side street proffered a small trattoria with an outdoor patio and excellent food. We all agreed Kelly had made an excellent college selection having Boston so close to her new school.

September 3

The wind howled outside the windows of our hotel, which was perched on a pier overlooking the Back Bay, location of the infamous, revolutionary Tea Party. Rain flooded the adjacent park's sidewalks and flowed into the bay's frigid water, now colored the dull, wet gray of a porpoise.

We had left Aspen, Colorado with the crystalline sky uncluttered by a single cloud; the aspen trees had begun their golden shift to fall. After a brief honeymoon with the local weather during last night's dinner, we were now greeted by winter in full regalia. Kelly made me a list of additional clothing I would need to ship and she wondered aloud if maybe she shouldn't have gone to a California school after all.

"OK, Mom, I think I'm going to need my old down jacket... I know we just bought a new one, but this East Coast weather is way too cold...I can wear it over the new one for backup. And then you can send three more sets of long underwear and my extra wool ski hats."

"As long as I'm sending things, what about Ni-night (her fluffy yellow and white childhood blanket)?" I suggested. "You can wear it on top of your jackets for extra wind-resistance. Remember, layering is the key!"

She nodded in agreement, "...and I think I'll apply to graduate school at Stanford...NOW."

Absorbing some of Boston's considerable history was on our pre-college checklist, so we were determined to hike the Freedom Trail, downpour or not. The Freedom Trail wandered through sixteen historically significant sites, a red brick line that conducted travelers through Boston's narrow streets. Since eating great food was one of our family's favorite pastimes, we would need sustenance before our two-and-a-half mile walk. John, Kelly and I struggled over the cobblestones of the North End, as slick and perilous as the bumpy back of a submerged alligator, using our umbrellas alternatingly as walking sticks and rain shields. My umbrella almost obliterated what remained of an old woman's eyesight in the process, but we finally found Pizzeria Regina, a culinary institution in Boston since 1926.

Being exposed to history (of places, people, or cultures) can be exhilarating, but I would much rather eat at a restaurant that has been in operation for a hundred years than touch the granite of yet one more iconic monument. A dining establishment lives and breathes in a way that bricks and mortar can't—recipes, ingredients, techniques passed from one chef to another; wooden booths scratched with initials of lovers long dead; high heels pounding paths into marble floors on the way to a glorious meal. That is history.

Even though what we eat now may not be exactly what was eaten in the past, thanks to the invention of refrigeration and microwave ovens, food links the present to the past more tangibly than bricks ever can. With a brick, you are always wondering what was, with food, there is never a doubt.

We waited in the mist to be seated. Our vantage point from the bar stool seating allowed us to view the tiny kitchen. It was half the size of what I imagined Kelly's dorm room would be, yet it housed three chefs, the pizza oven, a small shelf lining the room upon which sat thirty or forty puffy discs of pizza dough, and a minuscule space for assembling pizza ingredients. The only items on the menu were pizza, beer, wine and soft drinks. The bartender poured cheap red wine into sixteen-ounce dime-store tumblers for John and me, and we listened to his tales of how Boston had changed since he was a boy, a mere twelve years ago.

The pizza arrived, its crust brushed with fresh tomato sauce, ricotta cheese sauce on top of that, then mozzarella cheese, and prosciutto. Impossibly, the pizzaiola men had managed to inject hot air into the soft, succulent dough; it was the best pizza I had ever eaten.

After an afternoon spent following the Freedom Trail to

the U.S.S. Constitution, Paul Revere's House and the Copp's Hill Burying Grounds, we were done with history—and the freezing horizontal rain. By now, Kelly must have realized that tomorrow she would be starting her Dartmouth Outing Club trip, a four-day hiking expedition for first year students into the White Mountains of New Hampshire, a bonding expedition designed to teach the many traditions of Dartmouth and ignite the lifelong love affair for the school that all Dartmouth alumni seemed to have.

Nervousness appeared. "Dad, I'm not nervous, I'm excited," Kelly announced at one point, prompting John to launch into one of his notorious parental lectures, designed to guide her on her journey in life.

The most memorable of these talks occurred the summer after Kelly's high school graduation, just before she and a girlfriend left for two weeks in Europe on their own. I had panicked because I had encouraged her to go and then I wasn't so sure it was such a brilliant idea, so John jumped in with some helpful advice. "All its life," he began, "the little bird had been protected. Its parents had fetched worms for it to eat, had kept it sheltered inside the nest so it wouldn't fall to the forest floor below, and had taught it to fly when the little bird was ready. After it could fly, the bird began exploring the forest, and its parents taught it to hop safely in the bushes to avoid predators. The flock kept the youngster safe as they traveled longer distances, expanding the little bird's horizons beyond the forest."

Kelly nodded, her strawberry blonde ponytail bobbing up and down, while John continued. "As the bird grew, its parents allowed it to fly to parts of the forest with its friends, but never too far away. Finally it was time for the parents to set the bird free on its own flight path of life." Kelly and I smiled at that one, but John seriously went on. "The little bird and her friend planned to journey across the large meadow at the edge of the forest. Its parents advised her one more time to pay attention to the dangers of the world, and always be aware of what was on the horizon. With that, the excited little bird flew into the meadow...and...*wham*! A hawk plummeted out of the sky and ate her!"

Kelly's huge blue eyes widened, "What kind of a story was that, Dad?"

"Just think about it, honey," was all he said.

Kelly couldn't get to sleep that night. I watched as she rotated in her bed like the hands of a clock ticking toward morning...back to side, side to front, front to side and back for an hour before I finally heard the low rumble of her snore. For a long while I sat beside her bed and watched her breathe, the same way I did as an inexperienced mother, at the end of a long day with my new infant.

September 4

John and I awoke early and Kelly woke late. Sometime during the night, her Excitement Button had toggled over to her Really Nervous Panic Button and even the mention of a flaky lobster tail sweet roll filled with whipped cream from Mike's Pastry in the North End had no impact on the speed with which she would move—it was slow or slower.

As we approached the campus after a two-hour drive to eastern New Hampshire, Kelly began to grin like a Cheshire cat. Her new dorm, McClaughlin Hall, was technically "finished," but there were still hordes of construction workers painting, hammering and hanging temporary blinds on the windows. Her room was a "two-room double, basic" but one hundred percent better than most of the dorm rooms we'd seen on our college tours.

Kelly dropped her duffel bags on the floor of her new home, each large enough to conceal a Sumo wrestler, and we walked across the Dartmouth Green to find some lunch. On one of our college excursions, the head of admissions encouraged prospective students to stand in the middle of whatever constituted the gathering space for the college, whether it was a quad, a commons or a parking lot.

"Stand for five minutes, look around you, watch what the students are doing...feel the sense of place in your gut," he said. "That's the best way to decide which school is right for you." At each of the twenty-six schools we visited, we performed this task religiously, but I think all three of us were completely sold on Dartmouth after a minute and a half.

Its grassy Green, the size of half-a-dozen football fields, is described in Scott Meacham's *Notes toward a Catalog of the Buildings and Landscapes of Dartmouth College*, as "the collective living room, crossroads, multipurpose space, center, heart, and focus of celebrations, demonstrations, and fairs, used any time when collective joy or frustration is to be expressed." Gravel paths bisect the grass from the corners and the sides. The Green was laid out in 1771 as the original town square of the village of Hanover. Back then it was mostly forested with pine trees soaring up to 270 feet high. It took sixty years before all of the stumps were cleared, assisted in large part by the requirement that each incoming class had to remove one stump.

The school is one of the most technologically advanced colleges in the nation, with wireless access everywhere on campus. Students are required to own a laptop so that even on the Green they can study or BlitzMail (the campus-wide email system) with ease.

The Hanover Inn, lodging of choice for Dartmouth parents, is positioned on the south side of the Green and its rooms look north from the Green's expanse towards the boxy white tower of the Baker Memorial Library. The Inn's location on East Wheelock Street marks the line between the campus and the town of Hanover, which flow seamlessly from one to the other. Students cross Wheelock Street for a cup of java at the Dirt Cowboy Cafe, while townspeople attend Pilobolus modern dance performances at The Hop, the campus's performing arts theater. The Inn also serves as a quasi-official meeting place for professors, alumni and students. The Student Activities Office offers students a voucher to *Take a Professor to Lunch* at the Hanover Inn, and in the hall of the side entrance to the Inn is a wooden panel where alumni place cards with their name and year of graduation to instantly reconnect with old friends when they return to campus.

Our destination was Lou's, Hanover's favorite breakfast and lunch joint, which is located just around the corner from the Hanover Inn. Almost everyone eating lunch was a troika consisting of two parents and a freshman; the new students, Kelly included, tried to eat while subtly checking out their potential roommates, studymates, and playmates. After a few stops to purchase last minute camping items (just more delaying tactics) we finally arrived at Robinson Hall, the official meeting place for the start of the Outing Club trip. About thirty Dartmouth students of both sexes sported bright green Mohawk hairdos, pink tutus, and skin-tight Red Cross uniforms (we later learned this was called "flair"). They danced and screamed as a bus bearing freshmen from the previous Outing Club trip returned. The fresh parents and students stood rooted to the ground watching the scene as the exhausted freshmen disembarked; the parents wondering if the Ivy League was actually some form of very expensive cult and maybe this was the initiation ceremony, and the students not believing their good fortune in getting accepted to a school that encouraged cross-dressing and spontaneous outbursts of ribald singing.

Kelly stood in line to sign in for the trip and chatted with another freshman girl, my daughter's usual shyness overcome by the excitement of the day. Within moments the two girls were herded into an assembly line of new recruits learning the college's official dance, *the Salty Dog Rag*. John and I slowly walked away from the crazy scene—I walked backwards while taking documentary photos. I realized that this wasn't the Last Goodbye, even as one lone tear escaped down my cheek. Kelly was so excited she didn't notice our departure, and it was difficult for me to be sad. Without a doubt, I knew I could hold back the torrent. I was strong.

On the road again. John and I drove east out of Hanover, and back into the lives we had led before our intrepid freshman entered our world as a tiny, screaming infant. We had made reservations at a number of classic New England inns to keep us busy while Kelly was hiking. Our first stop was The Manor on Golden Pond.

An extraordinary feeling of lightness enveloped me at dinner. John and I laughed and giggled like teenagers over the four-course meal, accompanied by four courses of wine. I had successfully performed my job as a mother guiding my daughter through the basics of life. She could take over from here! I was free! Free at last!

At four in the morning, I hurled off the duvet and bolted upright, stark naked (I never wore pajamas to bed) and emotionally naked as well. Had she remembered to take her Xyrtec, Xantac, and EpiPen? What would happen if she had a reaction in the woods without them? She carried the medications for a mysterious allergy she acquired in her junior year of high school. It caused a rapid allergic reaction known as anaphylactic shock at inopportune moments. I assured myself that she was now an adult, of course she had remembered, and after thrashing about thinking of other grim scenarios (falling off concealed cliffs, escaping from furious forest fires, eating poisonous New Hampshire ground pineapples) a sane thought escaped from my weary brain. It was the sobering recognition that even though Kelly may have graduated from her mother's basic training, I might have a way to go before I gave up my position as leader of the pack.

I fell asleep at six a.m.

John bounded out of bed, refreshed and ready to go at six-thirty a.m.

Hell.

September 5

After breakfast, John and I walked hand-in-hand down the hill to Squam Lake, known to millions of moviegoers as *Golden Pond*, and attempted to romantically paddle a canoe around the lake. I volunteered to steer, although unfortunately I could only do it to the right, but the water was peaceful, calm, and thank God we weren't eighty-five years old and trying this. In all probability, Henry Fonda and Katharine Hepburn had more practice prior to filming than we did.

Having survived our outing, we drove north through countryside that was everything *Travel and Leisure* magazine celebrated in its advertising for leaf-peeping trips to New England in the fall. Two lane roads snaked between the compact rolling hills and periodically opened onto fertile emerald meadows decorated with what resembled elongated blobs of Ben and Jerry's Oreo Cookie ice cream. As John slowed the car I recognized them as Holstein cows. John, being a former ranch owner and cow lover, informed me that the Holstein is the world's highest production dairy animal. Obviously Ben and Jerry had located their production facilities in Vermont to take advantage of this fact.

The pristine white steeple of a country church announced an approaching town, its spire an exclamation point in the surrounding foliage, now quietly transforming from green to red. After passing gold and white ornately painted signs at the side of the road, tastefully welcoming us to "_____ville," we drove through blocks of unsightly commercial buildings, and then finally into the heart of a picturesque New England village.

One of our favorite communities (perhaps because it was food-related) was the stretch of towns named after John Montague, the fourth Earl of Sandwich. Due to a wicked gambling habit, he refused to leave the game table to eat, instead directing his valet to bring his supper of beef nestled between two slices of toasted bread. Sandwich, Central Sandwich, and North Sandwich were squashed between the Lakes Region and the White Mountains, New Hampshire's two major tourist areas; their perfectly square wood-sided buildings were painted white, with shutters and fascia trimmed in black, giving the impression that John Montague had flung a colossal handful of dice across the countryside.

Our accommodation for the next few nights was the Adair Inn in Bethlehem, New Hampshire. We turned off the highway and drove up the long entrance, maple trees arched overhead framing the stately home ahead. I was overcome.

"John," I exclaimed, "doesn't this completely remind you of the country homes we've stayed at in England?"

"Does 'New' England ring a bell?" he deadpanned.

The front door of the Inn was open, but there was no sign of either an English or New English bellman, so we cautiously stepped inside.

Under my breath I asked, "John, what if this is actually someone's house...where do these East Coast people stand on gun control?"

The gracious innkeeper emerged from his office to greet us. The interior of the inn seemed spare compared to the Manor at Golden Pond, which had been elaborately detailed with dark oak paneling, but after we had been at Adair a few days, its austere white walls and simple furnishings grew on us as did the engaging personalities of the innkeeper and his wife.

And then there was the food.

Our first morning's breakfast began with a bowl of fresh melon and berries, followed by popovers the size of grapefruits on steroids, and then fluffy pancakes. Day Two brought another fruit cup, more popovers and Eggs Dijonnaise, hard-boiled eggs in a mustard sauce ladled over spinach. On Day Three (although we were barely able to walk at this point we still arrived early for breakfast) we ate more fruit, more popovers and then a dish that layered sliced ham over freshly baked focaccia bread and was glazed with melted Vermont cheddar cheese.

I knew if we stayed more than three days, we would become very large-scale people.

Adair Inn Popovers

Yield: 6 large popovers

6 LARGE EGGS
6 TABLESPOONS BUTTER, MELTED
PINCH OF SALT
2 CUPS MILK (ANY KIND BUT SKIM MILK)
2 CUPS ALL-PURPOSE FLOUR

Beat the eggs in a medium bowl with a wire whisk. Add the butter and salt, and then whisk in the milk. Stir in the flour, leaving small lumps. Do not over beat. Cover the batter with plastic wrap and refrigerate overnight.

Place the oven rack on the lowest level and preheat the oven to 400 degrees F. Spray six ¾ cup ovenproof glass cups with cooking spray. Remove the batter from the refrigerator and stir until the batter is relatively smooth but still has some lumps. Ladle the batter into the cups, filling them three-quarters full. Place the cups on a baking sheet, allowing some space between them, and place the baking sheet on the lowest oven rack. Bake the popovers for about 50 minutes, until puffed and brown. To prevent the popovers from collapsing, avoid opening the oven door during the first 40 minutes of baking. Serve immediately!

Adair Inn Lemon Chiffon Pancakes

Yield: 6 servings

6 EGGS, SEPARATED
2 CUPS COTTAGE CHEESE
1 CUP FLOUR
¼ CUP FRESH LEMON JUICE
¼ CUP VEGETABLE OIL
2 TABLESPOONS MAPLE SYRUP
4 TEASPOONS BAKING POWDER
2 TEASPOONS LEMON ZEST
PLUS ADDITIONAL ZEST FOR GARNISH
½ TEASPOON LEMON EXTRACT
¼ TEASPOON SALT
CONFECTIONER'S SUGAR
SLICED STRAWBERRIES

In a mixer, beat the egg whites with the whisk attachment until firm peaks form. Set aside and refrigerate the egg whites until just before you are going to cook the pancakes.

Place the egg yolks, cottage cheese, flour, lemon juice, oil, maple syrup, baking powder, lemon zest, lemon extract and salt in a food processor. Process until the batter is smooth and fluffy. Pour the batter into a bowl and chill until ready to use.

When you are ready to cook the pancakes, heat a griddle for 5 minutes until hot. Spray with cooking spray or oil lightly. Gently fold the egg whites into the batter. With a ¼-cup measure, dollop the batter onto the griddle. Flip the pancakes when their edges are firm; these pancakes take a while to cook! As soon as they are browned and cooked through, garnish with confectioner's sugar and additional lemon zest. Serve with sliced strawberries.

We waddled to the rental car. Our plan was to drive a circular loop through the White Mountains, stopping first at the historic Mount Washington Hotel in Bretton Woods. Built in 1902, the hotel was an ornate example of Renaissance Revival architecture, holding court like a massive, reclining Spanish queen over the surrounding mountain peaks. The Bretton Woods International Monetary Conference, which established the World Bank, the International Monetary fund, and designated the gold standard at $35 an ounce, was hosted at the hotel in 1944. Saving both money and our waistlines, instead of eating lunch, we opted for an hour-long hike to the Upper Falls on the hotel's property, which according to my calculations worked off exactly one popover.

Driving south on the Crawford Notch Road through Notchland, we turned off the highway at Bartlett and drove farther south on Bear Notch Road. I had never heard of a notch, so John explained that it was a saddle point between two areas of higher elevation, usually a gap between two mountains.

"Why don't they just call it a pass like everyone else?" I would obviously have to read up on New England geography in the next four years.

We turned west onto the Kancamagus Highway, enjoying more erupting foliage through the misty windshield, and worked off half a popover on a drizzly hike to Sabbaday Falls. From what appeared to be an ethereal green punchbowl at the top of the falls three tiers of water plunged through a glacial gorge to land at the bottom into a peaceful pool.

Like horses dashing back to the barn, by the end of the day we were ready for the comforts of the inn, but we were sidetracked by a sign on the northbound highway announcing another famous notch. John couldn't resist and maneuvered the car into the Franconia Notch parking lot. We ran to the ticket booth, hoping to buy tickets for a walk through the Flume Gorge, but were met with a closed ticket booth and a sign asking us to return tomorrow. I had read in my AAA guide that Franconia Notch State Park was also the site of the Old Man of the Mountain, a natural rock formation rising

1200 feet above Profile Lake, its granite ledges forming an elderly man's profile. The photo in the guidebook bore an uncanny resemblance to Ronald Reagan. The Old Man was the New Hampshire State Symbol and had been imprinted on the New Hampshire quarter.

We walked to the viewing site in the park, studied the mountainside for the Old Man and saw nothing but a single protruding ledge. I finally read the guide's fine print and we learned that three years after the quarter had been minted, in 2003, the Old Man had collapsed onto the terrain below, leaving only his bouffant hairdo behind.

When I wasn't analyzing how many more popover calories I had to burn, I had spent most of the day subconsciously worrying about how Kelly and her fellow freshmen were faring in the day's nonstop drenching rain. There was still no word from her, even after I placed a stealthy phone call so John wouldn't chastise me for being a Helicopter Parent.

The scourge of college administrators, Helicopter Parents are identified by their pathological need to manage all aspects of their children's lives, frequently resorting to selecting their children's roommates, calling professors to change grades, and using that essential Helicopter Parent tool, the cell phone, to wake Junior up for class every morning. Hovering at close range and always being within reach are critical components of H.P. Behavior.

"Did you take your medications? Did you take your Epipen? Are you alive?" At this point, I was fairly certain that if she had already survived two nights in the wild, she would probably live. I slept well.

September 8

We bid adieux to the Adair Inn, a copy of their eponymous cookbook in my backpack, and drove northeast toward Stowe, Vermont, a step closer to Kelly and her return from the Outing. I prayed that the *Salty Dog Rag* would work its wonders on yet another Dartmouth freshman, convinced that her adventure would be a harbinger of her college years... please, please, please, let it be good!

Kelly was ebullient when she called to tell us her bus had returned to Hanover, and when I asked how the experience had been she screamed, "Excellent!"

We retrieved her at Robinson Hall, besieged by more flair-attired screaming students, and she spent the next two hours on the drive to Boston talking about the kids on her trip (the trippees), the trip leaders, the Hanover Croo, the lodge Croo, the *Salty-Dog Rag*, the Ice-Ice Baby dance, playing "contact" on the trail, hiking twenty-four miles, the Moosilauke Lodge, slipping and sliding using camping tarps, and playing Twister on a 20 x 20 foot game board. She emphatically pronounced that she couldn't wait to get back to school, and that Dartmouth was the perfect college.

"Mom, I'm so happy!" she said, a major statement for a child not given to overt displays of emotion and who kept her feelings in check until she had full understanding of a situation.

How can a mother be sad that her child is leaving home *(and is she really leaving or just taking a momentary breather from her parents?)* when she is precisely where she is supposed to be at precisely the right time? Is she starting a new journey, or am I?

September 9

Kelly was due back at Dartmouth in three days for Orientation Week and the official start of classes, so we returned to Boston to shop for dorm room essentials. Leaving John to explore more history, Kelly and I went to Best Buy to purchase a printer, ink, copy paper, and bags of cables to connect technological devices. Next up was the Container Store, where we bought containers of every kind—containers to store things in, hang things from, attach things to, and divide things from other things.

Midway through our power shopping expedition, Kelly and I stumbled upon a Legal Sea Foods Restaurant, a Boston institution known for their clam chowder. The menu upheld the convention requiring the words "Famous" or "World Famous" to preface the words "clam chowder" wherever those words appeared on any restaurant's menu…anywhere in the world. Being a clam chowder lover, I've always wondered who bestowed such congratulatory adjectives so consistently. The clam chowder was very good, not too many potatoes, lots of bacon, a hint of thyme, and not too thick.

Our final destination was the Bed, Bath, and Beyond store near Fenway Park, where every incoming student from the hundreds of colleges in the area was buying dorm room necessities. The boys were especially entertaining. They usually shopped by themselves, and instead of using a gigantic rolling cart like their female counterparts, they stashed their essentials in overflowing hand-carried baskets, with an 8 x 10 foot area rug rolled beneath one arm and a blender stuffed with margarita mix squeezed under the other. Coeds, on the other hand, accompanied by overanxious parents, filled huge carts with pink towels, matching pink sheet sets, pink laundry baskets, and pink plastic carryalls full of grooming aides ready for the inaugural walk to the shower room, past the boys' rooms, their blenders already whirring.

After stashing Kelly's pink acquisitions in the back of the car, we crossed the Charles River to meet John at a Boston Red Sox game at Fenway Park. Boston has the greatest baseball fans in the world; they sang every song the organist played, shared the batting averages of every player we asked about, and served the "World's Best" stadium hot dogs (I am the taste arbiter on that one), spicy kosher wieners on the squishy white buns usually reserved for lobster rolls. Unfortunately the fans' fervor wasn't enough to help the team defeat the bottom-of-the-league Kansas City Royals, even after twelve innings.

September 10

Prior to leaving Boston, Kelly and I unloaded the car, tore off every piece of extraneous packaging, and repacked the car to conceal the quantity of dorm room contraband we had acquired. Even though John is very understanding, men don't always grasp the utter necessity for coordinated under-bed storage units and matching laundry hampers.

I had recently read an article in *USA Today* on the best places in the United States to eat lobster. One of their recommendations, Brown's Seabrook Lobster Pound in Seabrook Beach, New Hampshire, was conveniently situated on our way to Kennebunkport, Maine and our arrival was perfectly timed for lunch. We ordered fried clams, scallops and shrimp at an outside window, then walked inside to decide how much lobster we each could consume. The order-taker scooped an eleven-pound crustacean with claws the size of a ham-fisted linebacker out of the tank for us to photograph while we pondered. We each opted for a petite 1½-pound model. We ate at rickety wooden picnic tables on the sunny deck, devouring the lobster's sweet flesh, its glaze of warm butter dripping from our chins through the deck's cracks into the saltwater marsh below.

Kennebunk is a town of 10,000 people, all living in immaculate white clapboard houses; blue, green, red, or black shutters winked at the mandatory pumpkins on their front porches, jolly orange advance men for fall's return.

Just beyond Kennebunk was its waterfront sidekick, Kennebunkport, where we checked into The Yachtsman's Lodge, a renovated ranch-style hotel, with a small marina in front. As we were waiting on the porch for our room to be readied, Kelly hissed to me, "Mom, I think that's the President!"

I looked up and recognized George Bush the First walking up the dock's ramp, surrounded by men in black. He waved, mouthed a quick hello, and made a hasty departure in his waiting convoy of black Suburbans. My thrill that she had grown up enough to recognize the former President was tempered by a disturbing thought. Up until this point, I had been excited for Kelly's journey into adulthood. I had trepidations, as I'm sure all parents do, about her ability to transition to a world where we wouldn't be there to guide her on a daily basis. So why was I suddenly feeling jealous, left-behind, as if I were missing out?

Maybe because ever since Kelly was born, we'd been at her side...taking her to the emergency room when she stuck a piece of gravel up her nose when she was two…quietly sobbing at the kindergarten door on her first day of school… picking her up from the bus stop every afternoon when we lived in Switzerland for a year...praying that when I said "How was your day today, sweetie?" she would say "great!" instead of just mumbling "OK,"…trying to alleviate her fears and ours as she struggled with a thirty-five pound backpack attached to her miniature frame for the eighth-grade field trip to scale three mountain passes…sending her, at age sixteen, to Ecuador to learn Spanish for a month…and then watching her leave the following summer for Thailand and Cambodia for six weeks, to hike between remote hill villages and live in a Buddhist monastery…and then on top of all that, enjoying and enduring the whole college application process…visiting twenty-six colleges, organizing SAT tutoring, applying to schools, waiting-waiting-waiting.... And now she has the nerve to go off to college without me???!!!

I'm not sure I really get this process. Maybe if I had six kids and this was the last one and I was sending him off to the Army just to get him out of the house, then I might understand.

As usual, food helped. We ate dinner at Striper's Waterside Restaurant, owned by The Yachtsman's Lodge. Assuming we would be dining at an upscale version of Brown's Lobster Shack, we were pleasantly surprised to be ushered into a serene blue room with plush upholstered chairs, white bead-board wainscoting, and a matching elegantly attired hostess. It looked as if *Food + Wine* magazine would be arriving at any moment for a photo shoot. The cuisine upstaged the décor; heirloom tomatoes picked that morning were layered with thick, creamy mozzarella cheese, and topped with an ice-cold tomato granita, all served in a deep round bowl splattered with basil oil and a balsamic vinegar reduction, with a presentation inspired by Jackson Pollack. And that was just the first course.

Tomato Granita

Yeild: 6 to 8 (light first course) servings

1 POUND BEEFSTEAK TOMATOES,
CUT INTO TWO-INCH WEDGES
½ CUP CREAM SHERRY
1 TEASPOON SUGAR
1 TABLESPOON PLUS 1 TO 2 TEASPOONS
SHERRY VINEGAR, DIVIDED
1 TO 4 TEASPOONS SALT AND PEPPER TO TASTE
2 CELERY RIBS
½ SEEDLESS CUCUMBER
2 LARGE RADISHES
½ TEASPOON EXTRA-VIRGIN OLIVE OIL

Blend tomatoes, sherry, sugar, 1 tablespoon sherry vinegar, and 1 to 4 teaspoons each of salt and pepper in a blender until smooth.

Strain and press through a fine-mesh sieve into a bowl. Discard solids.

Pour tomato mixture into an 8"x 8" or 9"x 9" nonreactive baking dish and freeze until partially frozen, about 1 hour.

Scrape and stir with a fork, crushing any lumps. Continue to freeze, scraping once or twice, until evenly frozen, about two hours more.

Cut celery, cucumber, and radishes into fine julienne strips, then toss in a bowl with oil. Add remaining 1 to 2 teaspoons sherry vinegar and salt and pepper to taste.

Serve granita with vegetable julienne.

Cooks' note: Granita can be made three days ahead and kept frozen. Cover with plastic wrap once frozen.

September 11

A day written in infamy, and yet the three of us were merrily off to Dartmouth at long last—at least in Kelly's mind. Every stop we made (Target to look for lamps, Bed, Bath and Beyond for more lamps, lunch at a roadside brew pub) were all roadblocks on the highway to her new life. We arrived late in the day and stopped at the dorm to unload both Kelly and the entire back end of the rental car, navigating around the workmen who were still painting and attaching maple baseboards. Soon after Kelly met up with friends from her Outing Club trip, went to a pizza party in a "schmob" (Dartmouth lingo for a large group of students), and then to a concert.

John and I, on the other hand, checked into a king-size room at the Hanover Inn, a suite that over the next four years should probably have had our name inscribed on its door. Tomorrow was the official Move-in Day for the class of 2010, and looking out our window over the Green, from every direction walked the Move-In Threesome of two parents and accommodating child, the latter ready to get on with his or her life, knowing that enduring another day of Mom and Dad was all that stood between them and freedom. (Except, of course, for those unfortunate few who were accompanied by the egregious Helicopter Parents.) Every member of these mobile family units wore a piece of Dartmouth green attire, so the overall effect was that of a giant, swirling tide of seaweed coursing across the gravel paths, out onto the streets, and into the crisp, white New England buildings.

September 12

I didn't want to miss one second of Family Orientation Day, so John and I woke at dawn to meet Kelly for breakfast at Lou's (their decadently evil Cruller French Toast was the special of the morning). Kelly had slept on the plastic-covered mattress of her dorm room, not quite ready to begin the unpacking and move-in process. Meanwhile the boys down the hall had already repainted their rooms, hung posters, laid down area rugs, and were on their fourteenth blender of margaritas.

Lou's Cruller French Toast

Yield: 4 servings

1 CUP HALF AND HALF OR MILK
4 EGGS
⅓ CUP ORANGE JUICE
1 TEASPOON SUGAR
1 TEASPOON VANILLA
1 TEASPOON GRATED ORANGE PEEL
¼ TEASPOON GROUND CINNAMON
⅛ TEASPOON GROUND NUTMEG
4 DAY-OLD CRULLERS, HALVED LENGTHWISE
2 TABLESPOONS (¼ STICK) UNSALTED BUTTER
POWDERED SUGAR
MAPLE SYRUP

Whisk first 8 ingredients in medium bowl. Add crullers to egg batter and turn until thoroughly coated.

Melt butter in heavy large skillet over medium-high heat. Add crullers and cook until golden brown on both sides, about 3 minutes per side. Sprinkle powdered sugar over.

Serve with maple syrup.

While Kelly registered for clubs, social activities, and sports teams, we attended lectures and information sessions designed to entertain (read: "occupy") parents and extricate them from their children's dorm rooms while their offspring were unpacking and forging exciting new relationships. The info sessions also helped parents forget the impending GOODBYE moment that for some would be that evening and others, like us, the following morning before the first Class of 2010 meeting.

John reminded me that Kelly wasn't leaving for good, "It's only eight weeks until we see her in San Diego for Thanksgiving…and remember, she was in Thailand and Cambodia for six weeks, and that wasn't such a big deal."

"John, I think you're missing the point. This is the BIG LAUNCH, the part where we push her out of the nest; it's the ultimate test of parenting. Even if we don't like it, we have to embrace it…feather by feather!"

At the end of the day, while John contentedly napped, I helped Kelly with some final organizing in her room. Up until this point, I had resisted my interior designer's tendencies to arrange her room, based on advice found in the Parent's Guides To Parenting Your College-Age Child books given to me by Kelly, as well as the advice of Harry, the father of Kelly's friend Lauren. Harry told me that at George Washington University, where Lauren was matriculating, it was said there were two kinds of parents: those who assist their children with making their beds and then leave, and those who commandeer the move-in and take over all activities up to and including organizing their children's underwear drawers.

"Shelley, we're supposed to be the first kind of parent," Harry said to me, and we forged a pact to see who could best accomplish this feat. I decided Harry wouldn't judge me too harshly, since Kelly had specifically asked me to help, her room was a mess, and she was arranging her own underwear. We organized her room in less than an hour and met John for The Last Supper at the Canoe Club restaurant. In the previous three weeks, John and I had bombarded Kelly with every scrap of parental advice we jointly possessed, so instead of agonizing over more What if's, Don't forget to's and Remember don't's, the three of *us* spent the evening joking about how the *other* threesomes in the restaurant were faring with *their* launches. I was very calm about the whole process and was fully confident that tomorrow morning after we had eaten our breakfast at Lou's, I would be dry-eyed, stoic and cheerily sending Kelly off on her new flight path.

September 13

Despite my promise to Kelly that I would be STRONG, midway through breakfast I felt as if I had been smacked on the head with a week-old baguette. THIS...WAS...IT. Moisture spewed from every orifice on my face. My body was as hot as a Buffalo chicken wing, while my lungs struggled to suck in air. While John paid the bill, after another therapeutic round of Lou's Cruller French Toast, I could see by the look on Kelly's face that my emotions, instead of being closeted discretely somewhere, had escaped from my body and were painfully exposed for all to witness. She kissed John, scurried me out of Lou's, gave me a long, crushing hug, and vanished, not allowing me to walk her to the corner and embarrass her in front of every other parent who had managed to keep it all together, at least until they reached the obscurity of their Hanover Inn room.

I ran up the back stairwell to our room four steps at a time, the sight of the board with the alumni names causing me to weep more furiously, and then I completely gave in to despair.

Sob

WRENCHING SOB

SOB, sob....

When John returned to the room, he took a quick look at my face, which now resembled an aged pomegranate, hugged me fiercely and decided he couldn't stand the thought of me erupting like Mount St. Helens for the next two and a half hours on the way to the Boston airport. He informed me we were going to take a quick walk through the campus.

From every direction came schmobs of students, five here, ten there, some accompanied by their undergraduate advisors, and all on their way to their first class meeting. Another Dartmouth tradition is the referral to classes by the year they graduate. Instead of freshmen, sophomore, junior or senior, Kelly would forever be a '10.

I eventually calmed down, and after a coffee fix (my usual grande decaf nonfat wet cappuccino) we headed off to Boston. I furtively left a message on Kelly's cell phone while John was at the Hertz car rental counter, just to let her know that everything was fine and I thought I would live.

SOB in the airplane restroom at 36,000 thousand feet.

WRACKING SOB in the Denver airport Red Carpet Club restroom at 5,280 feet.

On the way to our connecting flight from Denver to Aspen, I managed an appearance of calm even after meeting a friend from Aspen on her way to take her son to college in Washington State. She was relaxed and happy. *She couldn't possibly be aware of what was about to happen.*

Even after a four-hour layover at Denver International, a delayed plane and, when we finally arrived, a dead car battery, I didn't shed another tear. *I must be cured, hallelujah!* I went to bed exhausted but relieved that my illogical, irrational, roller-coaster emotions were now under control.

September 14

When I woke up, the snow-dusted mountain peaks across the valley wore a rosy pink veil and fall was imprinted on the hills, where brilliant yellow aspen trees vied with the rusty red oak brush for bragging rights. A new day had indeed dawned...and then I rolled over in bed, saw John's tear-stained face, and immediately burst into tears.

"Honey," he said, "I was wrong. I thought that Kelly going away to college was going to be like another summer trip. She'd be gone for eight or ten weeks, come home, and everything would be just the same. Only it won't be...this is it, major milestone time. She's really gone!"

I couldn't utter a response that didn't sound like a whale breaching. I crawled to the shower trying to make myself presentable before my dermatologist's appointment in an hour. Then it struck me. My solution-driven brain provided an out. I would allow myself to cry as much as I wanted in the shower, no fuss, no muss, and no witnesses to my misery. Walls of water would wash over me, my tears would blend with the hot water flowing from the showerhead and no one would ever know. Even if it meant taking twelve showers a day, I would be clean and cleansed at the same time. My eyes may look like shriveled craisins surrounded by puffy, white, unbaked cookie dough, but I would be in control.

This new method of coping seemed to be working well. The dermatologist didn't even ask why I looked like hell as he examined every old age spot and pre-cancerous lesion on my body. I was surviving.

On the way home I stopped at Jayne and Fred's house. They were the parents of Lacy, Kelly's closest friend, who had just left to attend the University of Colorado at Boulder. Kelso, our yellow Labrador retriever, had been bunking with them while we were gone.

Not one teardrop had fallen from my eyes in two hours; I just knew I was over the hump. I walked up the brick walkway, saw Jayne's infectious grin, gave her a huge hug, and cried as I had never cried before.

"Shelley," Jayne said, "look, I have a bottle of champagne for us to celebrate the girls' successful college launches!" *Could I really take any more of this?* Between my tearful outbursts, we polished off the bottle, accompanied by some Entenmann's sweet rolls. It was 10:00 a.m. and suddenly the world was looking a little brighter.

Kelly called twice that afternoon, the first time to see how we were doing. "Great," I lied. It was when she called again, to ask for her Uncle Jeff's telephone number for some computer help, that I realized that although she might not be sleeping in her room, under our roof, she was still here on the face of the planet. I could call her, I would see her again, and she was still my daughter, asking for my advice and needing me.

Relieved, I started cooking...roast chicken, barbecued sweet fresh white corn, asparagus marinated in balsamic and quickly grilled, and cheesy buttermilk biscuits. Why does everything feel the same and yet apocalyptically different?

> 11:17 p.m. sounds like you had a tough trip back. oh, i got my mac computer working, still not sure how most of it works, but it's tres cool, i love it. i have met some really nice people randomly, like at dinner last night, there was a huge line and i was talking to the people behind me, and we ended up hanging out all night. it was fun. i took the math placement test, i didn't take Spanish or French placement because they put me in the third level which isn't bad. i didn't take physics because the intro-courses sound like they cover a lot i didn't know. i also got a credit for biology and english! life is good.
>
> you should try not using capital letters in your emails. it's way easier!! i miss you, and love you mucho, more than all the green sweatshirts at dartmouth!!
>
> Kelly

September 15

I fully expected to continue my new shower-sobbing regime when I woke up. Instead, when I opened my eyes to a drizzly, grey day—and felt great—I was stunned. *When would it start?* No moisture flowed as I wandered to the shower. *Was my mental health restored?*

I chatted with three good friends throughout the morning, and all generously offered me their hard-earned pearls of wisdom:

Pearl #1: Close the door to your child's room when you leave for the LAUNCH and don't enter…for at least a month.

Pearl #2: Don't redecorate your child's room…until they graduate from college.

Pearl #3: Let your child call you…they have very erratic schedules, so email if you feel you have to make contact.

Pearl #4: Send a care package at least once a month… include food.

Pearl #5: If your child asks for your advice about an earth-shattering problem, respond, "Well, what do you think *you* should do about this?" Don't give them an answer; they must learn to figure things out on their own.

My eyes and nose were still dry by late afternoon when we departed for dinner at Sandy and Peter's house. They are also the parents of an only child, whose departure for an East coast college ten years ago had left them wallowing in the same mucky pond in which we now found ourselves. Sandy must have sensed that John and I needed help with our adjustment to empty nesterhood, and with a delicious meal of spicy chicken paprika, she rescued us from a silent dinner in front of the widescreen TV.

Kelly called after dinner and regaled us with stories of her orientation adventures. She was attending breakfasts, dinners, department open houses, all while making numerous social contacts. Kelly's life was good, so how could I cry?

And since yesterday, I hadn't. Too soon to tell for sure, but I think I might make it.

September 16

No tears, and no call from Kelly. In a moment of inspiration, I recalled that Pearl of Wisdom #3 allowed email contact.

> 3:30 p.m. hi angel! hope all is well in merry old Hanover! just a couple of questions for you (in true motherly style):
>
> 1. have you been able to make an appointment with the student health center about your allergic reaction situation? when you go, ask them about that new cervical cancer vaccine.
>
> 2. and remember - everything in MODERATION! sorry about the caps but I felt they were necessary in this instance. love you mucho too - more than all the people who have ever graduated from Dartmouth! love and kisses!!! your mom

September 18

Kelly called. "Hi Mom, how are you doing?"

"Great sweetie! How's Dartmouth?" I still got excited just saying Dartmouth.

"Super. I have to go to a lecture tonight called 'Consensual Sex is Hot'. It's required."

"What?"

"I've also got a bit of a cold."

"Well, honey," I was trying to be a supportive non-Helicopter Parent and allow her to feel her own way on the college scene, "Are you getting enough sleep?"

"Uhhhh...I haven't been to bed before 2 a.m. since I got here. But I have been able to sleep late every morning," she said.

I asked what had been happening until two in the morning.

"Oh, I hung out with friends from my floor, and then met up with some friends from my Outing Club trip, and then I ran into some other people from my dorm cluster."

Innocently, I queried how she met people. "Do you run into them walking across the Green, or in the dorm, maybe in town?"

A very long pause.

"O-H-H-H-H, " I said, "…at the fraternity houses?"

No answer.

"Well, how are they? Do you have a favorite? Are they well decorated?"

"They're pretty much alike," she said, and I read between the lines that they all had basements, frat boys, beer and ping pong tables. I wasn't quite ready for the next conversation, but I think she knew where Animal House was.

September 19

A few months ago, anticipating our new reality, John and I had considered taking a road trip as soon as Kelly left for college. Now that Kelly's room was as orderly as a sterile hospital suite (which was a sure sign of her absence) we thought a road trip might be just the cure for Walking by the Empty Room and Breaking into Tears Syndrome.

John and I dated for two years before we got married, informally meeting as we flirted in the security line at the San Diego airport, and formally meeting at the baggage claim carousel when we arrived in Salt Lake City, a meeting necessitated by my obligation to thank him for the glass of wine he had sent me on the plane via an obliging stewardess. He owned a real estate development company, and I was the head of design and business development for a large commercial interior design firm, so we knew immediately we had a lot in common.

Before Kelly's arrival, we took "280" trips. John owned two Mercedes Benz 280 convertibles; a 1969 model nicknamed Peaches, due to her warm, fleshy body color, and a 1968 version called Cloud, a cool white road goddess. I never understood why he needed two, but being an eligible bachelor, I assumed it had something to do with the Ferris wheel of femininity.

The concept behind a 280 trip was that there were no destinations, no timetables, and no reservations. With small suitcases stashed into Peaches' trunk, and a well-stocked wicker picnic basket squeezed into the cramped space behind the two sheepskin-covered seats, we drove where the roads weren't crowded, where the weather was good, and no one could reach us.

We would drive for two or three or eight hours on the uncrowded roads of California, Oregon, and Washington, pull into a picturesque bed and breakfast, eat a remarkable four-course gourmet dinner, sleep under fluffy duvets, and be on our way the next morning. Once we drove a paltry forty miles, found an interesting place to stay and called it a day at eleven in the morning.

After Kelly was born, the vehicle of choice was a 1987 burgundy Volkswagen Westfalia, alias the Big Baby Carriage. Not nearly as romantic riding in Peaches with the wind blowing in our hair, but certainly easier for breast-feeding.

This trip was going to be a modified 280. My white Land Rover SUV would transport Kelso, his cumbersome plastic dog crate, and us. We didn't have any reservations, but that wouldn't be a hindrance as we were traveling midweek in late September. We had a destination—the San Juan Islands in the Pacific Northwest, where we also lived—but our route to get there was unplanned...the freedom of the open road!

We left later than our anticipated early morning departure, but no timetable was the nature of a 280. Vernal, Utah, appeared to be the logical stopping point for our first night. Surrounded by the dreary grey hills of northeast Utah, Vernal is best known for the dinosaurs that used to lumber through its streets during the Jurassic age as well as the thirty-foot tall pink Tyrannosaurus Rex with long fake eyelashes that greets visitors on the edge of town. Two hours from Vernal, just to be on the safe side, I called the first hotel in my AAA Pet-Friendly Hotel guidebook, a three-star Best Western motel.

"Sorry ma'am," the southern clerk drawled in answer to my request for a room, "We are completely full tonight."

Strange, I thought, and moved down the list to the next three-star motel, with the same results. *Very strange.* John mentioned that perhaps there was a trucker's convention in town, as there were more trucks on the two-lane road to Vernal than usual. After the fifth phone call, this time sinking to a two-star motel on the outskirts of town, I asked the receptionist if every motel was full and she confirmed that yes, every hotel was at full capacity.

"There's a fossil fuel boom happening here," she said, "and the oil, gas, and construction industries have every room booked. I wouldn't even bother calling anyone else, because I know you won't have any luck, especially mid-week."

Evidently we were in the midst of the current Bush administration's efforts to extract natural gas and oil from the strata below. Undeterred, I called every motel, even the ones that didn't accept dogs. Not one room. As we left town, I spied a new Best Western not listed in the book. Frantically dialing their phone number before we passed out of cell tower range, I secured their last room, the Bridal Suite, and added as an aside that we had a dog, and that wouldn't be a problem, would it?

"Yes, it definitely would!" yelled the desk clerk. "My head will roll if I allow a dog in that room!" and she slammed down the receiver.

Our only option was driving two hours to the next town, Heber City, visually battling the sharp, golden shards of the setting sun the entire way. We pulled in to the Swiss Alps Motel at 9 o'clock at night, hungry and tired. The eighty-five-year-old desk clerk recommended the Dairy Keen next door for dinner, and helped out with a coupon for a free homemade milk shake. Hamburger dinners for two cost $8.69, and as we laid our weary heads on the flat, worn pillows, I smelled petroleum oozing out of the pores of the truckers next door through the paper-thin walls.

September 20

We had been driving for half-an-hour, fueled by a nutritious breakfast of convenience store Krispy Kreme doughnuts, when Kelly called.

"Mom, I met with my counselor today, and I have my classes figured out!"

"Great, peanut. What are you taking?" All of the books I had read, and Dartmouth's own parent orientation sessions, insisted on parents stepping back and allowing the student to make their own decisions, especially when it came to classes for the first term.

"I'm taking a Biology class called DNA and Diversity, Calculus, and the Anthropology of Islam."

"They sound amazing," I said, thinking that I might like to go back to college. I would probably learn a heck of a lot more than I did the first time. I was proud of Kelly for taking charge of her academic destiny, the way her best friend Lacy had.

Lacy had started classes two weeks prior to Kelly. Her course selections included the History of Music, English, Anthropology, and a women's issues class. When Lacy called home and described the first meeting of Women's Issues, which included the screening of a film about lesbianism, Jayne was supportive. Lacy, on the other hand, a demure and conservative eighteen-year-old, was thoroughly shocked. She dropped the course and enrolled in creative writing.

A few hours later, we arrived in Ketchum, Idaho, home of the Sun Valley ski area, Ernest Hemingway, and a small wine company we had an investment in. One of the benefits of having an interest in a wine company was that we could purchase great wine below wholesale prices, and indulge in a little wine tasting...*for the company's sake.* In our family, John was the wine connoisseur, I was the chef and Kelly loved to bake. A productive triumvirate.

The Best Western Tyrolean Lodge, overlooking Bald Mountain, was the only hotel in town that accepted dogs, and there were plenty of rooms available. Our hopes for a few romantic dinners and art gallery walks were dashed when we were forced to sign *The Pet Owner's Commandments* at the front desk, in which we had to agree to pay $200 if we left the loveable Kelso alone in the room.

We left Kelso in the car while dashing into a few galleries and learned that at least ten well-known restaurants had been shuttered in the Ketchum-Sun Valley area in the past few years, so we weren't quite as disappointed in our meager pizza and pasta take-out fare, knowing that our dining options were limited.

One afternoon John had the brilliant idea of taking Kelso to be groomed, so we succeeded in eating a delicious lunch at a French cafe without the sad hound-dog eyes of our pooch watching us from the car.

September 21

"Mom, I may not have planned my schedule very well," Kelly announced in her next phone call.

"Why not, sweetie?"

"Well, it turns out that the Islam class I wanted to take conflicts with the Biology section I need, and if I change the Biology section, my math class will be screwed up. It also turns out that if I want to take Chinese or Arabic, I have to start them this term, because the beginning classes aren't offered in winter or spring terms, but Italian is...and I've always loved Italian. And then they put me in Math 3, but I think I should really be in Math 8 because everyone else on my floor is in Math 8, and I'm really ticked off at IB (the International Baccalaureate program she graduated from) because all the kids who took Advanced Placement got tons of credit automatically, and I have to beg for every credit I can get."

I mentioned that maybe she should have a chat with her advisor and get some advice from him.

"But, Mom," Kelly pleaded, "What do *you* think I should do?"

Despite wholeheartedly agreeing with the Pearls of Wisdom, specifically Pearl of Wisdom #5, I felt like flying to Dartmouth and holding Kelly's hand as I, a mother needed once again, walked her across the lovely Green to her advisor's office, discussing all of her scheduling options with the distinguished white-haired counselor as we shared steaming cups of Earl Grey tea, my daughter gazing lovingly at me and in awe of my problem-solving skills....

Kelly said, "Bye mom, gotta go," to the sound of raucous laughter in the background. "I'm going to crew practice. I'll tell you what happens later."

Reverie ended.

Maple leaves crunched like golden corn flakes underfoot as we scuffled through Ketchum's streets. The Cavallino Lounge was a late afternoon find, its discovery necessitating another temporary incarceration of the sad-eyed Kelso. The Cavallino Lounge didn't serve food...it was not a kiddie bar. The menu consisted of six pages of exotic and classic cocktails and boasted an extensive wine list, all served in a hushed, brown and black interior, a contemporary cocoon that could have been transported from San Francisco or New York. We had French 75 cocktails, a drink popular when John's mother was the toast of the USO dances in the 1940s. The drinks were a blend of champagne and gin, and they went down cool and smooth from our perch at the bar, we kissed each other and laughed out loud. Maybe there were some positives to empty nesterhood. After all, every night could be a Friday night, and every day a Saturday.

French 75

Yeild: 1 cocktail

- 1 OUNCE GIN
- ¼ OUNCE LEMON JUICE
- ⅛ OUNCE SIMPLE SYRUP
- 5 OUNCES CHILLED CHAMPAGNE

Shake gin, lemon juice, and syrup with ice. Strain into a champagne flute. Top with champagne.

September 22

After an early morning hike to Chocolate Gulch, north of Ketchum, we arrived at the wine company to commandeer our yearly allotment of wine. John estimated eight cases would fit snugly into the SUV.

The company's knowledgeable manager helped us search the warehouse shelves for cases of our favorite red, Rosso de Montepulciano, and Chablis, a French white that pairs perfectly with anything, but especially with fresh oysters. After removing every item from the SUV, and without the aid of that indispensable man tool, duct tape, to wrap around the boxes, John systematically packed thirteen and a half cases of wine into the car, and we were still able to see out of the rear window above Kelso and his crate. As we stopped for gas in Stanley, just over the pass from Ketchum, my cell phone rang. It was Kelly.

"Hi peanut! Can you hear me now? How's the class schedule going?"

"Well, I think I have it all worked out. A friend and I went to the Islam class, which was way too confusing. The professor wrote the book, but I didn't like his teaching style. So then we heard about a class called Intro to Anthropology, so we audited the first class and it was amazing, so then we went to the registrar, who said there were fifteen people on the waitlist ahead of us, but they hadn't called her back yet, so she let the two of us in! It was so cool and serendipitous!" *Was this an SAT vocabulary word, or a recently learned college expression?* I thought to myself.

"So what happened with the math?" I said.

"That worked out well too. I went to Math 3 which was really slow and I knew everything they were going to be covering, so I decided to take Math 8 which went incredibly fast, but was much more interesting. I'll hope for the best. And I really like the Bio class, so I'll stay there." And she had handled it all herself. We traveled a circuitous route north through McCall, Idaho, looping through Hell's Canyon National Park and driving in the back door of Washington state through the southeast corner, with the goal of reaching Walla Walla before nightfall. Famous for the Walla Walla sweet onion, the town also housed Whitman College, one of the schools that had accepted Kelly, but which we hadn't visited on our college treks. Admittedly, John and I were more interested in seeing the nation's newest wine-growing hotspot than the campus. I anticipated the countryside on the outskirts of Walla Walla, an Indian word meaning "Many Waters," to be similar to Napa Valley's vineyards, but all we saw for miles were gentle rolling hills, like pregnant golden mounds swelling from the earth's underbelly. Not a grapevine in sight.

We learned later that most of the area's one hundred vineyards were miles away from the town and the primary crops of the region were wheat and green peas. Lewis and Clark had traipsed through Walla Walla's hills, following in the footsteps of the Nez Pearce Indians and blazing the route for the Oregon Trail.

Given our recent lodging experience, and the fact that it was a Friday night, I started calling for hotel rooms three hours before our estimated arrival time. There were no four-star motels that accepted dogs, but there was a classic old hotel in the middle of town, known as the Marcus Whitman. According to the guidebook, it housed tasteful (?) Victorian furniture in the lobby and was dog friendly.

"I'm very sorry ma'am," came the oh-too-familiar refrain, "but we have no rooms available tonight or tomorrow night."

Blankety, blankety blank....

"Shelley, I think these hotel situations are affecting your language," John said politely, noticing the increase in foul language ricocheting around the car in the past few days. When Kelly was a toddler we lived in Mission Beach in San Diego, and I was a freeway junkie. With Kelly strapped into her car seat behind me, we drove the freeways together, running errands, visiting friends, going to the mall.

It's all about the car in Southern California. And California drivers are fast and rude, so to relieve tension, I frequently screamed obscenities at them from the security of the VW van, my favorite expression being "shit." My obscenity-strewn days came to a screeching halt the day two-year-old Kelly saw a car almost sideswipe us. Before I was able to get my lungs in gear to utter my favorite oath, I heard her yelling from the back seat "Chit, Chit, Chit!"

Controlling my baser linguistic urges, I calmly asked the desk clerk, "Well could you please tell me what's happening in town? A weevil-harvester's convention, perhaps, or maybe a grape-picker's rendezvous? And are all the other hotels full too?"

"It is, in fact, an oncology nurse's meeting, and yes," she said, "you may have some difficulty finding a room, unless of course, you happen to be a nurse." Which, sensing my underlying hostility, she probably had a hard time believing I was.

Ten phone calls later, and not a bed to be had. In addition to the nurse's convention, there was a university soccer game, the opening of Walla Walla State College, and the weekend onslaught of winery tourists. The closest town was Pasco, sixty miles away, and visions of another late Dairy Keen dinner reared its cholesterol-laden head...just as I had been salivating over one of the excellent Walla Walla restaurants I'd found in my latest *Food and Wine* magazine. At the last exit before we departed for Pasco I spied the bright yellow sign of a Super 8 motel at the edge of the freeway.

John had been making the last round of calls while I drove. "I'm pulling in here," I said. "It's our last hope. By the way, did you try this one?" He replied that he hadn't checked any two-star motels.

"What?" I shrieked.

I jumped out of the car, ran into the harsh fluorescent light of the lobby. Dashing ahead of three other desperate travelers in the parking lot and panting like a contestant racing for the finish line on *The Amazing Race* I secured the last room. Leaving Kelso in our room, we dined guilt-free on seared duck breast perched atop a bed of duck confit hash. The meal was aided by a bottle of Spring Valley Vineyard Uriah Merlot, recommended to us by the couple sitting at an adjacent table. They suggested that a return trip to the Walla Walla wine region for a complete reconnaissance of the area's wine tasting rooms should be high on our empty nester To Do List. *Check*.

The mild, dry climate and rich volcanic soil of eastern Washington, combined with copious water from the Cascade Mountains runoff, provides a perfect palette for the winemaker's art. The first wine grapes were planted in the Walla Walla Valley as early as 1860 with the nearby Yakima and Columbia Valleys also becoming important regions for the introduction of varietals by Italian, French and German immigrants. The modern era of Washington wine making began in earnest in 1960 with the first large-scale planting of vineyards, led by the Chateau Ste. Michelle and Columbia Winery. Washington State is now ranked second in the nation for premium wine production, with more than 31,000 acres planted and a new winery opening every 15 days.

"John," I said, "we could be in eastern Washington for a very long time."

My grape-fueled reverie ended when I was hit with an immense pang of guilt—and it was not about the dog. I hadn't thought about Kelly in three hours…was there something wrong with me?…was I relinquishing my role as a mother? or…in a flash of brilliant insight…was I just claiming a place in the world of adults without kids at home?

September 23

Shoppers at the Saturday Farmer's Market in Walla Walla were being serenaded by a local barbershop quartet when we arrived mid-morning, hot javas in hand. Farmers with rough hands, calloused and dirt-stained, offered samples of sweet ripe pears and Honey Crisp apples. Oilcloth covered tables were scattered with ornamental corn and multi-colored squash ready for autumn centerpieces. We sampled buckwheat honey drizzled on nutty stone ground bread, pulled from an early morning oven. The ten-year-old salesman at the Onion World stand sold us a bulging bag of ultra-sweet candy onions, cousin to the Walla Walla Sweet, but with a higher sugar content and longer lasting. "So sweet you can eat 'em like an apple," he told us.

If our 280 driving karma held up, we would be able to reach the coast of Washington by day's end, with an outside chance of arriving at Anacortes, the terminal for the ferries serving the San Juan Islands.

Just after lunch in Ellensburg, halfway through Washington State, (highlight of which was the "Heavenly Bread" at the Yellow Church Cafe, a savory version of a cinnamon bun, swirled with cheddar cheese inside and out, and topped with fresh herbs—certainly not for the faint of hips), we began the familiar routine.

"OK, honey, I know that we're farther out than usual, but why don't you start calling now and see if we can find a place to stay in Anacortes? That way we can catch the 9:30 a.m. ferry tomorrow," John suggested. I noticed that faced with the next twenty years (actuarially-speaking) of living without an offspring in the house, John and I were becoming softer and gentler towards one another, even after twenty years of a great marriage and my unexplained panic attacks in the weeks before Kelly's eminent departure.

"John, what's going to happen to us? Are we going to be OK? How are we going to manage?" John was his usual calm and mature self, probably the result of his being born 17 years before I was and having had a family with three children as a young man.

"Nothing to worry about, darlin'...we'll be fine!"

I steeled myself for the first phone call, hoping that the Ship Harbor Inn near the ferry terminal would welcome us with open arms and empty rooms. "We have no vacancies tonight or tomorrow night, ma'am," the polite desk clerk explained, while I silently roared at the Almighty God of Empty Hotel Rooms Somewhere in the Universe, asking where an available room might be that was closer than Beijing, and calmly put down the phone.

Anacortes and all of the cities, towns, and Indian casinos in the surrounding area were completely occupied. After the third phone call, I discovered the source of the problem. It was the twenty-fifth annual Oyster Run, a Harley Davidson motorcycle event sponsored by Limp Lee Productions, whose official motto was "The first bike gets the oyster, the second bike gets the shell." *I should have known.* Seven phone calls later, we parked for the night at a budget hotel in Everett, an hour's drive south of Anacortes; our drab room and its bleak view of the parking lot mirroring our mood.

September 24

We have lived with some spectacular views. We always insist upon a great view wherever we live, when we rent hotel rooms, or at the restaurants where we dine. Our compulsion to view beautiful scenery has created many embarrassing moments for Kelly, but thankfully, she too is now afflicted with the family disease.

When Kelly was a toddler, we lived in a house on the northern coast of Oregon overlooking the Necanicum River estuary, where three rivers united before flowing to the Pacific Ocean. Just past the sand dunes in the distance giant waves broke against the shore. Bald eagles would plunge from the sky to steal salmon from the sea, sometimes braving eighty-mile-an-hour winter winds, while the clouds that brought the inevitable Oregon rain changed shape by the minute. In between storms, flocks of bridal-white swans vacationed on the placid cove below our deck.

Our house in Aspen boasts spectacular views of six dominant peaks in the Elk Mountain Range, each approaching 14,000 feet in height, towering and Zeus-like in their ability to gather clouds and toss thunderbolts on summer afternoons. The peaks surrender their jagged icy crowns to aspen groves, pine forests and the uneven stripes of the ski runs clawed by man through their midsections, finally ceding to civilization and the concrete ribbon of Highway 82 at their feet. The highway winds its way up the Roaring Fork Valley, ending in the town of Aspen, which spews glitter at night like a sparkler on the Fourth of July.

But the best view we've ever lived with has to be the view from our kitchen windows on Brown Island, a mile-long island perched at the entrance to Friday Harbor, the main town in the heart of the San Juan Islands of Washington state. Eight-foot tall windows rise unobstructed from a long butcher-block countertop and wrap around the corner, bumping into a vintage 1967 avocado-green stove. The windows overlook a covered deck, bereft of railings, which hover above a rocky, high bank cliff, the ocean licking at its base.

Blue robed and barefoot, I make a morning cappuccino and watch the sun's rays slither between the trunks of the one hundred foot tall Douglas firs. The light comes to rest on a small piece of forested land across the water to the west, on which there are a few scattered buildings owned by the University of Washington Marine Labs. Except for these structures, there are no other buildings in our view. Brown Islanders call San Juan Island the "Mainland" and the rest of Washington State, the part you travel to by ferry, is referred to as "America."

Across the sound to the north is Shaw Island, famous for, among other things, the order of Franciscan nuns who owned and operated the ferry landing and general store for three decades. They greeted each ferry garbed in long brown habits topped with bright orange and yellow safety vests and ran the only store on the island, the quaint Little Portion Store, which offered an eclectic array of essentials from imported French soap to Mother Prior's Mustard. With no new converts clamoring to greet the ferries, the nuns recently retired to a Franciscan center in Oregon to teach music and raise chickens.

Looming in the distance beyond Shaw Island is Orcas Island, the largest and most mountainous of the San Juan Islands. It is shaped like a massive set of lungs. Turtleback Mountain occupies the left lobe, and Mount Constitution, the highest point in the San Juans at 2,400 feet, the right. Orcas Island attracts hikers, bikers, and Microsoft millionaires.

From six in the morning until midnight there is a nonstop parade of Washington State Ferries coursing under our kitchen window, the almost primal throb of their engines slightly shifting the foam on my cappuccino. In winter when the dark comes early, the ferries look like giant floating hotels, their windows illuminated to reveal commuters playing gin rummy and reading books to pass the time.

After we purchased our home on Brown Island, a neighbor told us about the foggy night years ago when a junior mate, obeying the captain's orders, kept to his prescribed course and ran the ferry straight into the high bank in front of our house. The homeowners at the time were eating their supper at the dining table and were shaken both by the impact and the sight of the bloodshot eyes of the inebriated captain staring straight at them from his perch at the helm.

Below the windows on the high bank, a twenty-foot tall stump of a tree survives the noisy assaults of the redheaded woodpecker that visits daily, and adjacent to the stump is an aged pine that looks like a gigantic bonsai specimen arching gracefully out over the water. It was Ben White's favorite tree.

Ben was a tree hugger. He had an unkempt scraggly white beard and smelled like peat moss. He was also a member of the Green Party and last fall he had run unsuccessfully for a seat on the County Commission, despite the most rational political campaign platform I have ever read.

John invited Ben to our property to survey the trees to make sure they would survive. He and his crew climbed high into the treetops, swinging like monkeys, trimming random branches, cutting and snipping them into shape. Ben didn't make a lot of money. He spent as much time traveling to Costa Rica and the Amazon to save whales and other endangered species as he did trimming trees.

The sea below the kitchen window is a giant conveyor belt, its tides ebbing and flowing, moving boats of every description from north to south and east to west. Zippy little Sea Sports cruise at twenty-eight knots with fishing rod holders mounted on their sterns, loaded with salmon, spot prawns, and Dungeness crab in below-deck coolers. Sailboats with bulbous sails struggle against the currents and the wind, sometimes traveling backwards. Sleek white yachts with bulbous owners sashay into the harbor, drink holders replacing fly rod holders, while Ralph Lauren-clad crewmembers guide the multi-million dollar toys (some of which bore a striking resemblance to a pool of melted white candle wax) into the Friday Harbor marina.

My view often includes a local whale watching boat going by with forty or more tourists lined along the railings, all straining to glimpse a pod of Orca whales breaching. Captain Pete is usually the man at the helm. He and his wife Nancy live on a restored salmon trawler, the *Sandra Jean II*, which is tethered to a buoy in the middle of Friday Harbor.

We met Pete, whose bushy red mutton chops hide an impish grin, when John, Kelly, and I took a Trawler Training course with him before purchasing our boat, *Paradis*. We spent three days learning to drive a thirty-four-foot single engine diesel boat, conveniently already smashed up before we took the helm. Patience must have been Pete's middle name, as he never seemed concerned about our lack of steering skills while maneuvering around buoys, landing at fuel docks, and attempting to drop anchors in tiny coves. His patience might be the result of the six kinds of home brewed beer he and Nancy concocted aboard the *Sandra Jean II* in a galley the size of a dead man's locker.

Besides being a repository of knowledge about boat engines, celestial navigation, and knot tying, Pete was also a naturalist with a sense of humor. Once, while Kelly was at the helm, we were headed toward a rock outcropping surrounded by a huge forest of bullhead kelp when Pete gave the order to slow down. He stretched over the railing and pulled a thirty-foot piece of kelp out of the water. He sliced off eighteen inches of kelp adjacent to the round bulb-like head of the seaweed, which kept the kelp blades afloat on the surface of the water. Then he cut holes in the stem and played "Blow the Man Down" on his kelp flute.

Captain Pete was also responsible for telling us about eagles being able to swim. Neither John, Kelly nor I believed for a moment it was true, until a few nights later, as we were enjoying the sunset from our patio, Brown Island's bald eagle plunged headfirst into the sea below us. He emerged with a writhing thirty-pound salmon in his talons. Fully expecting the eagle to take to the sky, we were amazed when he remained on top of the water as the salmon tried to pull him below. The eagle's claws were locked into the fish's coral flesh. To escape a watery death, just as Pete had predicted, the eagle raised his mighty wings in an avian version of the butterfly stroke, swam thirty yards to shore, and dragged his prey onto the mussel-encrusted shoreline rocks.

As I look out of our kitchen windows to the east, the volcano Mount Baker will sometimes emerge above Lopez Island. In the early 1790s, Captain George Vancouver was commissioned by the British government to map every inlet and outlet of the northwest coast of North America. After entering the Strait of Juan de Fuca, between Vancouver Island and what is now Washington State, Captain Vancouver records his third lieutenant, Joseph Baker, sighting "a very high conspicuous craggy mountain...it presented itself, towering above the clouds: as low down as they allowed it to be visible it was covered with snow; and south of it, was a long ridge of very rugged snowy mountains, much less elevated, which seemed to stretch to a considerable distance...."

Captain Vancouver bestowed Baker's name upon the peak, usurping the indigenous native's moniker, White Steep Mountain. It is the northernmost volcano in the Cascade Range and last erupted in the nineteenth century. Even in the heat of summer, I have never seen it without its thick white glacial cloak. Sometimes the mountain will be invisible for days, suffocated by the Northwest mist, some days it will be at best a fleeting thought, but the best days are the days it flings off its damp grey blanket to bare its single alabaster breast to the sapphire skies.

The view from the far, far right of the kitchen windows is a wild, impenetrable thicket that lies between our gravel terrace and the distant neighbors. Two teak Adirondack chairs live on the edge of the terrace, ready to host any willing reader on a hot summer's day, but more often than not, the chairs are betrayed by the reader's reluctance to remove their eyes from the view of the sea, the boats, the islands. Much like the unwillingness of a mother to take her eyes from the most beautiful view of all— the face of her child.

September 25

When we finally got home, life back on the island settled into its delightfully predictable routine. After our first summer on Brown Island, our Aspen friends would ask what we had done for the past three months. All I could say was, "It wasn't about doing, it was about being."

Friday Harbor is the main port in the San Juan Islands and the only real town on San Juan Island. Brown Island is situated in the middle of the harbor. There is no ferry service to Brown Island, so our days revolved around taking our Brown Island dinghy into town, a five-minute ride, to get groceries European-style, shopping by the day, for the day.

The dinghy dock on San Juan Island is located adjacent to the ferry-landing terminal, which mainlines its cargo (foot passengers, bicyclists and cars) up Spring Street, straight into the heart of Friday Harbor. It is a workingman's town, not yuppified like some other island villages, Nantucket coming to mind. Spring Street runs from east to west, and is lined with stores that real people actually use. King's Grocery store sits dead center of town, an easy walk both for townspeople and the boaters. Six or seven good restaurants, a couple of clothing stores, an outpost of West Marine, and a few tourist traps selling T-shirts that read *Friday Harbor, a quaint little drinking town with a fishing problem* are bundled into a twenty block area where buildings from the late 19th century prevail.

San Juan Island has no stoplights and no fast food chains. It has three Shell gas stations, a Radio Shack, a Coldwell Banker real estate office, and a Wells Fargo bank branch, but that is the extent of globalization on the island.

There are always conversations to be shared and coffee to be savored on the deck of the Doctor's Office Café which overlooks the ferry landing. Sometimes days pass and I don't accomplish anything. This is probably what "being here now" is all about. That's probably why I love the island, because when I'm here, I'm more "here" than not.

September 26

After all the mostly mediocre meals on the road, I felt the need to cook. Cooking in earnest might take away the sting of realizing that the half gallon of milk I had just purchased would probably last two weeks, instead of three days, now that my teenager consumed her calcium half a continent away instead of at my kitchen counter.

Was she even drinking milk these days?

My kitchen frenzy produced fresh Alaskan halibut slathered with a sauce of mayonnaise mixed with Walla Walla candy onions and fresh tomatoes (sounds strange but was surprisingly delicious), fresh mesclun salad with a lemon/dill vinaigrette, and coral-colored cauliflower pureed with goat cheese.

Mayonnaise Baked Fish

Yield: 4 servings

- 1½ TO 2 POUNDS FRESH HALIBUT, CUT INTO 4 PIECES
- ½ CUP GOOD QUALITY MAYONNAISE (HELLMAN'S OR BEST FOODS)
- ½ TEASPOON DRY MUSTARD
- 1 MEDIUM ONION, CHOPPED INTO ¼-INCH DICE
- ½ CUP RED PEPPER, CHOPPED INTO ¼-INCH DICE
- DASH CAYENNE PEPPER

Put fish in a lightly greased shallow baking dish. Stir mayonnaise, mustard, onion, red pepper, and cayenne in a small bowl until blended. Spread mixture on top of fish. Bake in a hot oven (400 degrees) for 17 minutes or until fish just begins to flake when touched with a fork.

September 28

Our island routine now included daily phone calls from Kelly, usually initiated by her, since I had read in one of the college self-help books that it is easier for a college student to call between events in her highly erratic schedule. The calls usually came toward the end of our day, and at the beginning of her night. I didn't always ask what went on the previous night, but I did elicit a few details about beverages other than milk. Keystone was the beer of choice and the critical ingredient in Dartmouth's favorite evening sport, beer pong. It's like a game of ping-pong played with plastic cups of beer that are lined up on each end of the table. If your opponent hits their ball into one of the cups on your side of the table, highlighting your inadequacy as a player and probable inability to make the Chinese Olympic team, you and your partner must quaff the cup of beer. I was relieved to learn it was a team sport, as it might reduce the amount of beer consumed.

Each fraternity also had a signature drink, like tea.

"You mean Constant Comment or Lemon Zinger?" I asked.

"Uh, no, Mom," Kelly replied.

"You mean Long Island Iced Tea?"

"Whoa, Mom, how did you know about that?"

"Oh, I've heard it has a lot of different liquors in it—something to be wary of, honey."

Sometimes I listened to myself on the phone with Kelly and I sounded like a complete stiff. *Of course, she's going to try it, so why did I have to sound like such a bore?* Remnants of motherhood.

Not able to resist one more stab at teaching her about the evil ways of the college world, I blurted out, "And remember if you ever go to a party given by medical students, be really careful of the punch they make...sometimes they use grain alcohol, and it can be wicked!" Thinking back, of course, to the only medical school party I attended in college, and waking up the next morning, fully clothed, with three inches of sand deposited at the bottom of the bed sheets.

I didn't share this with Kelly, especially after she commented, "Oh right, that's pretty good stuff, but they don't make it very strong here." I was learning that good long-distance parenting also required a huge dose of self-control.

September 29

We drove onto the early morning ferry (definitely not my idea) to take Peaches to Bellingham to have her canvas top repaired. John had been a little too exuberant flinging it back one day and now the top wouldn't retract.

While the Mercedes was being repaired, we walked three miles to Fairhaven, the Old Town section of Bellingham, and discovered Fino, a contemporary wine bar and restaurant on the harbor front. We each ordered a salad. Mine was a Caesar with shaved manchego cheese, prosciutto, and pistachios. John's a tower of butter lettuce and spinach with walnuts and blue cheese doused with Spanish sherry vinaigrette. They were edible modern sculptures on a plate. For our entrees, we shared an order of tapas. There were melt-in-your-mouth potato croquettes, sherried prawns, a slice of manchego cheese with quince jam, Spanish almonds, albondigas, Serrano ham, chorizo, peppers, and olives and a basket of *pane e coperto* (European breads served with pesto butter, sun-dried tomato butter, and garlic chive butter). Over the years, we have developed a philosophy about dining; if a meal is excellent, the desserts will be too. So we skip desserts at restaurants that are ordinary, and go for broke at places like Fino. Our culinary nirvana ended with a rich roasted banana chocolate bread pudding.

The euphoria of the meal was deflated by the news that a new top for Peaches would cost $8,000. I guess we'd learn to drive with the top down, permanently.

September 30

Kelly's call today revolved around her weekend's activities. Like peeling away the layers of a Walla Walla sweet, I was slowly being allowed to get closer to the core of the college experience—and weekends were unquestionably the core.

"Did you have a good weekend, sweetie?"

"Yes," she laughed, "it was great, and you have to hear this one, it's all-time!"

"Go for it," I said, steeling myself for the worst.

"There are a bunch of us who usually go out on Friday nights," *OK, no early morning Saturday calls from now on*, "and there is a guy on our floor who always comes. Well, he got so wasted Friday night we had to walk him home and throw him in bed. When his roommate woke up the next morning, he was gone, and no one knew where he was. We all decided to chill about it, but he still hadn't returned Saturday afternoon. We were getting a little worried by this time, so at 4:00 a.m. Sunday morning," *4:00 a.m.?* "we called Safety and Security, they're the campus cops who are so much cooler than the Hanover cops, so if you get caught drinking, they're the ones you want to deal with. They just take you back to your dorm, not the police station."

How does she know all of this? She's only been at school two and a half weeks! Was there something I missed in the Parent's Handbook?

"So Safety and Security came to his room, and completely searched it from top to bottom, and still no sign of him anywhere on campus. They left a message for him to call on Blitzmail but we were convinced that something really bad had happened."

"Honey, this is serious," I said, "I'm glad you all had the presence of mind to call security."

"Yah, they are cool, and responded really quickly too. Anyway, still no sign of him the rest of the day. So tonight we were having a meeting with the Undergraduate Advisor, and in he walked, completely casual, like nothing was wrong. We all screamed, jumped up and down and he had no clue why everyone was so excited about him walking in the door. And this is the funny part...three days ago he had told a friend of mine down the hall that he was going to a music retreat all weekend, and she had entirely forgotten...it was so hysterical, we all just about peed in our pants!"

OCTOBER

October 1

A new month, a new life, and that meant it was time for a dinner party. Not that I was celebrating Kelly's departure. I was merely acknowledging a different state of affairs in our world. We hadn't entertained since we'd returned to the island. Since there weren't many islanders in residence in the fall and winter months (there are forty houses in all, but only six full-time residents) we decided to have the locals in for dinner. Compared to dinner parties in Aspen, where invitations are issued weeks in advance, the common island practice is to call a day or two ahead and see who shows up.

Our guests would be the caretakers for the island, Captain Pete and Nancy, as well as a couple who had just moved to Brown Island. Remembering we had a new raclette machine stashed in the hall closet, I decided to treat our guests to a Swiss meal. Raclette is a Swiss tradition, and ever since we lived in Switzerland for a year when Kelly was twelve, it was a meal we ate regularly and loved.

We experienced raclette for the first time in the town of Gruyere, the heart of the Swiss cheese region. Shortly after our arrival in Switzerland, we took a weekend train trip to witness the Desalpe, the descent of the cows from their summer pastures high in the Alps. We awaited the arrival of the herd with throngs of locals and tourists, rain pelting our newly purchased umbrellas. We heard cowbells in the distance over the blaring of the local brass band, and soon the cows emerged from the cold mist, drenched and dripping red, blue and green streaks from the soggy paper flower garlands strung between their horns.

That evening, we dined at a restaurant that served every cheese dish known to the Swiss. As we sat in the dim smoke-filled space, the family dining at the table next to us were served a piece of raclette cheese the size of a cow's head, impassively sitting underneath a raised heating element positioned directly above it.

"There is absolutely no way they can eat that," I whispered to Kelly and John. "That has to be at least four pounds of cheese!" We watched closely as the family used rounded knives to scrape the melted cheese onto small white potatoes, accompanied by cornichon pickles and tiny white onions. Before we could gawk again, the raclette was half gone.

We ordered a smaller portion for the three of us, but received just as much cheese as our neighbors. The potatoes were a perfect foil for the nutty cheese and before we knew it, we were finished. Only the crusty rind of the cheese remained, still sizzling under the heat. We were hooked.

Over the course of our Swiss year, we experienced at least seven different methods of heating raclette; from individual portions cooked by a chef in a wood-burning oven, to a half wheel of the cheese cradled in a wire basket and exposed to a heating element, to piles of two-inch thick squares of raclette brought to the table and heated on top of a hibachi.

Our raclette maker is a typical suburban Swiss model. Oval-shaped, it consists of a solid metal griddle with a heating element suspended underneath. Each diner places a one-quarter inch thick square slice of cheese in a small tray and cooks it below the heating element, while atop the griddle, we toss sausages, onions and sometimes shrimp to serve alongside the cheese.

Newcomers to raclette are usually nervous about their first melting attempt, but once they learn the consistency required to pour the cheese over the potatoes, they become raclette zealots. They are always amazed at how much cheese they can consume. Based on the advice of some Swiss friends, we add chopped red peppers, nutmeg, and cracked pepper to the top of the melted cheese, plus I often include cooked broccoli for the inevitable carbophobe in the group. Swiss tradition mandates copious amounts of white wine to ease the meal down; the Swiss don't drink water with raclette, as it supposedly hinders the digestive experience.

After the raclette, we polished off a plum tarte tatin for dessert. I promise I'll walk, energetically, around the island, and twice. Tomorrow.

October 3

Today I made thirty-seven jars of jam.

Three times a summer, the ladies at the St. Francis Catholic Church arrange for a faithful parishioner to deliver a truckload of just-picked berries from the Skagit Valley (from America) for a fundraiser to benefit the church. We get strawberries in June, raspberries in July and blueberries the size of holy wafers in August. By the time the berries arrive in their fifteen-pound white plastic tubs, stripped of leaves, washed, and smelling of the summer sun, the ferry ride has pulverized them into the perfect consistency for making jam.

As soon as I receive the blessed buckets, I head to my retro stove. This past summer I strayed from my tried and true raspberry jam recipe in favor of something more exotic. For one batch, Kelly and I concocted a base mixture of raspberries and sugar, then added thin strips of orange rind and fresh orange juice. For the second batch, we julienned fresh ginger, chopped crystallized ginger into nuggets and added both to buckets of strawberries to create strawberry-ginger jam. Delicious.

I entered the concoctions in the San Juan County Fair in August. Kelly and I returned to the fairgrounds after the judging to discover that we had won a Best of Show for the strawberry-ginger jam, and a first place for the raspberry-orange mixture. When I read the official commentaries and the judge's notations about the winning entry, "Is it always this runny?" we laughed. Who knew? We'd never made either jam before.

Since this past summer also brought an onslaught of forty-two days of house guests, I was left with little free time and a bucket of raspberries nagging at me from the depths of the freezer. Now, devoid of carpool duty for the first time in years, I had time to cook.

For the first fifteen jars of jam, I repeated the raspberry-orange brew. Then I made fourteen jars of lemon-infused raspberry jam, and finally, I clipped handfuls of the fresh rosemary outside my kitchen door to make eight jars of rosemary-scented raspberry jelly. For some reason it never fully set, so I renamed it *Rosemary Scented Raspberry Syrup* and decided to serve it over vanilla ice cream.

Raspberry Jam

Yield: about 7 (1 cup) jars

4 CUPS PREPARED RASPBERRIES
(ABOUT 2 QUARTS FULLY RIPE RED FRUIT)
6½ CUPS SUGAR, MEASURED INTO SEPARATE BOWL
½ TEASPOON BUTTER OR MARGARINE
1 POUCH CERTO FRUIT PECTIN

Bring a boiling-water canner half full with water to simmer. Wash jars and screw bands in hot soapy water; rinse with warm water. Pour boiling water over flat lids in saucepan off the heat. Let stand in hot water until ready to use. Drain jars well before filling.

Crush raspberries thoroughly, one layer at a time. (Press half of pulp through a sieve to remove some of the seeds, if desired.) Measure exactly 4 cups prepared fruit into a 6- or 8-quart saucepot. Add sugar, stir.

Stir in sugar. Add butter to reduce foaming. Bring mixture to full rolling boil (a boil that doesn't stop bubbling when stirred) on high heat, stirring constantly. Stir in pectin. Return to full rolling boil and boil exactly 1 minute, stirring constantly. Remove from heat. Skim off any foam with metal spoon. Ladle immediately into prepared jars, filling to within ⅛-inch of tops. Wipe jar rims and threads. Cover with two-piece lids. Screw bands tightly. Place jars on elevated rack in canner. Lower rack into canner. (Water must cover jars by 1 to 2 inches. Add boiling water, if necessary.) Cover; bring water to gentle boil. Process 10 minutes. Remove jars and place upright on towel to cool completely. After jars cool, check seals by pressing middles of lids with finger. (If lids spring back, lids are not sealed and refrigeration is necessary.)

Cook's note: To add orange flavor, add ½ cup orange juice and the zest from 4 oranges along with the sugar.

Proceed with instructions from there.

Strawberry Jam

Yield: about 8 (1 cup) jars

4 CUPS PREPARED STRAWBERRIES
(ABOUT 2 QUARTS FULLY RIPE STRAWBERRIES)
7 CUPS SUGAR
½ TEASPOON BUTTER OR MARGARINE (OPTIONAL)
1 POUCH CERTO FRUIT PECTIN

Bring a boiling-water canner, half-full with water, to simmer. Wash jars and screw bands in hot, soapy water; rinse with warm water. Pour boiling water over flat lids in saucepan off the heat. Let stand in hot water until ready to use. Drain well before filling.

Stem and crush strawberries thoroughly, one layer at a time. Measure exactly 4 cups crushed strawberries into a 6- or 8-quart saucepot. Add sugar; stir. Add butter to reduce foaming. Bring to full rolling boil (a boil that doesn't stop bubbling when stirred) on high heat, stirring constantly. Stir in pectin. Return to full rolling boil and boil exactly 1 minute, stirring constantly. Remove from heat. Skim off any foam with metal spoon.

Ladle immediately into prepared jars, filling to within ⅛-inch of tops. Wipe jar rims and threads. Cover with 2-piece lids. Screw bands tightly. Place jars on elevated rack in canner. Lower rack into canner. (Water must cover jars by 1 to 2 inches. Add boiling water, if necessary.) Cover; bring water to gentle boil. Process 10 minutes.

Remove jars and place upright on towel to cool completely. After jars cool, check seals by pressing middle of lid with finger. (If lid springs back, lid is not sealed and refrigeration is necessary.)

Cook's note: To add ginger flavor, add 3 tablespoons of grated fresh ginger and 1 cup candied ginger, diced into ¼-inch pieces, along with the sugar. Proceed with instructions.

October 4

Another cooking frenzy produced dinner: brown sugar baked salmon (Kelly's favorite fish preparation), Chinese risotto, and steamed baby bok choy.

There are things that happen when you become an empty nester that, prior to your newly liberated state, you have no idea will occur. I have always liked to cook, but becoming a cooking maniac was nowhere near the top of my anticipated Top Ten List of Empty Nester Things To Do.

Brown Sugar Baked Salmon

Yeild: 6 servings

6 SALMON FILLETS, 1-INCH THICK,
OR 2-POUND SALMON FILLET IN ONE PIECE

Marinade

½ CUP BROWN SUGAR
4 TABLESPOONS MELTED BUTTER
3 TABLESPOONS SOY SAUCE
2 TABLESPOONS LEMON JUICE
2 TABLESPOONS DRY WHITE WINE OR WATER

In small bowl combine all marinade ingredients. Place salmon on foil-covered baking pan that holds fish snugly in one layer. Pour marinade over fish. Cover and marinate in refrigerator from 30 minutes to 6 hours.

Uncover pan. Place on middle rack of preheated 400 degree F oven. Bake 15 to 20 minutes or until fish is done, basting every 5 minutes. Do not turn fish. Serve immediately.

October 5

Part of the rationale for our trip to the Northwest, in addition to escaping Aspen and Kelly's lingering absence, was our desire (no, let's be honest, it was guilt) to explore the Gulf Islands of Canada. This summer we had spent a total of only eight days on our boat, which included an adventure to Desolation Sound on British Columbia's Sunshine Coast with one of my Canadian cousins. (I was born in Canada and lived in Vancouver, BC until I was ten years old, when my father uprooted us and we immigrated to the United States in pursuit of the American Dream.)

All well and good, but certainly no justification for keeping a forty-foot power boat around, with all its attendant expenses. Underlying the whole cruising dynamic was the realization I was also afraid of the boat. When *Paradis* was built a few years ago, we were inspired by the hardy Northwest islander mentality. Her twin Volvo Penta 300 diesel engines ate up the sea at the rate of twenty-eight knots an hour. As John liked to say about navigating it, "Think of it as trying to tame a bull."

Yesterday we lightly provisioned the boat, as we planned on staying at marinas with good restaurants. By mid-afternoon we were ready but the weather wasn't. A fire in the fireplace and a glass of Zinfandel sounded better than fighting low hanging clouds and gusty winds. We delayed our departure by a day.

Today there was sunshine and glassy water. By 9:30 a.m., with Doctor's Office coffees in hand, we checked the oil levels, cleaned the water filters and verified that we had enough fuel to make it to Sidney, the customs clearing port on the east side of Vancouver Island. It was a mere half-hour away in our aluminum rocket.

Driving from the fly bridge with Captain John at the helm, we entered the Port of Sidney, and I prepared to calmly step off the stern. In our Trawler Training course, Captain Pete had insisted, "You must never jump off the boat to tie the lines, the captain of the boat should be able to bring the boat in slowly so the mate can step off the boat like Johnny Depp in *Pirates of the Caribbean*. You always want to look good!" That was my game plan...slowly step off the boat and stylishly tie off the lines of the raging 22,000 pound bull, *alias boat*, under the adoring gaze of my husband.

"What the heck are you doing?" John yelled. "Grab the spring line, the stern's hitting the lamp post! Now go up and tie off the bow line, the bow is getting away!"

Apparently my demeanor was a little too calm for the captain, because while I had slowly and gracefully tied the stern line, we both realized I had also tied the fenders too high, so the deep blue aluminum hull of the boat was smashing against the dock. Hopelessly, I pushed against the tonnage of the boat and struggled to retie the fenders. Other than that, I was certain my technique had been flawless...except for the part where the front of the boat-bull was escaping from the dock. Fortunately, no one saw my valiant attempt to fling my body across six feet of fifty-five degree frigid water to grab the bowline. The unhappy captain abandoned his position on the fly bridge, and scrambled onto the wharf to tie off the spring line to save the boat from additional damage. A little dockside harangue was all that was necessary to send our marital glasnost off into the sunset with the alacrity of Osama Bin Laden escaping to his cave in Tora Bora.

We cleared customs and made our way to the Brentwood Bay Marina, where our next landing attempt was executed impeccably; the marina manager handled the lines, Captain John drove, while I sat in the salon with Kelso and read a good book.

For a little post-landing relaxation, we piloted the dinghy across Tod Inlet to the back entrance of the world renowned Butchart Gardens, a botanical sanctuary planted by Jennie Butchart over one hundred years ago. Her industrialist husband had built a cement factory at the inlet to take advantage of its plentiful limestone deposits that were vital to the production of cement. When the limestone quarry was depleted, Jennie lined the floor of the desolate pit with soil brought by horse and cart from neighboring farmlands and created the Sunken Garden, filled with lush floral displays that change with every season. From the elevated garden viewpoint, we spotted a solitary brick chimney, the last remnant of the cement plant's kiln. Jennie was passionate about gardening. She transformed the family tennis court into an Italian garden, planted a Japanese garden on the ocean side of their family home, and replaced the kitchen vegetable patch with a rose garden. I assumed her prodigious efforts were propelled by her first child's departure for college.

October 6

A gull's lonely screech sliced through the calm of a morning mist that flowed like softly whipped egg whites down the mountainous shore opposite the marina. Kelso and I walked through a neighboring park, plucking an acorn and its hat from the ground to send to Kelly as a reminder of her Canadian roots. Strolling down the dock back to the boat-bull, I casually glanced at the water to our left where the largest starfish I had ever seen was attached to a crusty piling. It was bright orange, at least twenty-four inches across and had twenty long, squiggly legs. The marina manager passed behind me and informed me that the creature was a sunflower sea star. It could grow up to three feet across and when under attack by predators like the king crab it could shed its arms, which would, over time, grow back. The sea star was also a predator, devouring sea urchins, sea cucumbers, clams and even other sea stars found on its undersea travels. The 15,000 tubelike feet on the underside of its body propelled it through the water at a rate of three feet per minute.

Kelso and I returned to the boat, greeted by John with another quick lecture on proper docking technique. We were the picture of marital perfection as *Paradis* slowly departed the marina, but then, reversing into open water is not usually an insurmountable challenge.

When we arrived at the town of Chemainus, just north of Brentwood Bay, the public wharf was empty and this time *Paradis* smoothly attached herself to the dock, as if colossal underwater magnets were sucking her to the wooden structure. I was the epitome of tranquility and efficiency, handling lines in perfect order, a proper Stepford boating wife.

Chemainus, fifty miles north of Victoria on the west side of Vancouver Island, was historically a lumber town, fueled by the construction of the Trans-Canada Railroad in the 1800s. Chinese, Japanese, and East Indian laborers joined forces with Scots and Germans to work on the railway, and after its completion, stayed to work either in the area's mines and forests or on fishing boats. In 1983, with British Columbia already in a recession, the lumber mill was shuttered after 120 years of operation, which further eroded the area's economy. The town's inventive citizens attempted to revitalize the town's fortunes by painting a series of giant murals on the exterior walls of the downtown buildings, with the hope of attracting tourists and their disposable incomes.

Fortunately the plan worked. We wandered through the town's core, admiring each of the forty-one murals, most of which depicted scenes from Chemainus's colorful past. We saw depictions of Hing Hong, a Chinese merchant, standing in front of his grocery and liquor store, loggers standing on a springboard to fell a monolithic tree, and tugboats pulling log booms into the harbor. The murals attracted close to half a million visitors a year and every year a new mural was added to the collection.

As we were admiring a mural of the Copper Canyon Railway, my friend Kathy called from the Parent's Weekend she was attending at Bowdoin College in Maine. Kathy, whose black hair is as wild as licorice cotton candy, operates a Pilates studio in the remodeled former family room of her basement and is the spouse of the town surgeon, Bill. Her daughter, Elissa, was one of Kelly's best friends and in her first year at Bowdoin. Kathy was her usual ebullient self, bubbling on about Elissa's activities and the Bowdoin Parent's Weekend party circuit, sending stabbing pangs of jealousy into my weakened heart, since the Dartmouth Parent's Weekend wasn't held until the end of April.

Kathy told me her daughter was having a great time in college. Because Elissa had attended a private boarding school before college, it seemed she was controlling herself far better than Kelly appeared to be. Since both girls were on their respective college's Nordic ski teams they'd be competing in Dartmouth's Winter Carnival in February, so Kathy and I decided we should all attend together. Hopefully the fact that Kathy, Bill, John and I would be traveling en masse would be an acceptable reason for our daughters to allow us to attend the biggest college party of the year.

John and I made a perfect exit from the Chemainus Marina and an even better landing at the Page Point Marina in nearby Ladysmith, mostly due to the assistance of the resort's chef, who scrambled to retrieve our lines as his chef's hat skewed to the portside. Jumping off the boat-bull, I noticed a torrent of water spewing out of an opening on *Paradis's* starboard side and called out to John. He raced down into the engine room and discovered a leaking hose that was flooding the bilge. He made a panicked phone call to the boat's builder, who offered to retrieve the boat the next day and take her off our hands by storing her for the winter in his boatyard. Suddenly we were relaxed again. With no worries about crossing the deadly Straits of Georgia ahead of us, we shared a merry dinner in front of the fire in the Page Point dining room. We were even more amused when Kelly called and told us about her interview for the Dartmouth Ski patrol.

"I don't think I made it onto the ski patrol, but I had an insane interview! There were two outrageous ski patrol guys who asked how I would market a product."

"What was the product?"

"A tampon!" she giggled. This is a very Dartmouth-style of question to ask—they all aim to shock.

"No way! What did you say?"

"I told them they could use it to stop a nose bleed in a pinch! Probably for the best I didn't make it, because it would have interfered with Nordic skiing, but it was so funny, I couldn't stop laughing! And thanks for the goodie box, I love the bucket of trail mix, it'll be great for workout snacks. Bye, gotta go to a study session, so I'll talk to you later!"

October 7

Today was the start of the Canadian Thanksgiving holiday, a three-day weekend that celebrated the European tradition of harvest festivals. Back at the coffee shop in Chemainus, the clerk had been perplexed that Americans observed Thanksgiving in November, when crops had already been harvested and the trees were leafless voids of color. Though the actual holiday is on a Monday, Canadians are flexible about what day they eat their holiday meal.

By 10:00 a.m. the Old Town Bakery in Ladysmith was a hub of Thanksgiving activity. Patrons were queued out the door, and our wait to the counter was an impatient one. Ten flavors of cinnamon buns, from orange poppy seed to almond cream cheese shared counter space with cookies and squares, a Canadian staple. When I was growing up, squares were my mother's favorite dessert. She made date squares, lemon squares, and my favorites, rickety-uncles, a crispy blend of rolled oats, brown sugar, and butter.

The racks behind the counter housed freshly baked bread, sliced on request on an old-fashioned bread slicer. Warm whole-wheat buns sweated inside plastic bags, while pumpkin pies, coconut cream pies with fresh meringue tops and spice cakes were ready to be purchased for holiday tables.

The chef-dockboy prepared a complete Thanksgiving meal at the restaurant that night. It was a great meal, improved by the fact that I didn't have to cook it, that it was October, and that we were surrounded by the bounty of fall, overlooking the calm waters of the Ladysmith inlet...and we didn't have to drive the boat back to America.

Rickety Uncles

Yield: 12 bars

- 4 CUPS ROLLED OATS
- 1 CUP MELTED BUTTER
- 1 CUP BROWN SUGAR
- ½ TEASPOON SALT
- 1 TEASPOON VANILLA

Mix all ingredients well. Place in an 8"x 8" or 9"x 9"pan. Bake at 350 degrees F for ½ hour. Cut when still hot, and then cool.

October 8

Yesterday I awoke to air as sweet as brown sugar spread on warm buttered toast and water so reflective I could have used it as a mirror to pluck my eyebrows. Today was a different story. A dark mist hung low over the water, draping the boats at the marina with a thin film of moisture that, over the course of the morning, thickened to rain. Kelso had developed a hacking cough, courtesy of his visit last week to the kennel. Instead of the morning call of the lonely gull, this morning my alarm clock was Kelso's rendition of a forlorn foghorn.

A taxi arrived to take us from Ladysmith to Sidney, where the Friday Harbor ferry was scheduled to depart in the late morning. The cab driver and John had an engaging discussion that flitted from politics to oil drilling to natural disasters. The driver also told us a story about his 23-year-old daughter who had been in Thailand two years ago. She was on a day hike to get groceries at a small mountain town outside of the village of Khao Lak. She and a friend took the high road instead of the flatter route. Halfway up the hill, as the noisy jungle around them suddenly hushed, they looked out to the ocean and watched the sea quickly recede from the coastline, "like lips pulled back from the fangs of a snarling dog," the driver added. Her friend had heard this could be the sign of an impending tsunami. They bolted up the hill and watched in amazement as, indeed, a tsunami's fury engulfed the village. The cab driver and his wife had had no communication from their daughter for ten days. They were preparing for the worst when she finally emailed that she had survived.

Suddenly my feelings about Kelly's college departure were put into perspective.

October 9

The morning sun lay low on the horizon as if to deceptively con me into thinking it was late afternoon as I steered the dinghy across the pond to visit the local dentist. Courtesy of a sticky Italian candy, I would now be the proud owner of a new porcelain crown. The dentist thought he was very cool as he worked in hip street clothes and crooned, "*I'm turning Japanese, I think, I'm turning Japanese, I really think so,*" into my gaping, defenseless mouth as he installed the crown.

I wandered around town with nothing else on my schedule except a few errands to accomplish. The pavement undulated beneath its icing of dried maple leaves, their decaying odor a familiar, comfortable, once-a-year smell. The morning dew melted through the back pockets of my jeans as I sat on the Doctor's Office deck savoring a cappuccino. I was happy.

Until the phone rang at 11:00 p.m...that would be 2:00 a.m. in New Hampshire. It was Kelly. She had just returned from the Dartmouth-Hitchcock Medical Center where she had spent the previous two hours as a result of an allergic reaction.

She had been rowing in the warm New England fall on the Connecticut River with her crew team, eaten dinner, and returned to her dorm room. Then she felt the onset of the familiar abdominal pains, rash, and nausea.

The anticipation of Kelly's first allergic reaction at college was, for me, the most terrifying part of her departure. I had recurring nightmares about receiving a panicked phone call from her in the middle of a reaction, no EpiPen at hand, miles from nowhere on a Nordic trail, screaming, "Mom, help me!" and I was 2,000 miles away. I knew I would keep having that dream until the real moment came.

Fortunately, Kelly had handled it well. She told me she had quickly swallowed her medications, grabbed four friends to go with her to the college's Health Center, where she was dispatched in an ambulance to the Emergency Room at the hospital. She was alive and well, if not exactly kicking.

I felt a sudden shift in the responsibilities. She was now in charge of her health, not me. I wouldn't be there to hold her hand when they put the IV into her arm in the ER, flooding her veins with epinephrine and prednisone. She was the one who was going to call National Jewish Medical Center in the morning and discuss her case with them, not me. And that meant that, down the road, she would be the one responsible for her life, not me.

And I knew that was exactly how it was supposed be, but I was still not quite ready to accept it.

Time to head to the shower....

October 11

Our days have a ritualistic quality about them, full and simple...

Walk around the island loop

Soak in the hot tub and watch the ferries pass by, in the morning, at dusk or sometimes both

Dinghy over to the Doctor's Office for coffee and pick up the daily newspapers

Workout on the exercise bike

Do dreaded paper work, make phone calls to friends and family

Go to town for lunch and/or more errands

See an occasional late afternoon movie

Cook a gourmet dinner or eat at a local restaurant

Watch TV, usually a recorded episode of the latest "Best New Show on Television"

Get the latest college report from Kelly

Go to bed

...and boring. I missed having goals. I missed my Aspen friends.

And I really missed my kid.

October 12

Today was Lakedale reconnaissance day. A year ago last April, John and I exchanged some apartment buildings we owned on the outskirts of Portland, Oregon for a resort called Lakedale on the San Juan Islands. The Portland apartments were in constant need of repair and there was nothing sexy about replacing dry-rotted siding with new plastic shingles. So John scoured the Northwest and discovered Lakedale, an eighty-acre oasis of towering fir trees, verdant meadows, and three swimming lakes in the heart of San Juan Island, ripe for the picking. Or so he thought.

The resort consisted of 120 campsites, a new ten-room log lodge, and seven rustic log cabins that cozily accommodated four adults and a passel of kids. The Seattle management firm we hired to manage the resort projected a rosy economic scenario after a few years of seasoning. The best part was the fact that it was an over-the-top beautiful piece of land and John had never met a piece of land he didn't like. It was also a quick commute from our island home, so Lakedale seemed like a reasonable economic adventure. John reasoned with me, "...and don't worry, honey, if things don't work out here, we'll just sell everything and move to Lakedale!" *Right-o! Me and 400 campers using the communal restrooms. But, as they say, for better or worse.*

John soon discovered the monthly commute to Lakedale wore thin, especially in the middle of winter. His body overheated when he wore wool sweaters in the dry cold of

Colorado's snowy months, but in the bone-chilling Northwest winter he needed four layers of wool underneath his down jacket to stay warm while boating from Brown Island to Friday Harbor. A wool fisherman's cap protected his tender ears and scalp.

Lakedale's revenue projections proved far less accurate than anticipated. We decided to try to jump start them by analyzing what we could do with the design to enhance the Lakedale experience and as a result increase the bottom line. The aging washrooms, originally a concession stand, had been given a new coat of paint at the beginning of the summer, but they were in need of much more maintenance. Spiders spun sticky webs in every corner, faucets dripped, fluorescent light fixtures flickered uncertainly and the fresh paint had been scratched off to impart intellectual messages starting with the letter "F". This was not a Four Seasons encounter.

In the cabins, gigantic futons with brown, patterned upholstery dominated the log living rooms. The futons rested on brown, patterned area rugs. Adjacent were mismatched side chairs. I had found a goal. Revitalize Lakedale with an attractive, yet affordable, design.

October 13

In our late night Kelly Chat, she reminded us that the upcoming days were Dartmouth's Homecoming Weekend.

Not revealing that I had the entire Homecoming schedule memorized from scouring daily the Dartmouth website, I asked, "What's happening?"

"This is the weekend we build a gigantic bonfire in the middle of the green and all of the freshmen run around it the same number of times as their class year."

I asked if it was ten times, to correspond to her class year of 2010.

"Well, it's either ten or a hundred and ten," she said, "they haven't decided yet. And I have to wear some wild clothes that the crew team is going to get us. There are a ton of cool events happening, the football game is against Holy Cross, and then there's the soccer game against Harvard, so I'll be pretty busy." In four years of high school her social life had consisted of attending two football games, no soccer games, and an occasional movie with girlfriends. This was a definite improvement.

"Didn't you say you have midterms next week?" I said.

"Oh, right...but I think I did pretty well on my bio quiz last week, so that should be okay. The appalling (*appalling?)* part is that our calculus professor is not letting us use calculators or formula sheets, how bad is that?"

"Have a great time sweetie, and try not to wear polyester near the fire—you never know about sparks flying around from those things." *Will I ever learn to shut up?* On the positive side, at least I didn't tell her about the bonfire I'd read about at Texas A&M in 1999 that collapsed and killed twelve students.

We missed viewing the Dartmouth bonfire on the college web cam, aimed at the Green from its perch atop the Baker Library tower, because we went to a late afternoon showing of Martin Scorsese's most recent film, *The Departed*. We should have watched the bonfire instead...even with a massive disaster there would have been fewer bloody bodies in Dartmouth than Martin managed to kill off in two and a half hours of screen time.

I turned on the web cam after we returned to the island from Lakedale, John driving the dinghy cautiously as he tried to avoid buoys in the dense fog. The bonfire was still burning and a few hardy souls were walking across the Green, but no sign of Kelly. The night was still young and as the web cam didn't extend to Webster Avenue, alias frat row, I had to assume she was safely there, enjoying campus life.

October 15

On a late August afternoon, Kelly and I had hauled two of our kayaks behind a golf cart from the Brown Island marina to our house. The dry and dusty road swirled plumes of dirt up my nose and onto every surface. Today's hauling trip back to the marina was the polar opposite. John drove the golf cart while I shivered in the rear, clutching the bow of the kayak between my legs, its stern attached to a set of rolling wheels trailing behind the cart. This time the island road was damp, and the deep blue of the kayak was a study in color wheel contrast to the brilliant orange maple leaves, the size of elephant's feet, that whirled under the golf cart's wheels. Kelso galloped alongside, chasing life.

I continued my afternoon's exertion by spinning on the exercise bike while watching the Food Network. It was Guinness World Record Week. I watched as the record for most number of pancakes cooked in an hour (555 to be exact) was set.

The phone rang and in a raspy voice Kelly recounted her weekend's activities, from the bonfire (110 laps around with the Nordic team, dressed in a sports bra and green spandex tights), to the frat house dance parties, to the football game against Holy Cross (which Dartmouth lost in overtime), to crew races against the alumni. She was exhausted.

In high school we had been her official pacemakers, helping her schedule activities, and reining her in when we knew she needed rest. Obviously, she was in need of some help. Her conversation darted haphazardly from one topic to another, but with a little prodding I unearthed the fact that she had been to the original *Animal House* fraternity, Alpha Delta Phi. A Dartmouth grad who had been a member of that august body had written stories based on his experiences that eventually became the movie.

"Don't worry, mom, I won't be back. It was truly disgusting!"

"Why is that?" I asked.

"There was a gutter along the base of one entire wall that the fraternity brothers pee into and there was a hole in one corner to puke in!"

This was far too much information for me. I had been willing to give Kelly some leeway on her college journey, but I was honestly starting to worry if she could break out of the "freshman freak-out" period and succeed. Midterms were next week, after all.

And then she emailed photos of Homecoming Weekend.

Standing arm-in-arm with friends in front of the bonfire (a three-story tall structure that looked like it was fabricated from oversized Lincoln Logs) in their Dartmouth green 2010 sweatshirts, wearing hard-hats from building the bonfire and looking like they owned the world.

The hell with academics, let her have some fun.

October 16

Although the siren song of Aspen was calling, leaving Brown Island at the end of summer was, as always, like leaving the arms of a new lover...I haven't had enough, it tears me apart to leave, and I don't know when we'll be together again. This was the first time I was ready to exit the warm embrace, the romance having settled into a long-term affair. John and I were driving back to Colorado for the winter.

We stopped for gas and a coffee at one of the numerous coffee kiosks lining the Washington State highway system. As I exited the car to buy our cappuccinos, the strong odor of gasoline overpowered the aroma of coffee. John peered underneath the car to see gas spewing from the tank.

"Get away from the car!" he warned.

"But I have to get the dog...and my computer!" I said.

"Don't touch anything, it may ignite a spark and blow up!" John was panicked. I felt like I was in an episode of Law and Order with the law enforcement officers closing in on us, shackling our wrists as they dragged us screaming from the car, and then watching as the car exploded, our dog trapped inside, incinerated by the massive blast fueled by the gas pumps.

Fortunately, I had my cell phone in my pocket, so I ran fifty yards from the car and called the Land Rover dealer to politely ask what would cause a gas tank to burst. The service manager reassured me that we wouldn't blow up, but cautioned us to fill the gas tank only three-quarters full until we returned home, when we should bring it in to the dealership. His advice was hardly comforting with 2,000 miles yet to drive.

Listening the entire time for pre-explosive noises, we drove an hour north to Blaine on the way to an appointment with the Canadian and U.S. customs departments to get Nexus cards. The cards were sort of a border-crossing honor-badge. They would allow us to cross the border with just a phone call, which would no doubt prove helpful, since keeping landings at docks to a minimum was now a marital imperative.

The intense questioning from the barrel-chested, dour and bald Canadian customs agent made is feel like hardened criminals. He was the antithesis of the American agent, who was thin, jovial and nearing retirement age.

"Have you ever been arrested?"

"Of course not!" I laughed. The Canadian glared at me.

"How many other names have you used? Have you ever been convicted of a DUI? Do you know where your children are? And your dog?" He carefully went through a list of items that were forbidden to take across the border, such as apples, cherries or beef. "And if you are caught with even one apple, you will be banned from the Nexus list for life! 1,200 people were banned last year alone." He stared at us again. John's lack of hair seemed to carry more weight than my Canadian birth. My husband appeared to be immune from the agent's ire and even eked a smile out of him.

Relieved to have our Nexus cards in hand, we drove south. Almost forgetting about the potential fireball beneath us we detoured to Chuckanut Drive, a scenic two-lane road just past Bellingham, where in early "280" days we had eaten a memorable lunch that involved oysters.

That café was closed now, but a mile farther down the road we found The Oyster Bar, a wooden structure cantilevered over the oyster beds of Samish Bay. With immaculate white tablecloths and an expansive view, it was treehouse dining at its best.

We began the meal with a glass of Muscadet which we paired with a dozen Kumamoto and Samish Bay oysters. Then we shared a roasted beet salad. For the entrée we each ate a King crab napoleon, a tower constructed of whisper-thin layers of mango and avocado, roasted starfruit, crowned with sweet King crab meat, with a delicate vanilla vinaigrette on top.

The Oyster Bar King Crab Stack

Yeild: 4 servings

1 LARGE MANGO
(PEELED AND SLICED ABOUT ¼-INCH THICK)
1 LARGE AVOCADO
(PEELED AND SLICED ABOUT ¼-INCH THICK)
1 POUND KING CRAB (COOKED)
½ CUP WATERCRESS LEAVES
VANILLA BEAN VINAIGRETTE (RECIPE FOLLOWS)

Layer two rows each of mango and avocado in four 3-inch ring molds, starting with the mango on bottom and finishing with the avocado on top. Fill the leftover space in the ring mold with king crab meat. Place serving dish over ring mold, carefully flip over and lift ring mold away from dish. Top with watercress and drizzle with vanilla bean vinaigrette.

Vanilla Bean Vinaigrette

1 TABLESPOON LIME JUICE
1 TABLESPOON ORANGE JUICE
3 TABLESPOONS RICE WINE VINEGAR
½ TABLESPOON BLACK PEPPER
½ CUP CANOLA OIL
¼ CUP OLIVE OIL
1 TEASPOON VANILLA BEAN
(PULP SCRAPED FROM THE INSIDE OF THE BEAN ONLY)

Whisk lime juice, orange juice, rice wine vinegar and black pepper together and slowly add the oils to emulsify, then whisk in the vanilla bean pulp.

It was too bad we had to inhale the meal in half an hour in order to catch our ferry. The food was so deftly prepared and sophisticated, it would have created a food buzz in a big city restaurant. I stopped in the restroom on the way out, and being in a state of food rapture, felt it was my obligation to pick up a paper towel from the floor of the otherwise spotless lady's room, in partial thanks for such exceptional cuisine.

This was probably the same compulsion that drove me to buy misshapen red peppers (and some other odd-shaped vegetables) while I was grocery shopping. What a waste for the plants to have taken someone's time and energy to cultivate, taken space in the earth's rich soil, and then been discarded for no reason other than cosmetics. Kind of like people. People who are afraid to be that glorious, imperfect, sweet red pepper, the one that tastes a whole lot better.

Our goal today was to reach the west coast of Washington, midway down the Olympic Rain Forest peninsula. We drove through flat green farm fields dotted with ruminating cows and leaves still changing on the birch trees. We reached the Keystone ferry at the foot of Whidbey Island with no time to spare, claiming the last space on the three o'clock boat. I had called the Kalaloch Lodge in America three days ago to ward off any unpleasant lodging surprises, being midweek in October after all, and was assured they had availability and loved dogs.

The ocean front cabins were rustic, like don't-walk-barefoot-on-the-carpets rustic, but they did have wood-burning fireplaces, hot water, and an onsite restaurant that we walked to through the dusky drizzle.

October 17

Kalaloch was sweating under a blanket of rain and fog. John set a fire in the brick fireplace, we drank tepid push-button lattes from the general store, and I started my new book club read while John scanned the first of his three daily newspapers. He didn't read many books, but he was religious about reading current events, and he often recited excerpts he found interesting to me, which I occasionally ignored.

Later in the day, as we drove south down the peninsula, we saw that the sides of the highway had been shorn of major trees. Through the heavy mist we glimpsed the aftermath of a logged forest, strewn with thirty foot high piles of log debris. Some were burning, some smoldering. A string of miniature hell fires decorated the two-lane road.

At Ruby Beach we detoured for a walk, crossing large, flat river rocks slick with moisture. The beach was strewn with carcasses of trees. Kelso ran like a puppy on steroids through the water, legs splayed, tongue flapping, with a huge dog grin on his face. He was so excited that we stopped for another excursion a few miles farther down the highway.

We entered an adjacent beach via a trail that wandered through a forest of spruce and burls. I envisioned Harry Potter and his pal Hagrid emerging from between the tall, thin spruce trees, the grotesque blobs scattered on their trunks. Some were crowned with ferns like feathers on a fancy lady's hat. Our umbrellas didn't protect us from the relentless humidity, so our jeans were soaked when we returned to the car, and the pungent smell of wet dog scented the air.

It was nearing four o'clock when we passed the Ocean Crest Resort. John sensed that he had once stayed there. Even though it was still shy of our anticipated destination of Ocean Shores about twenty miles away, in true "280" style we stopped. We discovered they had available rooms, were dog friendly and had a 5- star restaurant on the premises. We were skeptical, but after inspecting six rooms to find the perfect floor plan (a favorite pastime denied us on our journey to the island due to the completely full occupancies) we settled in.

While we ate dinner, wind and rain howled outside the restaurant's windows, whipping the firs into a frenzied tango, but the meal was delicious. The clam chowder was easily as good as that of Legal Sea Foods', with an unusual pink color and an unusual ingredient (evaporated milk). John's newspaper scouring had revealed that spinach was safe to eat again after a recent recall, so he ordered a spinach salad, strewn with strawberries, applewood-smoked bacon and mushrooms. The bow-tied sommelier recommended a bottle of Oregon Chehalem 2002 Ian's Reserve Chardonnay, a complicated lemon-scented wine, to complement our entrees of curried scallops and seared halibut. Lastly John, possessor of the family sweet tooth, ordered bananas foster crowned with puff pastry and a huge white tongue of Madagascar vanilla ice cream. I hadn't officially begun a diet yet, but the starting line was looming closer.

Grandma's Ocean Crest Clam Chowder

Yeild 4 servings

- 1 CUP DICED POTATOES
- 2 CUPS WATER
- ⅓ CUP DICED ONIONS
- 1 TEASPOON SEASONING SALT
- ⅓ CUP DICED CELERY
- 2 SLICES BACON (CHOPPED)
- 2 (6½ OUNCE) CANS CHOPPED CLAMS
- 1 (12 OUNCE) CAN CARNATION EVAPORATED MILK
- OYSTER CRACKERS

Cook vegetables and bacon in water with seasoning salt (a salt, pepper, onion powder and granulated garlic combination works well).

When vegetables are tender and water has been absorbed, add clams including liquid. Pour into a 13"x 9" baking dish and chill in the refrigerator (chowder base should be no more than 2 inches deep).

Once chilled, place in crock pot or double boiler and mix in Carnation evaporated milk. Heat on low to medium for 1 to 2 hours but do not boil (the longer you heat the chowder, the more the sugars in the milk will caramelize which delivers a bisque-like flavor).

Pour hot chowder into warmed bowls and serve with oyster crackers.

October 18

"Hi Mommy." From the demoralized tone of her voice, I knew immediately that Kelly was off her happy Dartmouth feed. Her first set of midterms had begun, and my initial impression was that they were not going well. "I've only had one, and it was math, and not so good." There was no sparkle in her voice at all.

"It can't be that bad, and it's only the midterm," I said in my optimistic Mom voice.

"Well, let's put it this way...we couldn't use our calculators, we had no formula sheets, and I sucked."

"How badly did you suck?" This was not an expression I usually encouraged her to use, but now was not a good time to correct minor linguistic infractions.

"Let's just say that with the curve, I got a C and I'm happy for that." *Whoa, she had never had a C in her life, she must be in a state of shock.*

I asked, "Do you remember last year when your high school buddy was in her first term at Carleton College and her mom told me that she had never worked harder to get a B than she did in her biology class?"

"...I know." I could tell she wasn't convinced but she wanted to believe that it would be OK. I recognized that this was a new experience for her, she needed to figure out how the system worked, adjust to it, and that it was part of the learning process. You know, it's all about being a life-long learner.

> 8:56 p.m. hey mom, forgot to ask how the pooch is doing? give him a big hug for me!
>
> 9:17 p.m. do you think I should get some more highlights in my hair, its starting to look a little dull...is that something i have to pay for out of my budget or do you want to??? hint, hint, love ya! Kelly
>
> 11:01 p.m. did I tell you about the paper I'm writing for bio? think its going to be really good...sweet dreams!

October 19

A good night's sleep hadn't cured the coast's drizzles, but the Ocean Crest's breakfast of a tower of avocado, house-smoked salmon and scrambled egg topped with crème fraiche added some culinary sunshine. Soon after we were driving down the coast and for about thirty miles we debated which direction to take. South along the coast meant more rain, while going east meant sunshine and a city stop in Portland. City and sun won.

As we drove through hazy valleys filled with poplar trees turning the color of lazy marigolds, the sun appeared, returning my curly permed hair to its normal frizzless state.

The Riverplace Hotel sits on the banks of the Willamette River in the heart of Portland, America's most environmentally-conscious city. The hotel rated four stars, had plenty of vacancies and they loved dogs, even providing Kelso with his own ceramic water bowl on a tray atop a starched white napkin, with two gigantic dog biscuits on the side.

We abandoned Kelso to have a drink in the upscale bar. John sipped a Hendrick's martini, up, dry, two slices of cucumber please, and I ordered a mango mojito. We felt like adults again, our furry "child" out of sight.

I'd been worried all day about Kelly's low morale, calculus, her other midterms, and conjured up doomsday scenarios that I didn't know how to solve. I really needed that mojito.

"John, what if she flunks out?"

He said, "So what, it's part of her education."

"Flunking out? What are you talking about? After everything she did to get admitted to Dartmouth, how can you even utter those words?"

"She'll figure it out."

By now the mojito had kicked in and my mood was significantly altered. She'd be fine—so what if she did ended up working the La Marzzoco machine at Starbucks? What about the Peace Corps, did you have to have a college degree for the Peace Corps? She loves dogs. Dog walker? I was back on the empty nester road again. All that training we had drilled into her for the past eighteen years would work, I was sure of it. *I'll have another, bartender!*

When we returned to the room, my cell phone rang...it was Kelly.

"Hey guys, how are you?"

"Suuuuuuuuuperb, honey!" I said, major mango relaxed. "How did you do today?"

"Great! Bio went better than usual and I think I did really well in anthro. Five short essays, and they were easier and shorter than I thought they'd be. Just wanted to let you know. I have to catch a nap now, I was up until 1:30 studying last night. Oh, and I thought I'd go to Boston this weekend to the Head of the Charles races with some girls from my crew team, is that OK with you?"

"Sounds like great fun," I said. It still pleasantly surprised me when she asked our permission to do something, half a continent away. "Have a great time, and watch out for those Hahhhhvahhhhd boys!"

October 20

In the past twenty years, the riverfront in Portland has been rejuvenated—bridges rebuilt, walkways installed, and more of the city's famous ever-flowing water fountains positioned to hydrate pedestrians.

Like Seattle, there are espresso bars everywhere. After a two-hour morning walk along the river, I stopped at Tutto Bella to purchase two coffee drinks to energize John and I for the next stage of the drive. The foam on my cappuccino was ultra-smooth and creamy, so I complimented the barista and we were soon chatting coffee. He was excited because that afternoon he was competing in the *Northwest Regional Barista Competition,* the precursor to the Barista Olympics to be held in Long Beach later in the year.

"All the best baristas in the Northwest will be there," he said. "They have fifteen minutes to prepare four standard coffee drinks and one signature drink, all while talking nonstop with the emcee about coffee."

I knew what we'd be doing this morning. I speed-showered and hustled John and Kelso out the door to the Wonder Ballroom, in a tree- lined neighborhood east of the Willamette River. We bribed Kelso with some biscuits and raced to the ballroom entrance, anticipating huge crowds and plenty of the free coffee drinks the Tutta Bella barista had promised. There were a handful of people milling around the booths lining the old restored dance hall, free samples of coffee beans, breath mints, and brochures that expounded the benefits of coffee, but there was virtually no one in the audience's folding chairs, and worse, not a soul manning the four illuminated espresso stations center stage. John, who was not as excited about this expedition as I was, asked a bystander when the competition started.

"One o'clock," was the reply. "You only have to wait an hour and forty five minutes!" With the prospect of at least 400 miles to drive I knew we didn't have that much time to spare, so John bought a t-shirt, we gathered up a handful of samples, and we were soon back on the road again.

"Honey, what do you think about going to Long Beach in the spring?"

No answer.

We lunched in the Columbia Gorge Hotel dining room, famous for their two foot high waterfall of syrup which poured onto breakfast pancakes—but not so famous for their clam chowder.

After eating we headed towards Baker City, which was about half the way back to Aspen. We were going to stay at the historic Geiser Grand Hotel. An old Beach Boys song about the end of summer blared from the radio as we drove through the barren landscape of eastern Oregon.

October 21

I could taste the cold as I woke. The ancient hotel had no heat to battle the first regiment of winter's chilly army. The equally frosty attendant who delivered our room service breakfast warned us that the temperature outside was a bitter eighteen degrees. We snagged our coffees at the Coffee Corral, washed the car, and headed down the highway for another long day on the road.

Midway through Idaho we turned off the interstate to meet our friends Bob and Chris for a leisurely lunch at their new home. Bob is the managing partner of our wine import venture, and he has the amazing ability to taste a clot of dirt from a vineyard and tell you precisely what grape grows there. Seven years ago, he and Chris planted two acres of Syrah grapes in Hagerman. They carefully tended them in every moment they could carve away from the wine company. He had hoped to garner enough profit from the grapes to retire from the wine business, but in three out of the last seven years the crop had frozen and there were no grapes to sell.

"Maybe I should have planted Riesling," he said while we ate. "Hey, John, have you ever considered going into the grape business?"

After two bottles of wine at lunch and some off-key singing of *You Can Eat Crackers In My Bed Anytime* in the car, we thought it might be wise to stop driving for the night. We found a brand new Super Eight Motel and a local pizza place that delivered a pizza as good in its own way as the pizza from Pizzeria Regina. This pizza had soul, Regina's had finesse, but both were equally good.

October 22

Like a horse heading back to the barn, once we were within an eight-hour drive of Aspen, we were ready to get home quickly. We were up at dawn and on the road again. Over the radio the Mormon Tabernacle Choir serenaded on the Sunday morning drive through Salt Lake City, home of the fastest drivers in the west. We stopped in Salina at Mom's Cafe, whose claim to fame was a write-up in Gourmet magazine in 1997. Teal-clad waitresses matched the teal-clad booths, and served homemade fare like chicken-fried steak, patty melts and Indian fry bread which we ate drizzled with honey butter squeezed from a bottle.

Rusty colored mesas and drippy hoodoos stonily observed from afar the parade of trucks and cars carried by I-70 as it wove its way across the broad plains. Small green junipers were the only visible sign of life other than an occasional pocket of orange-clad fall hunters gathered around their trailers by the side of the road, ready to hunt for elk. Utah couldn't have been a starker contrast to the flourishing emerald wetness of the Northwest. We pulled off the highway at Spotted Wolf Canyon so I could relieve John at the wheel and it was there we discovered the San Rafael Swell.

According to my trusty AAA guidebook, "the Swell is an oval shaped uplifted area of layered rocks - geologically termed an anticline - about 75 by 40 miles in extent, most of which has been eroded away, forming the mostly flat central plateau, while the strata at the edges are left exposed and angled near vertically (the San Rafael Reef); here are found most of the spectacular canyons." It was spectacular—barren, lifeless, red and beautiful.

Aspen was within shouting distance of the highway as it joined the Colorado River by Fruita, just outside of Grand Junction. The river was draped on both sides with a lush cloak of golden cottonwoods, which changed the river's usual hue of blue into a stream of gold, painting the entire valley floor with a beautiful intenseness usually reserved for the final aria of a Puccini opera. Farther up the Roaring Fork Valley, trees shed their color and exposed naked grey branches which looked like anorexic arms reaching for the cold.

On McClain Flats road, five hundred feet below the elevation of our house, snow was on the ground. "Sticking," John said. "Winter is here."

Kelso walked into Kelly's room and headed straight for the closet. I peered in. The room was painfully empty, the absence of its occupant as real as the scraggly junipers clinging to life on the ledge of a Utah canyon.

October 23

Monday morning arrived and John and I both had cases of "mountain nose." This was our friend Jayne's term for the phenomenon peculiar to dry mountain climates, in which you woke up, blew your nose, and a piece of organic matter the size of a small elephant stampeded out. I stared disgustedly at the elephant and wondered how it ever fit inside my sinus cavity.

I walked past Kelly's bedroom on the way to the kitchen to brew a cup of coffee. I kept expecting her to pop up, but there was no sign of her in the house. It was glaringly apparent that it was time for some radical new thinking. When Kelly was growing up, there didn't seem to be a need to define goals, classify outcomes, or elucidate objectives. She was the goal, the outcome, the reason for doing whatever I did, whether it was copying spelling sheets for her first grade teacher, traveling to Mesa Verde with the fourth grade class (who all caught the flu and upchucked their way through the cliff dwellings), designing and building the sets for the sixth grade play, or, when she was in high school, becoming the head of the district accountability committee (a full-time and unpaid suicide-provoking position). This agenda was perhaps not the politically correct career path for a mother with an MBA who had enjoyed a high-powered career, but I didn't care.

I didn't think, I did. I defined myself as Kelly's mom. Maybe setting some goals would give me the focus that had been on autopilot for so many years…or maybe it was time not to set goals and just see what happened. I decided to err on the side of having goals, but not worrying about the outcomes—the best of both worlds. After careful consideration, I settled on eight easily accomplishable goals:

> Goal #1: Lose fifteen pounds and get down to high school fighting weight. Not being an aficionado of scales, I didn't know exactly how much I weighed, but since John had gained five pounds after leaving the island, I couldn't be far behind. Plus, I had needed to lose a few pounds before we left. I would diet this week and get on the scale next Monday.
>
> Goal #2: Break a sweat every day. I gleaned this valuable piece of exercise information from a *People* magazine interview with Matthew McConaughey. It seemed to work for him, so

hopefully I could lose inches as well. Three inches per thigh would be ideal.

Goal #3: Print all the photos from my last five years of digital photography and put them into photo albums.

Goal #4: Redesign the facilities at Lakedale.

Goal #5: Find a gallery to show my artwork.

Goal #6: Do enough artwork to get into the above gallery.

Goal #7: Finish the Christmas wreath needlepoint pillow I started seven years ago. Have it ready to hang on the front door by next Christmas.

Goal #8: Start a personal contest for the Best Clam Chowder in America. Current contenders were from the Lime Kiln Café at Roche Harbor (where we had had lunch before leaving the island), Legal Sea Foods', and Ocean Crest, in that order.

Goal #9: Eliminate my foot fungus.

I figured these ought to keep me seriously busy.

October 24

I stopped carrying my cell phone whenever I was out of reach of a landline. I knew I would talk to Kelly most days, but if we missed a day, it wouldn't be the end of civilization, which in the United States just before the midterm elections was not so civil. I decided to call Kelly to settle on dates for her flight home for the Christmas holidays.

"Hey, Mom," she was huffing and puffing, "I'm on my way to crew practice—how are you?"

"Great," I said. "I'm really happy to be back in Aspen."

I had to admit it's home, even though the island is a lot more real. I love the fact that everywhere I go in Aspen, I know someone and have some history. I'll probably be hiking up Buttermilk Mountain with my petrified girlfriends when I'm eighty.

"Well, I'm glad you're feel good, because I have a little something to run by you." *Pregnancy, illicit drug use, an "F" in calculus?*

"There is a crew camp right after finals, and I love crew and really want to go, and it's in Miami and I have to let the coach know today if I'm going!" *Whew…nothing serious.* I asked her when the crew camp would take place.

"I'll check with the coach today, but I think it's from December sixth until the tenth." *OK, I can deal with that, she'll improve her crew technique, get some sun, and be home just a few days late. We'll still have three weeks with her at Christmas.*

"OK, just let me know today, so I can make the reservations for your trip out here," I said.

"Will do, love ya, Mom!"

She called back after practice, informed me that she had told the coach she was going, and that the dates were a little different than she had originally thought. It was now December seventh until the fifteenth.

"December fifteenth?" I winced. My brain did the math and I knew I was getting screwed. John and I had anticipated having her all to ourselves for a good long month, time to get all the gory details about college life, time to go to the movies, and to chat in the hot tub as the snow flew while we watched the Christmas lights in town below, time to…*buck up, you wimp!*

"OK, hon," I said," sounds good. I'll check with United."

"Thanks, Mom! Love you, bye."

October 25

Dinner tonight was with the Gourmet Group we had been invited to join last spring. The purpose of the group was to prepare a themed dinner at one member's home every month. The host couple prepared the main course and the rest of the group contributed appetizers, side dishes and dessert. And could these couples cook!

This time it was spur of the moment, so we decided just to meet for drinks and then to go to an Italian restaurant. After the group had downed a few martinis and some wine in our host's new underground pub, replete with pool table, card table, theater room, dartboard and fireplace, the Italian eatery was scratched in favor of pool and appetizers. We caught up on everyone's recent travels: the Bahamas, the Mediterranean and a run-in with a TSA agent in Las Vegas who had confiscated an obscene quantity of expensive make-up all figured into the evening's discussion. Sometimes I wasn't quite sure how we fit in. Since a blizzard swirled outside, and John had minor surgery to remove a pin in his knee from a previous operation scheduled the next day, we left on the early side.

October 26

At daybreak, the roads hadn't yet been cleared by the snowplow, so we slid our way down the hill through six inches of fresh powder on the way to the hospital. John was his usual perky morning self when I dropped him off, but I needed caffeine to be dragged into consciousness. I drove to town for coffee at our favorite espresso bar, and then headed home.

Posted on the side of our subdivision's gatehouse was the annual notice warning residents to lock their trash in bear-proof containers and secure their doors, as the bears were out in full force so they could feed before they hibernated for the winter. Having had bears in our kitchen more than once, we knew that their favorite foods were ice cream, sweetened breakfast cereal and butter. The guard on duty mentioned that one homeowner (eighty percent of the homes are secondary residences, and most homeowners are city-dwellers) had just tried to board a plane in Chicago with a loaded shotgun in order to be prepared for the scavenging bears when they raided his home. I bet airport security probably had more fun with him than with the expensive cosmetic bag.

I had just finished sweating through fifty minutes on the exercise bike, part of Goal #2, when the hospital called and said John was ready to go home. I slid down the hill again and prepared for a few days of nursing duty.

> 5:02 p.m. hi Kelly! working hard here, had a ton of snow last night, and it has been snowing all day. looks like a good winter shaping up! we have eight inches on the ground so far! i transferred $$$ to your account today as you were down to $56...books appear to be expensive. here is what you spent (I'd give you the info as to how to get online and check yourself, but it's tied to all of our accounts and I'm not sure i want that info disseminated around the dorm. if it somehow got out to a math whiz and he pilfered all our funds and sent us into bankruptcy, you wouldn't be at dartmouth - sorry for the digression!) luv ya lots! Mom
>
> PS. am going to the new warren miller movie on saturday with jayne and fred and...Lacy! will try to get the 411 on how college is going for her!

October 27

My patient relieved me of nursing duty for a few hours to attend a coffee for my friend Gail, who was running for a Colorado State Senate seat currently occupied by a "good old boy" potato farmer. Gail had boundless energy. She had helped started a foundation to raise money to benefit the public schools, been appointed to The Commission on Higher Education at the state level by the governor, and was now a Regent for the University of Colorado. She had spent the past six months canvassing the district (which encompassed a swath of 17,000 miles) to drum up support for her vision of change in the statehouse. In the months since I had last heard her speak, she had transformed herself into a true politician, able to dissect meaty issues and graciously request donations to fund her quest.

In the spirit of the event, I agreed to make some phone calls and pound the pavement to "Get Out The Vote for Gail" in the election. Of course I wanted to support Gail, but I also wanted to get back into the social swing of things and catch up with my friends. It seemed a small price to pay for a good get-together, even if it did involve politics.

October 28

Three positive reasons for Kelly to go to college (besides academics):

> No piles of books, sweatshirts, and miscellaneous junk on the kitchen counter where she used to do her homework.
>
> Only two loads of laundry to do each week, instead of three.
>
> Lower Chinese food bill.

> 10:12 p.m. guess what, a new issue of *People* magazine arrived today, yippee! thanks for the subscription! love and kisses, your literary mother (please don't send the national enquirer, it would ruin my intellectual reputation.)

October 29

Every year, as autumn fades and winter readies its icy siege, the Warren Miller Movie comes to town. Skiers and snowboarders await the event as anxiously as children anticipate the coming of the circus, for it means that soon the snow will arrive.

Warren's traveling road show (Warren had retired to Orcas Island in the San Juan Islands a few years ago) filled the Wheeler Opera House to capacity for six shows. Everyone in town attended at least one, welcoming each other back after off-season trips to Mexico and Moab and talking about next week's ski swap and the new ski gear they planned to purchase.

I tagged along with Jayne, Fred, Leif (their son and Kelly's "adopted" brother) and Lacy, who had returned home from CU for the weekend. She good-naturedly endured my weepy hug. John stayed at home to protect his tender knee from the crowds. We filled out raffle forms for the prize giveaway to be held at intermission and settled into Miller's *Off the Grid*. Daredevil skiers jumped off cliffs in Alaska, snowboarders materialized from chest deep powder in Utah, and extreme athletes taught astounded native children in Kashmir to ski, all to the ear-splitting pulse of rock and roll.

At dinner, I pressed Lacy for a few details about university life, which she seemed to be enjoying, though not with the same wild abandon as Kelly. She had returned to Aspen every weekend and I had to bite my tongue not to tell her to stay at school and have some fun, but, as Jayne says, she'll learn to fly one feather at a time.

October 30

Weigh-in day. I can't imagine what monstrous number the scale would have registered had I weighed in last Monday before my week of careful eating and religious exercising. My daily workout consisted of frantic pedaling on the stationary bicycle, then half an hour on the Nordic track, all the while watching cooking shows on tape like The Next Food Network Star and Iron Chef America. Seeing chefs sear puff pastry on the grill and braise wild boar had to temporarily replace the actual eating of gourmet fare. A strenuous afternoon walk with Kelso rounded out my exercise regime.

October 31

A few days before Halloween, Kelly requested I send some flair, Dartmouth's term for the brightly colored (neon was especially popular) and unstylish clothing worn while participating in college social events. As I was rummaging through the storage closet, I realized this would be the first time in eighteen years I wouldn't be sewing a Halloween costume for her. I got a twinge in my heart as I came to realize that that part of my life was over. Some holidays are just quintessentially about kids, like Halloween as well as Christmas and Easter (the egg part). It was a good thing I was in the closet under the stairs where I could have a good solitary cry.

I usually buy a few bags of Halloween candy for trick-or-treaters, but having never had one (living twenty minutes outside of town in a gated community wasn't conducive to drop-in guests) I skipped even that formality this year. Jayne and Fred had invited us to celebrate in town with them, dressed as pirates, but John still wasn't ready to expose his knee to rowdy Aspen revelers, so we were enjoying dinner in front of the TV when the phone rang.

"Hi Mommy." Since I had only one child, I figured the scratchy sound coming out of the receiver had to be Kelly.

"Kelly, what's wrong with your voice?" I asked.

"Well, I have a cold, but it's a lot better than it was a few days ago," she said…we hadn't spoken in almost three days, a new record. "I can barely understand you! Have you been to the health center?"

"Mom, it's all right," she croaked, "although the health center is useless. I'm taking Tylenol and Benadryl."

I asked her how long she had been sick.

"Just a few days. It got worse when I went to crew practice a couple of days ago at five in the morning. We were having a practice race, so if I hadn't gone, the entire team wouldn't have been able to row."

Five in the morning? Was this truly my daughter, the one who loved to sleep in until noon? She was doing this voluntarily?

"How long were you out there?"

"Oh, the usual, two hours. But it was raining the whole time, so that could have been part of the problem." *Holy Jesus, mother Mary…I might have to convert to Catholicism to get through the next four years.*

"It's OK though, because we won. And then I went back to my dorm and slept for three hours. Don't worry."

There wasn't much I could do but worry.

> 10:42 p.m. forgot to ask you this, but the Nordic team doesn't provide wax for skiing, so i have to buy about ten dollars worth. is that ok? hope so! here's another question, whether or not to buy the team spandex, its $175. yikes! and also, a fleece or something? oh, i went to the trainer today and she thinks I have tendonitis in my knee, so she told me to do some stretches/ice and take advil twice a day. should i? is tylenol anti-inflammatory? love you!
>
> Kelly

10: 51 p.m. i don't think you can race in your aspen RED spandex, given that dartmouth's color is green, so go ahead and get the dartmouth spandex, and a fleece or warmup, whatever the team wears. why don't you wait on taking the advil until we can figure out if it affects your allergy situation? according to my tylenol box, it's good for muscular aches, but you need to be careful because if you have three or more drinks per day, it causes liver damage! hint, hint.

xoxoxoxoxoxo

mums

p.s. try some hot lemonade for your cold...old Canadian remedy!

11:01 p.m. yep, and can't remember if I told you, but I signed up for a little buddy through the school's buddy program. i am meeting with her and her family on Sunday. she has a twin, is in the third grade, and lives in norwich, vermont, just across the river. i will get the spandex then, yay! i went to a program tonight called "Major Enlightenment" about different majors, and then went trick-or-treating! wahoo. love you!

bye!

Kelly

NOVEMBER

November 1

The mechanics at the Land Rover dealership in Glenwood Springs analyzed the car's erupting gas tank for five hours while I waited. The Service Manager finally sent me home in a loaner car so he could replace the fuel tank with a new plastic version. He thought it was exceptionally funny that for 2000 miles driving across the country we were convinced we were going to be blown sky high.

November 2

I went to my Pilates class for the first time in four months. Kathy was her usual sunny self while exhorting us through an hour of core-busting exercises. I must admit, I was getting a little tired of America's Iron Chef and Top Chef, and the bike seat was forming calluses; I knew I would feel my abs tomorrow.

The rest of the day I spent with doctors. The dermatologist zapped a scar on my arm with his laser gun to try to make it look less obvious, I was injected with the new flu vaccine, and then my teeth were cleaned. I felt like a cow on a feedlot being readied for slaughter.

The day's levity was provided by my book club, the WOWS (Women of the Western Slope). Over the summer we had read *The Willow Field* by William Kittredge, suggested due in part to a great review I had read in the Seattle Times. One of our members had recently become religious and thought the book was soft porn disguised as literature.

I had thoroughly enjoyed it.

So instead of discussing the book's plot structure we discussed recent school district events, (one of our members was a high school teacher), our children and their abilities to adjust to college life. Our next selection would be *Thirteen Moons* by Charles Frazier, a story about the Cherokee Nation and one less erotically charged than my suggestion had been.

November 3

John and I ate at a new restaurant in town, DishAspen, located in a basement space that John had frequented for over forty years. The subterranean location had once housed a Mexican restaurant, an Italian trattoria, a Mediterranean bistro, and now DishAspen was serving contemporary American cuisine. We shared an order of lobster corn dogs, which were tempura-fried chunks of sweet crustacean on a stick, which we followed with an olive-smashed Caesar salad, and then, in a feat of self-control, feasted on half-orders of fiery Shrimp Diavolo layered over fresh pasta. We threw aside any pretense of restraint when we ordered the "Deconstructed Ice Cream Sundae." It was almost half a gallon of homemade ice cream accompanied by a plate piled high with decadent toppings, by far the most wicked item on the menu. We ate the entire thing. And somewhere under the happy haze of the smooth red Barbaresco was the vague recollection that tomorrow I had pledged to step onto my scale and weigh-in.

> 11:54 p.m. yikes! we are racing tomorrow! the varsity crew team made us t-shirts, then dropped off bags of power bars and Gatorade and candy in front of our dorm room doors! and i am soooooo nervous/excited!!!

> 12:00 a.m. good luck, good luck, good luck!!! had another nice day here - no sign of snow. looks like instead of an early winter, it may be late! remind me never to eat ice cream again... xoxoxoxoxoxoxo M

November 4

The weigh-in had not gone too badly—I can probably lose twenty pounds by the time Kelly returns from her first year of college. She called, fresh from the finish of the crew race. The meet was headquartered at Dartmouth's Ledyard Boat House, perched on the banks of the Connecticut River. By mid-day, the cold morning had become frigid, pelting the Ivy-League rowers with frozen rain. Kelly's team placed third, another Dartmouth team finished second, so overall, Dartmouth's novice crew had taken first place in their division.

"Mom," she wailed, "Harvard sent only one team, and stacked it with all of their best girls, so they took the first place in the overall meet. Oh, well, what can you expect from Harvard?" Ivy League rivalries formed quickly and strongly. Apparently the memory of Harvard's freshmen taking two campsites instead of one on the Appalachian Trail during the Outing Club trip was still a fresh wound that apparently might never heal.

"I need to know what you think about something," she said. By the way Kelly phrased the question, I knew she already knew what the answer should be to whatever she was about to propose, but she wanted to get at least one more opinion before making a final decision. "I'm supposed to go to a cabin with the Nordic team tonight for a bonding session, and we have to walk in three-quarters of a mile through the snow... but there's a crew formal tonight, and I think we're going to get initiated or something, and it's supposed to be really fun... and then there's this other factor."

Probably a six-foot tall, broad-shouldered, good-looking Other Factor.

"Well, he's also rower," she said, "and I think he likes me and this could be the night where SOMETHING happens, and I really don't want to miss it!"

I don't think it had dawned on her yet that she could do whatever she wanted to do, and I was still pleased she was asking me. I jumped into parent mode.

"Did you already tell the Nordic team you were going? And by the way, when are you supposed to go?"

"Yes, I did, and I'm supposed to leave for the cabin in half an hour."

I told her that she probably knew exactly what she should do.

"Yeah, I figured that's what you'd say, but I thought I'd just check anyway. Ok, I'll call you tomorrow when I get back from the mountains! Love ya, bye!"

Diligently trying to accomplish Goal #4 (redecorating the resort) I spent the rest of the afternoon drafting plans for Lakedale. In the process, I determined I needed more design ideas to be truly effective.

As we dined on a new low-calorie invention, Tilapia Milanese with Sicilian relish (olives, tomatoes, and garlic), buttered squash, and spinach sautéed with garlic, I mentioned to John, " Honey, we need to go to the Denver Merchandise Mart on Monday so I can find ideas for the cabins and the Lodge's Great Room. It's too tough to try to do all of this online. And the Mart is having something called Super Monday and all of the showrooms are open. What do you think?" Unfortunately, he had a doctor's appointment to remove the stitches from his knee that day, so I would make a solo trip.

November 5

Taking advantage of the fact we had no youngster to get off to school, we ate a leisurely breakfast at Montagna, the restaurant at the Little Nell, our favorite Aspen five-star hotel Breakfast was amazing. It featured steaming hot churros, the Mexican version of a doughnut. It's a fried stick of lightly ridged dough, bathed in cinnamon and sugar. I followed them with perfectly poached eggs on fresh chicken hash, while John indulged in a plate of Huevos Rancheros that practically mariachi-ed across his palate. John declared that this was going to become a weekly tradition. It was as if we were back in Europe...dining.

Later in the day, Jayne and I braved fifty-degree weather for a bike ride up Castle Creek towards Ashcroft, a nearby ghost town. Snow thickened along the road as we pedaled higher, but a fervent discussion about our common menopausal hot flashes made us oblivious to the weather.

Six weeks ago I had stopped using a Vivelle patch, a hormone replacement therapy. I had decided that being on drugs, no matter how helpful, was not a good long-term strategy. Then again, I hadn't experienced any menopausal hot flashes or anxiety attacks in the two years I had been taking it. *Of course, you idiot, that's what the drugs were for!* My breasts had also been incredibly tender and for five weeks had looked like ripe cantaloupes. Since harvesting them was not a viable option I knew something had to be done.

I didn't discuss this decision with my doctor since he was on vacation, but decided (on his behalf) that this was the course of action he would recommend. The first three weeks were uneventful, but after that my face flushed, my body became engulfed in sweat at regular and uncontrollable intervals, and I was miserable, especially at night, when I couldn't easily stick my head into the freezer or run out outside in my underwear.

A typical nighttime scenario:

> 12:00 a.m. Throw off the covers and sweat into the refreshing night air (a brisk fifty degrees inside) for three minutes. Sweat evaporates on my naked body, turning me into a human popsicle, and grasp for more than my share of the duvet. Try to sleep again.
>
> 3:24 a.m. Same drill as above. This time John gathers the covers closer to his exposed head, and mumbles, "Flounder, is that you?" in response to my mad flopping around the bed.
>
> 4:47 a.m. Sweat. Covers. Popsicle. I pray this will be the last wake-up call for the night, and hope I can get three more hours of sleep.

This nocturnal routine completely threw me off my empty nester strategy of getting up at the crack of dawn to exercise, eat right, and accomplish manageable chunks of my goals so that I could laze around all afternoon reading great literature. I need eight hours of uninterrupted sleep to function and this schedule was not working. Ashamed, I called my doctor, told him what I'd done, and begged for the miracle patch back. He could see me next week.

November 6

At 7:00 a.m. I was on the road to Denver, my GPS programmed to take me straight to the Denver Merchandise Mart. I had plotted my excursion to the minute to make the most of my limited time. As I drove into the vast parking lot I couldn't find a parking place in the first few rows, so I continued farther on, eventually going up and down every row of automobiles, probably forty rows in all. Not a single parking spot. *This must be a really popular mart.* I started following people with ID badges swinging from their necks and hauling shopping bags, hoping they were leaving, but no one was. They responded to my "Are you leaving?" query with a "No, just dropping things off. Sorry!" I finally found a spot on the far side of the Mart, but this unexpected delay would wreak havoc on my carefully planned day.

The Merchandise Mart was a massive complex of buildings, about 300,000 square feet and home to wholesale exhibitors of giftware, furniture, jewelry, resort and lodge products, and apparel. Shoppers were everywhere, bags of merchandise slung over their shoulders, carried in their hands, and most had small rolling suitcases they pulled behind them as they traversed the four-story circuit of vendors. Every showroom had signs at the entry announcing either "Samples Here," "These Samples Not for Sale," or "Everything for Sale."

I was impressed by the turnout at Super Monday, and finally asked an exhibitor if it was usually this crowded. She laughed and said this was the busiest day of the year, a once-a-year sample sale, when the showrooms cleared out their outdated merchandise.

While searching the showrooms for ideas for Lakedale, I was entertained by older women drooling over samples like ravenous hounds, their nametags swinging like dog collars, identifying them as "Mildred Smith, Red Hot Mama's Boutique," "Mavis Peabody, Blanche's Bargain Basement," or "Isabel Jones, Espresso Heaven of Sioux Falls." When I called John from the hotel that night I told him that the Mart was THE place to go for women who owned Menopause Shops, the admittedly slightly derogatory term we used for knick-knack shops that were run by women of a certain age.

"Yes, honey, but doesn't it sound a little like you?" he chuckled. *He may be right.*

I plunked my aching feet on the leather ottoman in my hotel room, sipped a glass of Pinot Noir, and dove into a stack of Menopause Shop catalogs, as excited as if I were reading a new *People* magazine.

November 7

Election day 2006. After scouring the Denver Design Center for more ideas, I raced back to the mountains in time to reach the polling place before it closed. I was surprisingly excited to cast my ballot for someone (Gail) I actually admired and knew would make a difference if she managed to win the election...and we were going to watch the results with her and Alan.

November 8

"Hey, Mom, what are you doing?" Kelly cheerily asked.

"Oh, the usual, except that last night we went to a party at Gail and Alan's to watch the election results."

"What happened? Did she win?"

"Well, we left before midnight and she was behind by two points but only half the votes were counted. When we got up this morning, she was ahead by two points, with all of the votes in. She won by a thousand votes out of forty-eight thousand. It's pretty amazing!"

Kelly sounded quite excited. "Cool, I can't believe we know someone who's actually a senator!"

Of anyone I knew, what with her charm and determination, Gail was the one to do it. She was embarking on a completely new journey, one that no one else I knew would probably ever be on. Hobnobbing with the governor, lobbyists, and according to her daughter, already looking ahead to the national level. *What in the world was she thinking?* Being a politician is the last thing on earth, other than a disgraced television evangelical minister, I would ever aspire to be.

It's all about honesty. Even if he started his political career with the purest of intentions, no politician ever seemed to emerge from the process more honest than when he began. At the end of the day, whatever good intentions he had always seemed sacrificed on the altar of political compromise. I think Gail will be different.

I asked Kelly how the weekend's activities went.

"I guess it's a good thing I didn't go to the crew formal.

The crew team had some pre-party festivities, and then got dressed up," Kelly answered.

"As what?"

"Cowboys and Indians."

"What's wrong with that?" I said.

"Nothing...unless your formal is in the same building as the Native Americans of Dartmouth annual meeting." Dartmouth was originally established as a school to educate Native Americans, and this responsibility was still taken seriously, to the extent that Dartmouth graduates more Native Americans than all the other Ivy League schools combined. "Well, the Native Americans were completely offended and called Safety and Security about the crew team, who were then hauled in to the Health Center for some re-education. I was actually glad to be at the cabin, even if it meant I froze my butt off and didn't get to see the Hunk. And I am now completely bummed, because I don't get to go to Princeton this weekend for crew."

"Why not?" I am finding that in many of our conversations, my role has become that of the sympathetic ear, the sounding board that questions bounce back from to give my daughter a non-college perspective on her life.

"Because some girls who haven't been coming to practice have shown up again, and since they rowed in high school and have more experience, four of us can't go this weekend."

"That doesn't seem very fair, you've been at every practice even when you were coughing your brains out!" I was incensed at the athletic injustice of it all.

Kelly sighed resignedly, "I know, that's what the coach said. But she said she wants to have a winning team, and we don't have the experience." *Bummer*. Motherly advice ensued about sticking it out, being a member of the team, and everything would work out and she'd be on varsity next year.

> 2:01 p.m. say mom, can you look for some classes for me for next term? i'm not sure what to take? I really need your help! love you! Kelly

> 3:11 p.m. hi hon! aren't you supposed to figure out classes

with your advisor? lots of love, your loving, whirly blades on vacation, mom

3:45 p.m. pleeeeeeeeease? i'm a novice at this, I need your help.... Kelly

3:48 p.m. OK, but promise me you won't tell your father, I am supposed to be cutting the apron strings! I just got out the course schedule - how do these classes sound?

American Foreign relations

Linguistics (could be interesting)

Music Theory

Western Art Music

History of Jazz

Intro to Philosophy

Physics - Understanding the Universe

Astronomy

Intro to Psychology - one of my college favorites!

let me know how it progresses! we are going to Fiddler on the Roof tonight, if I can remember where I put the tickets, love and kisses, mom

3:59 p.m. oops - forgot a few more:

Intro to Public Policy

Patterns of Religious Experience

Intro to Sociology

Sex, Gender and Society

Into to Art History (a good background to have)

I can't believe it, but they have a section entitled "Queer Studies" in the schedule – did you see that? good luck!

6:14 p.m. I think Economics would also be a good background course to have, good for math and also probably a prerequisite for most international relations classes! luv ya, mom

10:35 p.m. was thinking about your classes - did you decide to do a language? which one? spanish might be easier since you've had it more recently, but then you also have to consider where you might want to go on your study abroad. have you been able to talk with another advisor? that would probably help! I found the tickets and Fiddler was great! love ya, sweet dreams! your mama!

i am parking the helicopter for the night...

November 9

I padded into the kitchen to make my morning beverage only to find that the gallon of milk I purchased two weeks ago was sour. It was still half full.

I poured the acerbic milk down the drain and thought about routines. The routine of making coffee in the morning, getting Kelly ready for school, attending parent-teacher meetings, going to Kelly's tennis matches and cross-country ski meets, while seeing all of the accompanying parental units along the way. Picking my daughter up after school, and after she could drive, waiting for her to come home and hear what had happened in her day. Making dinner while she studied at the kitchen counter. To the routine of now...which is no routine. It is hard to conjure up a meaningful routine out of thin air. I am feeling less productive now than when I had 300 projects on my plate. Weird. Maybe Gail has the right answer...politics.

4:06 p.m. what department was the american foreign relations class in? i didn't see that one...what do you think about econ?

4:08 p.m. hmm, still not seeing it...there's american political systems...your confused daughter, Kelly

4:15 p.m. take a look at the government section...did you look at international politics? love and kisses, your helicopter mom (who is not supposed to be doing this...)

4:20 p.m. can't take that because it's at the same time as my writing class...otherwise believe me i would, but i am

> thinking about "the many faces of latin america," it deals with art and history and other stuff, or econ, or patterns of religious experience. and fyi, and as much as i appreciate your exceptional help, i just made an appointment with an advisor for tomorrow. I'll let you know how it goes. your ever-more confused daughter, Kelly

November 10

I've found the solution. I need a job. One with flexibility, creativity, no boss, and excellent pay. When I mentioned my decision to John, he rolled his eyes, no doubt realizing my newfound quest for meaning might throw our usual travel plans haywire.

"What about Lakedale?" he asked. *Oh my God. It's all there in one package, AND I'm my own boss. Well, I do have to deal with John, but there's nothing we can't solve with a little pillow talk.*

Every day I had spent more and more time redesigning the interiors for Lakedale. I had expanded the scope of work. I was excited about the new design elements I'd unearthed in Denver. Maybe it was just getting back to interior design, which I love. It was my major in college and the field I'd practiced for twelve years before John and I were married. The solution was right in front of my nose.

As we were leaving the house to have dinner with friends, my cell phone rang. Kelly on the line, still upset about not going to Princeton, but with a burning question for me.

"Mom, do you think it's OK for the girl to make the first move?"

"Well, what do you consider the first move?" I asked.

"I don't know...that's why I'm asking you. The Short Kid (a nickname we had bestowed in high school) said he likes it."

I was a little worried about Kelly following The Short Kid's suggestions, as he had asked her out in the sixth grade via an intermediary. Kelly was quick on her feet and said she couldn't possibly go out with him because her parents wouldn't let her date until she was thirty-five. He was now studying at an eastern college and enjoying a robust social life, apparently his middle school training years had given him the skills required to navigate the college hook-up scene. Kelly continued, "He says guys like it when you come on to them, that it's hard for them to make the moves all the time."

"Just remember to behave in a lady-like fashion, and don't be too aggressive. Guys still like to feel that they're in control and they're the pursuers." *Was I really saying this? My mother's voice ricocheted around my brain, but I couldn't think of anything else to say. I've never been as good at doling out precious gems of parental counsel as Kathy or Jayne. Note to self: Call them tomorrow and ask what they would say.*

"OK." She seemed to accept my pitiful advice, even though she could probably hear John chattering in the background, "What is she going to do? Haven't you taught her what to do around guys? All they want is one thing! Doesn't she know that yet?"

"I'm going to see the Hunk tonight, and have decided that he should at least know I like him before he goes to the race in Princeton. Things seem to move fairly fast here, and he may be hooked up with someone soon, if I don't let him know."

"Good luck, honey, love ya!"

November 11

Time for me to check in on my goals:

> Goal #1: I am watching what I eat, getting on the scale occasionally, and have lost four pounds so far, although this is certain to change as we have two dinner parties in the next week and Thanksgiving is on the horizon.
>
> Goal #2: I'm doing really well on this one, I'm up to forty-five minutes a day on the machines, thighs slightly firmer, and am almost caught up on the first season of Top Chef.
>
> Goal #3: I've downloaded eight CD's worth of photos in preparation for taking them to the local camera store to print.

Goal #4: Lakedale is going well, probably my most successful Goal so far. Cabins, lodge, and restrooms are all designed although nothing will be ordered until we visit Lakedale after Thanksgiving. One of the front desk clerks is enthusiastically helping with ideas for the new retail store in the Great Room.

Goal #5: I have found no galleries in which to display my art, but then again, it may be because I haven't had the nerve to call any gallery owners. Maybe I should take the Short Kid's advice and just go for it.

Goal #6: I haven't created one piece of art (I am blaming this on my new "job"), and early stages of panic are setting in due to the art show I have to curate in mid-February. Ongoing night sweats and sleepless nights are actually helping with this situation. I try to think of new sculptures to fabricate as I lie awake at 1:37 a.m., 3:46 a.m., and 5:03 a.m. respectively and occasionally an image will resurface when I wake up. I'm realizing this is a far more effective sleeping aid than counting sheep.

Goal #7: I haven't picked up a needle to stitch even one color on the needlepoint wreath. As a matter of fact, I don't even know where the needlepoint canvas is. I'm not too concerned as I have all of next year to work on this before Christmas comes again.

Goal #8: No new chowder contestants.

Goal #9: The foot fungus has spread to my other foot.

November 14

All morning, I anxiously awaited my afternoon appointment with my doctor and soon-to-be savior. So anxiously in fact that I left home early and even after getting lost on the way to his new office I arrived early. His nurse drew a blood sample to test my estrogen levels to determine how hormonally deprived I was. When the results arrived, he calmly announced that my estrogen levels had fallen off the charts. *No kidding.*

"How far off the charts?" I asked.

"You are at 7.9 millimeters (or some other medical-speak amount), and the normal level is 50." I curbed my impulse to yell, "*Holy shit, no wonder I've felt like the newest inductee to the Northwest Sweat Lodge Society!*" but he was a gentle soul so I restrained myself. In retrospect, I realized he had probably heard far worse in the delivery room. He continued, "And I think there is a problem with the Vivelle. I've had quite a few patients recently who have been experiencing recurring menopausal symptoms, so there may be a manufacturing defect with the product."

He wrote me a new prescription and I felt 100% better already.

November 15

Tonight we would host the Gourmet Group for the first time. Our theme was Swiss food and the entrée was raclette, a meal I had made so many times I could prepare it blindfolded.

John wanted to be prepared. "Are the candlesticks clean?" he asked. "There is so much on the table with the raclette, we don't have room for them," I replied.

"Have you got the coffee maker ready?"

"It's automatic, darling, no worries."

"Have you...."

Time to tune in to the cooking, which with raclette was minimal, and since the group was bringing the rest of the dinner, I was completely relaxed. I was also unperturbed because half the group would be missing. One husband was on a hunting trip, hoping to snag his first elk. Another couple was out of town, and a third had double-booked themselves and were only going to arrive in time for dessert. No problem at all. On the other hand, I had not considered that maybe these were merely excuses and that they all abhorred cheese.

The phone rang at five o'clock, and it was Bo, husband of the beautiful Cheryl. "Hey, Shelley, it's Bo," he said in his languorous voice.

"Bo, how are you?" He answered that he was not doing very well.

Drat! This was starting to feel like a lot like the Worst Dinner Party We Ever Had. We had arranged a dinner to introduce a never-married bachelor buddy of John's to a sixty-year-old unmarried friend of mine after months of careful behind the scenes maneuvering. They arrived, met each other, had absolutely no chemistry and studiously avoided each other the rest of the evening. Our other guests were new acquaintances who arrived an hour late after getting lost on the circuitous route to our house. Then the last four guests arrived and casually mentioned that they happened to be vegetarians. I had spent three days preparing Beef Bourguignon, a recipe from Thomas Keller's *French Laundry* cookbook, which started with homemade beef stock made from roasted bones.

I drank a lot of red wine that night.

"I hope you're still coming!" I said to Bo, trying to be sympathetic, but thinking about the ten pounds of raclette cheese I had sitting in the refrigerator.

He answered, "If it's OK with you, I'll still come, but Cheryl won't be able to make it."

"Why not?" I queried.

"Unfortunately, last night our deaf and blind dog was run over by a car."

"Bo, I am so sorry!" I was feeling some guilt about being worried about the cheese.

"She was our son's dog, so Cheryl is going to stay at home with him. But I'd love to come…do you have any gin?"

"Absolutely, can't wait to see you!"

The dinner went well after all. Everyone consumed a lot of cheese, and Cheryl's dessert (oeufs a la neige), prepared under Bo's watchful eye, was an ideal light ending to the cheesy entrée.

November 16

Kelly's cheerful voice rang out on the other end of the phone, "Hi Mom, how are you?"

"Great, sweets, how are you doing?"

"Oh, the usual, but I've been so busy, I barely have time to eat. Did I tell you what I did this week?"

"No, what happened?"

"OK, do you have a minute?" she asked. *Of course...I had hours for Kelly.* "On Monday, I had lunch with an astronaut as part of the freshman seminar lunch series, then on Tuesday the Dartmouth Ends Hunger group sponsored a Homeless Awareness Week and I helped organize a movie screening for them. Then on Wednesday, we had a Hunger Banquet. It was so cool. Everyone got a ticket when they entered the room, with Low Income, Middle Income or High Income written on it. If you got the Low Income ticket, you had to sit on the floor and eat rice, if you got the Middle Income ticket, you sat in a chair and ate rice and beans, and if you got the High Income ticket, you sat at a table with a tablecloth, and ate as much pasta and meat as you wanted. It was meant to show what most of the world deals with on a daily basis as far as what they have to eat."

I asked her which group she ate with.

"I got the High Income ticket, but all my friends were in the Low Income group, so I sat with them. And then the professor who started the language program at Dartmouth gave a lecture on hunger."

"Unbelievable! I am so proud of you...it's amazing how many opportunities you're taking advantage of at school!" I gushed.

"I'm not done. Then on Friday I went to a lecture on the Sudan, and about the horrendous events going on there. I think I might have to resurrect my non-profit and try to raise some money for them." *Whew! To have that much energy, and go to two hour crew practices at 5:45 a.m. every morning too.*

I nonchalantly asked if she had managed to attend any classes this week.

"Yea, but it's been tough! And guess what? I get to go with the crew team to row in Boston at the Foot of the Charles race this weekend!"

"Yippee!" *I can't believe I actually still say things like that.*

"And the coach had two of us row, and then selected me to go because I rowed a little better with the team, but then another girl on the team sprained her foot, so both of us get to go anyway. We're leaving this afternoon, so I probably won't talk with you for a few days."

"No sweat...have a wonderful time and row well!"

November 17

We held our second dinner party of the week. Fortunately for this one, I didn't have to do anything except spread out a tablecloth, arrange flowers and invite the guests. Last winter John had gone a little overboard at a charity function we attended with Fred and Jayne for a local orchestra Lacy belonged to. "Compared to Aspen fundraisers," he whispered as the bidding got underway, "this is so cheap, we've got to bid on something!"

For fifty dollars, he won a flouncy black chiffon party outfit, size 14, which was paired with a fake jeweled red heart broach and bracelet. Next was a round of golf for four with lunch (definitely more useable) and then the opportunity for someone (like me) to conduct the symphony the following Mother's Day in front of five hundred of my closest friends. But his most inspired purchase was an evening hosted by a chef who would prepare a five-course meal in our home, match the courses with wine, and I wouldn't have to lift a finger. The chef would bring the china, silverware, and wine glasses, and all we had to do was invite five couples to join us. No dishwashing guaranteed.

The chef's wife and their sous-chef arrived forty-five minutes late, causing us to scour the freezer for backup dinner ingredients, but in half-an-hour, the table was set, oyster quesadillas were cooking and everyone arrived in a jovial, ready-to-party mood.

The chef introduced every course in the southwestern-themed meal with aplomb, starting with the quesadillas, charred corn and shrimp salad, and chile relleno appetizers. These courses were followed by black sea bass encrusted in corn, followed by beef tenderloin napped with two spicy sauces, and finally, rich chocolate tamales for dessert. No one left the table until the meal was over four hours later. As we learned in Europe, "there is no time at the table."

We did have to wash two cases of wine glasses, which I delivered to the Starwood gate for the guards to give back to the sous-chef. Despite that, I am now completely spoiled and may never cook again. This could prove to be a problem with the gourmet club.

November 19

Whenever we fly in to San Diego and emerge from the aging terminal, I feel like I've arrived in a foreign country. Gone are the sanitized Aspen-clone women, their identical bobbed noses framed by long, blond hair, with their D-cups balanced atop skinny legs in stilettos. In San Diego the women are black, white, tattooed, and sometimes obese. Bronzed breasts are over-exposed; perfectly aligned alabaster teeth sparkle in the sun. Pot-bellied old men in Mercedes' wait at the airport curbs and watch crew cut, frightened teenagers pass by in civvies, as they marched off to their first drills at the Marine Corps training depot. Sweet smelling jasmine-perfumed air disguises the film of smog that coats the city.

We drove north along the coast to the L'Auberge Del Mar, granting ourselves a mini-vacation at a nice seaside inn to mentally prepare for the upcoming family Thanksgiving. I've resisted going back to San Diego for years, a Jekyll and Hyde situation; hating the city I had lived in for so long because of its paralytic traffic, slavish obsession with expensive cars, superficial lifestyle, and bad air (caused, of course, by all of the above) and yet feeling a need to be there to visit my parents, as well as John's two grown children and five grandkids. Only now have I started enjoying La Jolla and Southern California, since I don't have to live there anymore and know I can leave after three days.

Del Mar's beach was awash in hundreds of Sunday strollers. The air was unseasonably warm and still, and with the stillness came an almost edible layer of brown haze that sat on the surface of the sea, north to Orange County and south to La Jolla. At dinner that night with a friend, she commented, "Wasn't this the most beautiful day?" John arched his eyebrow, silently warning me to be tactful, I replied, "Absolutely, they don't come much better than this." And I was telling the truth, at least as far as Southern California went.

November 20

My husband is nuts. Either that or his cholesterol medication is really having an effect on his brain. After a perfectly relaxing, great day...walking the Del Mar beaches, lunch on the hotel's terrace, scoping out retail shops for ideas for the Lakedale retail shop (Goal #4), we relaxed with drinks at the Poseidon bar, overlooking the ocean. While waiting for dessert and coffees to arrive from room service, I mentioned that maybe we should invite an old San Diego friend who had recently divorced for Thanksgiving dinner.

John mentioned that he had asked him to come to dinner weeks ago, and didn't I remember the conversation? Truthfully, I didn't. This is becoming a more common occurrence. John remembers an entire dialogue that I swear never happened, and I'm caught totally unprepared for his ensuing exasperation. John, on the other hand, won't remember entire events that I guarantee have happened. For example, I ordered a new umbrella online last week at his request. When it arrived, he asked me why I had ordered it. When Kelly was at home, she was witness to what events in our lives actually occurred and straightened us both out; another reason for my sense of loss at her departure. I am tempted to sew a microphone into my underwire bra to record what really takes place. Then again, maybe menopause is driving me nuts.

November 21

The day I had been waiting for since we dropped Kelly off at Dartmouth finally arrived. Like so many other milestone occasions in my life, including my wedding to John, I was late. How this consistently happens I don't know, but it happens so frequently, I believe I am genetically programmed not to be able to arrive for significant events on time. On the other hand I was only five minutes late, a testament to Kelly's importance in my life.

My young niece Alaina and I drove to the baggage claim exit at the airport, and there stood Kelly, unmistakable, clad in comfy Dartmouth green sweat pants, T-shirt, and flip-flops. She had never looked more wonderful. I squeezed her as hard and as long as I safely could before airport security caught on and waved us off.

Because we had communicated so much over the course of the previous two months, we didn't have much exciting news to share. Alaina filled the space with ten-year-old crazy chatter and I gazed lovingly at my daughter, all while trying to drive and avoid the Botoxed, cell-phone obsessed, twenty-something females on the road.

On the way back to my parent's house, we stopped at the meat market to retrieve the Turducken, a recent family Thanksgiving tradition. Originating in the south, some say by Chef Paul Prudhomme, the Turducken consists of a boneless chicken stuffed inside a boneless duck, which is then stuffed into a turkey, with layers of two different dressings sandwiched between the meats. The entire assemblage is then reshaped to look like a whole turkey, with legs and wings remaining. It is then thrown in the oven, baked for four hours, and "Voila!", turkey dinner.

Thanksgiving is the holiday in which our entire family comes together, usually at my parents' house. A holiday with nothing to get in the way of cooking, eating and drinking—very appropriate for a family of amateur chefs and food-lovers.

Countless movies have been filmed, hundreds of books have been written, and untold country western singers have crooned about families, especially families at the holidays. What untold sins would be reheated along with the leftover dressing? Who would be reduced to tears, simmered on the back burner, then salted and hung out to dry like familial beef jerky? The joy of reunion tempered by the icy reality of the family's sharp blade. One never knew what would happen at the annual family get-together.

As families go, ours was somewhat benign. We had learned not to discuss the current occupant of the White House, his misguided foreign policies, religious zealots, and recently menopause had been added to the list.

An Abbreviated Family Profile:

Doug: 82-year-old mercurial patriarch and ultimate authority; booted out of high school for writing a nasty yet creative poem about the principal; emigrated from Canada with us in tow; lives in comfortable retirement, having had the adventure of restoring and captaining two large boats.

Jean: 82-year-young matriarch and benevolent soul; nurse who met and married Doug in Nelson, British Columbia, Canada; mother of three daughters; giving, unconditional, perfect mother and grandmother; bridge and golf lover; and the syrup that keeps the family bound sweetly together.

Shelley: Me, eldest daughter; design major with an MBA; mother of one; recovering school volunteer; artist; pianist; writer.

Lea: Middle daughter, one and a half years my junior; former tomboy; petroleum geology major; mother of two; made the transition from granola-eating earth mother to sophisticated, golf enthusiast living in Utah.

Dave: Lea's husband; handsome former minerals exploration geologist turned bankruptcy attorney, having switched fields just before the oil business in Utah dried up; business interests have included air-bag manufacturing, and a luxury adventuring company.

Sienna: 24-year old beautiful blond; Lea and Dave's eldest and recent college graduate; applying to medical school; the

Imelda Marcos of Salt Lake City with hundreds of pairs of stylish shoes in her closet; dating a PhD candidate seven years her senior.

Nik: Lea's 22-year old son; a blond copy of Dave; sophomore business major at Northern Arizona University; avid rock-climber teetering on the edge of rock-climbing fame.

Julie: Youngest daughter of Doug and Jean; conceived eight years after my birth, probably as a result of a diaphragm failure (since Lea and I had discovered the diaphragm in our mother's nightstand and used it as a mini-Frisbee); mother of two daughters; chef and hostess extraordinaire; able to get along with every member of the family.

Jeff: Julie's husband; hysterically funny Texan with PhD in biomedical physics from UCLA and an MBA from Stanford; founder of a Silicon Valley high tech medical firm that went public; at work on developing another high-tech firm; soccer maniac, managing his girls' teams with the zeal of a Catholic priest teaching catechism to twelve-year-old boys.

Katrina: Julie and Jeff's 14-year-old eldest daughter; water polo star; high school freshman who always walks with a lilt in her step; the cousin Kelly is closest to.

Alaina: Ten-year-old daughter of Julie and Jeff; soccer player and creative artist with a sense of humor like her dad's (when Kelly mentioned at Thanksgiving dinner that she didn't like gravy, Alaina commented, "Well, obviously you can't be related to me."); at the 95% mark on the doctor's height chart, so will soon tower over the shortest member of the family, me, a rite of passage that every family member besides me awaits with glee.

The dinner conversation started out innocently until I stepped outside to cool off as another wave of heat engulfed my body. When I returned the subject quickly turned to menopause and whether or not a woman had to pay her dues and tough it out or succumb to the joys of modern pharmacology as I had done. Fortunately, Jeff jumped to my rescue, describing in great detail the time he had witnessed me drenched in sweat in the space of a minute, water oozing from every pore, face wet as a slick pickle. Menopause in action.

The rest of the weekend passed in a blur; most mornings were spent walking with assorted configurations of family members down the steep back bank of my parent's yard to reach the bicycle trail, which in turn leads to the village of La Jolla and the deck of the Pannikin, the nearest coffee shop. The dusty trail, fragrant with the licoricey smell of anise and bordered by dangerous knee-catching prickly pear cacti overlooks the ocean, high enough to avoid potential tsunamis, and yet close enough to hear the screams of the seagulls at Windansea beach.

The flat plane of land below is covered with World War II cottages, now being renovated by a new generation intent on profiting from the Southern California real estate market. John's daughter and son-in law had purchased one of these 1,600 square-foot quaint abodes (with one bath) a few years ago and are in the process of remodeling.

One afternoon we walked into the village to eat lunch at George's at the Cove. George's is a favorite family destination. It's where Jeff proposed marriage to Julie and where John proposed to me, having been a confirmed bachelor only an hour before. The rooftop terrace overlooks the La Jolla Cove, where jagged rocks that encircle a picturesque beach the size of a postage stamp provide perches for hundreds of white pelicans. Scores of swimmers, some in wetsuits, wade into the frenzied surf for the daily workout of the La Jolla Swim Club. In our family, betrothals aside, George's is Mecca, because it is here that we eat George's famous soup; a mixture of smoked chicken, broccoli and black beans suspended in a rich creamy base. A soup worth every sinful, luscious bite. A soup that has probably launched a thousand marriages.

George's at the Cove Black Bean Soup

Yeild: 4 servings

½ CUP UNSALTED BUTTER
½ CUP DICED CARROT
½ CUP DICED ONION
½ CUP DICED CELERY
1 CUP BROCCOLI STEM, PEELED AND DICED
2 TEASPOONS DRIED THYME
2 TEASPOONS DRIED OREGANO
1 TEASPOON DRIED SWEET BASIL LEAVES
¼ CUP DRY WHITE WINE
4 CUPS CHICKEN STOCK, HOT
1 TABLESPOON WORCESTERSHIRE SAUCE
½ TEASPOON CHOLULA SAUCE
1 CUP DICED SMOKED CHICKEN (RECIPE FOLLOWS)
1 CUP COOKED BLACK BEANS
1 CUP BROCCOLI FLORET
2 CUPS HEAVY CREAM
SALT AND FRESH GROUND PEPPER TO TASTE
2 TABLESPOONS CORNSTARCH, MIXED WITH A SMALL AMOUNT OF WARM WATER (OPTIONAL)

In quarter-cup butter, sauté carrots, onion, celery and broccoli stems for five minutes.

Add thyme, oregano and basil. Sauté five minutes more.

Add wine and deglaze pan. Add hot chicken stock and reduce by one-third.

Add Worcestershire sauce, Cholula sauce, smoked chicken, beans and broccoli florets. Simmer five minutes.

Add cream, simmer five minutes more and salt and pepper to taste (thicken with cornstarch if desired).

Drop in remaining butter, piece by piece, stirring until melted. Serve immediately.

Smoked Chicken

On a covered grill, slightly smoke boneless chicken, cooking to medium rare (about 30 minutes). Use applewood chips and don't allow the grill to become too hot.

Kelly spent most of her time with her cousins, although I received an occasional hug, usually when no one was looking. From my voracious empty nester reading, I had learned this was typical behavior for college students returning home for the first time. They had to demonstrate to their parents that they had established their own identity and were independent, except of course for that monthly tuition check and spending money. She made a few remarks here and there about drinking, but she didn't imbibe anything stronger than two-percent milk at the family dinners.

Another flash: for me, Kelly leaving the nest wasn't just about her being gone. It was about the loss of having a baby, a little girl, a teenager at home. And if she did return, it would be on her terms, not ours. I found myself staring at families with small children, impatient mothers reigning in wild toddlers, exasperated fathers calming crying infants, and wondered if they knew that in no time at all, they too would have an empty nest. "Enjoy every screaming, slobbery second!" I wanted to yell at them. Because you can't go back.

We cooked together, meals large and small, the most important, of course, being Thanksgiving dinner. Julie prepared fresh ricotta cheese for an appetizer, baked pumpkin, pecan and apple/cranberry pies, while I took charge of all the side dishes. Lea roasted the Turducken and produced her traditional sausage and apple dressing. Mom was pleased to relegate the cooking chores to us, having mashed more than her weight in potatoes over the years, and was content to scurry around the house, punctuated with occasional breaks to relax in her "action-rocker" on the patio. Kelly and her cousins constructed a floor-to-ceiling tent to hide the dining table in order to keep their table decorations a secret. As dinner was about to be served, they cast aside the tent and revealed the table décor of handmade turkey place cards, towering orange and yellow flower arrangements, and dozens of twinkling candles.

After the requisite holiday gorging, we knew we wouldn't have enough leftovers for the next few days, so we roasted a second Turducken after dinner. We managed to work off a few calories with a family bike ride to Mission Beach, weaving in and out of bikini-wearing middle-aged women who shouldn't have, and beer-drinking lushes lounging on the boardwalk.

After a few more menopause comments, some about global warming *(the number of menopausal women being a causative factor that might have been overlooked by our esteemed climatologists)*, the long weekend was over. Before Kelly, John and I parted ways at 5:00 a.m. on Sunday I wrapped myself around my daughter in a boa constrictor-like hug. As we parted, she, bound for Dartmouth, John and I traveling back to the Northwest, I expected the ever-present tears, and was shocked when none arrived. Maybe it was because it was five in the morning and my emotions weren't yet turned on, or maybe I was just getting used to life without Kelly.

When we arrived in Seattle, cold wet air penetrated our bones. Our hotel was built atop the icy waters of Elliott Bay; erratic, storm-fueled waves slapped the pillars upholding the structure while a fireplace glowed warm in our room. At a French restaurant just up the hill from Pike's Place Market, I ate a soothing cassoulet while John dined on an omelet aux fines herbs. We watched snowflakes swirl outside the windows overlooking the alley and didn't talk much. We staggered back to the hotel, exhausted after our 4:00 a.m. wake up call and the previous weekend's emotions. We were ready for a long night's sleep.

November 27

We had flown to Seattle for the annual Lakedale meeting, where we would be presented with the projected budget and marketing plans for the upcoming year by the management company's executives. I was now in the thick of the business of Lakedale, far beyond anything anticipated in Goal #4. I was up to my eyeballs in spread sheets—analyzing problems, trying to find solutions, and all in all, having more fun than I'd ever had in business. It was far more interesting to be the owner of a property rather than a client trying to serve the needs of an owner.

"Shelley and John, would you like some coffee?"

"How about a fresh, warm carrot cake muffin?"

"Here, let me get you some mineral water." They were in the hospitality business, after all.

John did most of the work, leveling with them about the state of the property, laying his many concerns on the line before they had a chance to execute their carefully scripted meeting. While they went back to the drawing boards we had lunch next door at Anthony's Seafood House. Anthony's "Famous Clam Chowder" was on the menu. Great flavor, a little too thick, overall a grade of 7. I had made some conclusions about Goal #7, the personal chowder contest I had instigated (John was now a willing participant), and was more firmly establishing the criteria for what I considered the "perfect" chowder.

1) It couldn't be too thick, that is, the consistency of wallpaper paste was unacceptable.

2) It had to include bacon, thyme, and onions.

3) There shouldn't be more potatoes than clams.

Shelley's Northwest Clam Chov

Yeild: 10 to 12 servings

1 8-OUNCE SLAB BACON, CUT INTO ½-INCH DICE
2 TABLESPOONS UNSALTED BUTTER
2 LARGE ONIONS, PEELED AND CUT INTO ¼-INCH DICE (ABOUT 4 CUPS)
3 STALKS OF CELERY, CUT INTO ¼-INCH DICE (ABOUT 1 CUP)
¼ CUP UNBLEACHED ALL-PURPOSE FLOUR
4 6½ OUNCE CANS WHOLE (OR CHOPPED) CLAMS, DRAIN CLAMS AND RESERVE JUICE
2 CUPS CLAM JUICE
6 POTATOES, PEELED AND CUT INTO ½-INCH DICE (ABOUT 4 CUPS)
1½ TEASPOON DRIED THYME
FRESHLY GROUND BLACK PEPPER, TO TASTE
2 CUPS MILK
2 CUPS HEAVY OR WHIPPING CREAM
¼ CUP GOOD SHERRY (NOT COOKING SHERRY)
3 TABLESPOONS CHOPPED FRESH ITALIAN PARSLEY

Cook the bacon in a soup pot over low heat until fat is rendered and the bacon is wilted and slightly browned on the edges, about 5 minutes. Add the butter, onions and celery and cook, stirring until the onions are wilted, 10 minutes. Add the flour and cook, stirring, another 5 minutes.

Add both the reserved clam juice and additional clam juice along with the potatoes, thyme, and pepper. Simmer 5 minutes longer or until potatoes are tender.

Add the clams, the milk, the cream and the sherry, and stir well over very low heat until hot. Do not boil, or the soup will curdle. Adjust the seasonings to taste, stir in the flat-leaf parsley, and serve immediately.

After lunch, we hailed a town car to take us south of Seattle to meet with Rainier Industries, a yurt manufacturer. We had recently become enamored with town cars, reasoning that the drivers smelled better and the back seat was roomier than a taxicab's. Indeed the car looked better, but our driver wore a baggy pair of sweat pants, barely spoke English, and had no sense of direction. He had the wisdom to ask the valet at the hotel for a map, which he read while driving the town car down the freeway through rush hour traffic. We arrived at Rainier an hour later, after three missed intersections and a speeding ticket for the driver. Since it would be difficult to get another driver, he agreed to wait for us. He was excited to be able to listen to the Monday night Seattle Seahawks football game on the radio, which was being played on the home turf.

John was interested in building yurts at Lakedale as an alternate form of lodging, and as part of our research, the Rainier salesman gave us a tour of his 100,000 square foot manufacturing facility. Giant eighty-foot long vacuum tables were fed yards of canvas that were then marked and cut by a computer-controlled arm. Immense canvas awnings were stretched over large aluminum frames. Rainier also had a print shop with scores of commercial printers that spewed out fifteen-foot wide graphic images onto fabric, plastic, and whatever else could be fed into them. The woodworking shop fabricated beautiful four-foot diameter rings that cradled the skylights to illuminate the yurts, and also made the lattice panels that encircled and supported the interiors of the yurts. We were impressed.

Night was falling as we left the building, the Vietnamese seamstresses that stitched the canvas having long since departed. A light snow was falling as we knocked on the town car's window to rouse the driver who was sound asleep.

I inquired what country he was from.

"I from Eritrea," he answered.

"Have you ever seen snow before?" I asked.

"Once before, it very cold."

John asked him if he knew the game's score.

"I not sure, but good game," he said.

Not that I was worried, but the snow was beginning to pile up. I talked John into stopping at the nearby IKEA store to do some research for my Lakedale cabin redesign project. I was in seventh heaven, sitting in sleeper sofas, turning on lighting fixtures, analyzing duvet covers, all because everything was so utterly inexpensive, inexpensive being my mantra these days. Half an hour later, at John's insistence, we exited IKEA and found ourselves in a snowstorm of epic proportions, even by Aspen standards. Even as the car slid across the parking lot to reach the exit turnstile our driver remained confident.

"No worry, ma'am," he laughed. After three more wrong turns trying to locate the freeway on-ramp, John found a map in the car, and forcefully told the driver that he'd help him navigate. The roads were slick, snow immediately turning to ice as it contacted the pavement, like a warm tongue sticking to a frozen signpost. There were no snowplows to intervene as cars slid across the slippery road, occasionally meeting car partners in a chaotic dance across the median. Just as we were about to enter the on-ramp heading north, an immense semi-truck started his waltz, backwards down the ramp, jack-knifing into another hapless truck right before us. Dance over, and the on-ramp was closed for the night.

Above us we could see the taillights of vehicles that had managed to successfully navigate onto the highway, but like cold molasses, nothing was moving. We slowly continued via surface streets, avoiding the other vehicles that were trying to either make it home or to the safety of the nearest bar to see the end of the Seahawks game.

Another on-ramp appeared to have the potential of delivering us to the northbound freeway, but as we were negotiating the wide right-hand curve, a white Lexus ahead of us lost its grip and, in slow motion, slid to within six inches of the low barrier's edge. Two airport vans in front of us nudged gently into the Lexus and then all forward motion ceased. We were stuck on a freeway on-ramp fifty feet in the air, while the blizzard of the century engulfed us.

After a few minutes, all of the drivers emerged from their vehicles, including John and our fearless driver. They carefully shuffled across the ice, like chilly Indians in moccasins stalking some elusive reindeer, and powwowed with the driver of the Lexus. He informed everyone that his car was worth $185,000 and he had no intention of trying to drive it off the on-ramp until the tow truck he had called arrived.

"Don't worry," he reassured the crowd gathered around him. "He'll be here soon." I thought to myself, *If the tow truck arrives in the next three days, it will be a miracle...kind of like the Virgin Mary appearing on a grilled cheese sandwich.*

John and the driver reconvened with me at the town car to analyze the situation. I had taken a quick visual inventory of nearby hotels on our way up the ramp, and determined that we could slide down the ramp to a nearby Super-8 Motel and wait out the white night there. If that didn't work, I had visions of us stranded all night, stars of a new reality TV series called "The On-Ramp."

Suddenly we noticed the cars behind us backing up, turning around and driving off the ramp. Using sign language and wildly waving arms, John gesticulated our driver into a 180-degree turn and we inched down the road, squeezing by the oncoming cars unaware of the Lexus roadblock ahead. Once again we turned north onto a surface street. John sensed that we could probably make it all the way to Seattle on this road, so we plowed on, literally.

The driver was getting more confident maneuvering on the ice, so he pressed exuberantly on the acceleration pedal. I'd had enough mental stimulation at this point, my fear/sweat/self-preservation glands working overtime, and I shrieked, "We'll be in pine boxes soon if you don't slow down!" realizing that he had no idea what I was talking about and completely violating driver-passenger taxicab etiquette. Normally I just clutch John's hand, grit my teeth, close my eyes, and pray for the best outcome, never uttering a word about the cab driver's erratic or excessively fast driving.

"No problem, Missy," he said as he slyly looked at me in the rearview mirror and pushed a little harder on the accelerator. The ice had softened, now squishy under the car's tires, there was a little more traction, and suddenly the pavement was merely wet. Miraculously, we were back in the city. Our driver delivered us to the door of our hotel, charged us $300 and wished us well. We staggered into the warmth of the bar and joined the other Seahawks fans watching the first game ever played at Qwest Field with snow underfoot. John ordered me a "Lemon Drop," my sister Julie's favorite drink. The silky tartness of the lemon juice and vodka encountered the sugarcoated rim of the martini glass in a perfect marriage, and soon the memory of the perilous drive was almost gone.

November 28

In the morning John turned on the television and the weather-heads described last night as the worst storm in 200 years with the most precipitation Seattle had ever received in a single day. People were still stuck in their cars on the freeways, having spent the night huddled in chilly isolation, waiting for their tow trucks to arrive. Mr. Lexus included I bet.

The normally quiet street in front of the hotel pulsed with the sloshing beat of more rain and sleet. We waited half an hour for a taxi to take us to Boeing Field for the flight to the island and arrived with barely ten minutes to spare, due to another directionally-challenged taxi driver. As our six-passenger plane flew above the islands, what lay below us was a scene unlike any other I had ever seen. The islands looked like puffy white meringues floating in a vast sea of churning chocolate. Every rock and every island (of which there are estimated to be 450 in the San Juan archipelago) was dressed in white.

The main road into Friday Harbor was unplowed, concealing a sheet of treacherous ice below. The Victorian houses that lined the streets wore elegant white robes. The snow had revived their weary wood frames like a fresh coat of paint. Fruit still clung to the wizened branches of ancient apple trees, dangling like withered red baubles on icy necklaces.

Only two tire tracks wove through the snow-covered Brown Island road. Just three homeowners were in residence, the rest having fled to safer ports of call to weather the storm. The roadside was strewn with massive branches that the storm's winds had ripped from the trees that covered the island. The north sides of the 100-foot tall pines surrounding our house still bore a sheet of white ice which would remain for the next week, the temperature never rising above freezing. And the fire burned all day, all week, in our large stone fireplace.

November 29

Emboldened by our recent town car ride, every morning we endured the frigid dinghy ride to town and ran to our VW van, which, lacking snow tires, caused us to slide all the way to Lakedale. The wind had strewn dismembered trees across roads and onto the resort's cabin rooftops, leaving in its wake unanticipated view corridors and small mountains of kindling for next summer's campers. After a sub-zero morning spent standing for two hours with the contractor in the gutted remains of the campground washrooms, my toes went missing. They returned a few hours later, and for the rest of the week, I sheathed my feet in three layers of wool socks stuffed into rubber knee-high Wellingtons.

A few Lakedale employees stranded in the storm were taking a busman's holiday at the resort. The head housekeeper was holed up in the Lake House with her two daughters, enjoying a break from school. Midway through the week we discovered her wandering around the lodge's great room at noon, glass of wine in hand, admitting that there wasn't anything better to do than drink, since we had no guests, and she was sick and tired of the damned cold. It was getting to everyone.

I spent my days inventorying the cabins, determining what we could reuse, what we would have to replace, and how we could add more lighting to brighten the dark log interiors, while John worked with the contractor on the new bathhouse. We left Lakedale by late afternoon, to better escape the sea's chilly embrace on the dinghy ride, and to get back to the warmth of home.

DECEMBER

December 1

John's phone rang. It was Kelly, laughing hysterically.

"Did you guys read the *Dartmouth Review* today?" she giggled.

We didn't get the newspaper, but I made a mental note to get the online version to be better informed about campus happenings.

"No, we didn't," John answered, even though he had read his three other newspapers that day. "It must not have made the national news."

Kelly continued, "I just attended a rally with 500 other people to show support for the Native Americans, who are completely ticked off again because the *Dartmouth Review*'s headline today was "The Natives are Restless." It showed an image of an Indian warrior with a scalp in his hand. Can you believe it?"

John asked her what they were restless about, but she wailed, "Dad, that's not the point! The point is that they feel they are being persecuted and aren't welcome members of the Dartmouth student body!"

I told Kelly I was very proud she was becoming politically active and asked what had happened at the rally.

"The college president spoke and said that all students at Dartmouth, whatever their background, should feel welcome here. And then he brought up the fact that the University of North Dakota's president had just rebuked the Dartmouth athletic director for refusing to schedule a hockey game with UND because their team still uses an Indian logo."

Dartmouth's mascot had historically been an Indian. Since the 1920s, the school was also unofficially called the Big Green. During the early 1970s, the Indian mascot was declared to be "inconsistent with present institutional and academic objectives of the College in advancing Native American education," and since then, the students had been trying to garner support for a new mascot, since it was rather difficult to dress as a Big Green. Keggy-the-Keg, an anthropomorphic beer keg, was the most popular choice, but the Dartmoose was running a close second.

> 6:03 p.m. i just went to the tree lighting, it was pretty cool, except for the fact that it was raining and 60 degrees outside…it's supposed to snow soon…but the glee club sang and there was a reception with the president with cookies and egg nog and other yummy goodies. so cool. yay college. i don't think stuff like this happens at other colleges. and then ken burns, the guy who makes all those history movies, is coming tonight and i want to go, but i have toooo much studying to do! sigh. love ya! Kelly

December 3

After years of traveling, John and I have two rules we follow religiously to maintain our sanity while traveling.

> Rule 1: *For each leg of a trip, you are required to stay twice that number of days at your destination, or the trip will be too physically taxing to be worth setting foot on an airplane.*

For example, driving from Aspen to Denver, then flying from Denver to Seattle, and then flying from Seattle's Boeing field to Friday Harbor counts as three legs. Therefore, you would need to stay in Friday Harbor for six days to get the maximum benefit from the aggravation of traveling.

> Rule 2: *Any flight that departs or arrives after dark counts as two legs.*

Flying in the dark is not enjoyable, especially in coach, which has become the equivalent of traveling on a Mexican bus. The passengers are jammed together, knees up to their noses, their odiferous fast food bags sandwiched overhead along with live chickens so at least there is access to provisions should they be stranded on the tarmac after ten hours.

We arrived in Aspen late in the evening, having survived five legs (one leg counting double due to night flying) only to find my Land Rover's battery was dead. A major snowstorm had blanketed it with two feet of snow, and the Automobile

Association said they thought they would arrive in six hours... at 3:00 a.m. We took a cab home and decided to deal with the car in the morning.

New Rule 3:*Dead batteries count for an additional leg.*

December 4

Our attempts to jump start the car with John's car elicited not even a whimper in response from my engine. AAA now said they would arrive in three hours, so I called the Land Rover roadside assistance number for some alternative advice. After telling us to leave the charging cables on for a minimum of fifteen minutes without turning on the key, the agent offered a creative idea.

"Madam," he asked in his proper English accent, "you are at the Aspen airport, are you not?"

"Yes, I am," I said.

"Well I am aware that there are quite a number of Rovers in that vicinity. It is quite apparent that even though your car is turned off, when other Rover owners open their cars with their remote key devices, the transmission going through the air wakes up your car's battery. If this happens frequently, as I'm sure it must in Aspen, your battery will eventually go dead." It was a good answer but no solution to my problem.

1:54 a.m. just a heads up...freddy and the fishsticks are playing at the Belly Up Tavern on December 22! wonder if it's sold out?

love you! Kelly

12:15 p.m. who are freddy and the fishsticks? love ya, mom

1:12 p.m. that's the name for jimmy buffet and his band when he doesn't want anyone to know he's playing a small venue...

1:29 p.m. I just checked- it was sold out in seconds! bummer!

4:15 p.m. ooo, is it snowing??? CAUSE ITS FINALLY SNOWING HERE! YAAAAAAAAAY. granted it's not sticking much, but every little bit counts! love ya, Kelly

8:29 p.m. congrats!!!! at least you'll have a little white before you hit the beaches! are your finals done yet? luv and kisses, m

December 6

The snow that had buried my car had also provided enough snow to lay tracks on the Starwood cross-country ski trails, so I strapped on my Nordic skis and set out for my first ski of the season with Kelso running alongside me. Sandy arrived later for an afternoon "art day," a way to jumpstart the creative process for the art show I curate every year at the Aspen Chapel Gallery. My day consisted of watching Sandy arrange cut-paper collages and organizing my art table; moving stacks of drawings to the top of my under-utilized etching press, moving bath fixture catalogs to the shelf underneath my art table and trying to find the wire I would sculpt with. I did manage to roll out some Sculpey clay, emboss it, form it into a ball, encircle the ball with wire and bake it in the oven. Not a promising start.

When I start working on new art, the first projects off my table are initiated with utmost confidence and the unwavering belief that they will propel me to the top of the New York art world and I will be smiling from the cover of *ArtNews* magazine by next February at the latest. I usually end up throwing these first efforts in the trash as soon as the show is over.

December 7

After a cross-country ski at the Aspen golf course, a group of friends met for lunch in Aspen. Gail, with her Senator name badge attached to her lapel, joined us for fifteen minutes, sandwiching us between a meeting with the mayor of Aspen and a meeting with her new oil and gas constituents. Even though she hadn't been sworn in yet, she was already working eighty-hour weeks. Inevitably, the subject turned to our children in college. Four of us had freshman daughters and all of us were suffering from separation anxiety. I was one of the lucky mothers, as Kelly was still thrilled with her choice of school and as far as I could tell, she hadn't flunked out yet.

Another friend's daughter, on the other hand, was not as fortunate. She had been accepted via early decision to a college in upstate New York, the choice of many theater, art and music students, and after being accepted, she had had second thoughts about her choice.

"She knew it was a relaxed school before she went," said her mom, "but then she met her roommate. My daughter is a real girly-girl, so her bedding ensemble was perfectly coordinated in shades of pink, with matching posters on the walls, under-bed organizers, her clothes organized by color and style. Her roommate, on the other hand, brought virtually no clothes, the ones she does wear are black, and *her* bedding ensemble consists of black satin sheets. Nothing on the walls."

Gail, the mother of three daughters, commented that at this age, everyone is experimenting, and satin sheets aren't all that bad...except in the dead of winter in upstate New York. My friend rolled her eyes and continued. The two new roommates got along fairly well for the first few weeks, until my friends's daughter woke up one morning and saw two mounds in her roommate's bed instead of one. As she put her eye shades back on to think about how she would get out of bed and to the bathroom inconspicuously in front of the male visitor (the college version of the Ostrich Syndrome) she suddenly she heard a female giggle. And it wasn't one she recognized. She slowly lifted her eye shades, and saw another girl in bed with her roommate.

A few days later, the roommate returned to the dorm room with her hair shaved into a crew cut and announced that she had decided to change her name to Leo. At this point my friend's daughter decided she was through with her east coast school and was now planning on finding another, more conservative school to transfer to, hopefully in California.

December 8

There are now only ten final contestants on Top Chef, and while I rode the exercise cycle on the easy setting, my inner thighs still reminded me that they may never do Pilates again and the chefs bickered at each other while they cooked a fifteen minute Quick-Fire Challenge using canned foods. The winner prepared a dish involving deep-fried anchovies, canned asparagus, and fruit compote. As much as I love food, there are times when I'm grateful I am not a judge on that show. The rest of the program was devoted to the preparation of the Christmas dinner from hell; screaming and yelling contestants, vats of mashed potatoes, cranberry foam, and pumpkin brûlée that wouldn't set.

I was glad to leave the house and have a great bar meal with John at Pacifica, a seafood restaurant. We had small, black and grey gigamoto oysters from British Columbia, still exuding the sea from their ugly, crenellated shells, French fries tossed with fresh truffles, tuna tartar, and a crisp Caesar salad topped with flash-fried shrimp and calamari, accompanied by a glass of French chardonnay. An excellent meal. Dessert was Casino Royale, the new James Bond movie. All was well in the new adult world of Shelley and John.

> 12:08 p.m. hi sweetie!!! how are you doing in miami? did you have a good flight? how's the weather down there? no snow on the horizon so start praying for snow! hope all is going well!!! love, mums
>
> 1:02 p.m. miami is good. the weather is kind of icky right now...it was super windy when we were rowing and rainy. but its going pretty well. i am soooooo tired! love ya! Kelly
>
> 10:12 p.m. too bad about the weather! it'll prevent you from getting sunburned. James Bond was really good - i liked it better than your dad because it wasn't nearly as violent as that last one we saw, and the new JB is quite a hunk, in a rough-around-the-edges kind of way! get some sleep!!! and we can't wait to see you - am holding off on cookie baking till you get here! luv ya, mums

December 9

I woke up...another Saturday, a day like all the recent others, a day different from all the recent others. No clock, no meetings, no child to wake and prepare a healthy breakfast for, just me lounging around until the warm flush starts and I conclude it is safe to get out of bed in the bracing twenty-three degree bedroom air. Another Aspen periwinkle sky, clear, cloud free, a perfect palette for soaring contrails of the jets flying to Miami Beach at 30,000 feet.

"Buon giorno!" I chirped my morning greeting into the intercom letting John, who was sipping coffee in the kitchen, know that I was awake.

"Beautiful morning," he said. "I know we have work to do, but tomorrow it may be snowing. What do you say we have breakfast in town and take a few runs?"

After poached eggs and corned beef hash at the Weinerstube, a local restaurant frequented by many of the Austrian ski instructors who had come to Aspen in the 1950s, we boarded the brand new gondolas at the base of Aspen Mountain. They were spotlessly clean and boasted inward facing seats for more "interaction," that is, as long as the passengers weren't talking on their cell phones. Glass from floor to ceiling afforded an up-close-and-personal view of the unfortunate skiers wiping out on the notorious Dumps a thousand feet below.

My first ski run of the winter was in the sunshine atop perfectly groomed corduroy snow. We skied 10,000 vertical feet before noon, and left the mountain as last night's partygoers were wiping the sand from their bloodshot eyes.

Goal #10: *NO, NO, NO, you can't make any more goals until you make some headway on your other nine.*

Yes, but this is such a good one, and it would be so easy to do.

OK, scratch one off the list and I'll let you add this one. What is it, anyway?

No scratches, I've made a commitment to them, and some progress, even if it's only in a cerebral way.

What's the goal?

Get out on the snow every day, either on Nordic skis, alpine skis or hiking up the mountain.

Hmmmmmm. I could almost buy it, sounds like fun. How's the foot fungus coming, can we get rid of it?

Not yet. I'm making progress. I read an article that said to use a solution of 50% hydrogen peroxide and 50% water solution and spray it on your toes every day. I think it's working.

What about the needlepoint?

As soon as I finish designing the Lakedale campground washrooms, I'm going to pick that up again. And anyway, I have until next Christmas to finish it.

You're hopeless. Make it five days a week, and you've got yourself a deal.

Ahhh, the delicate art of self-negotiation.

Later in the day Kelly called as I returned from my daily walk with Kelso.

"Hi, Mom! It's me." I asked how our Miami girl was faring.

"Tired, as usual, but we're having fun. It's really windy... rain all day yesterday, really yucky rowing when it's wet, but at least it's not as cold as New Hampshire." Knowing she was probably ready to get back to Aspen I tried not to tell her how great our ski day had been, so I concentrated on what the crew team was doing.

"How's the food?" I asked.

"OK, we're cooking in most nights, and snacking a lot between practices. Kraft macaroni and cheese, burritos, that kind of stuff. I am so ready for a home-cooked meal! But listen to this, tonight we saw the space shuttle launch!"

"No way!" I realized that I had been so involved in all of the Lakedale planning, I hadn't read a newspaper in a week. In fact I didn't have a clue that NASA was still in operation.

"The team walked to the beach and we were able to see all the way to Orlando where it took off. It took about fifteen seconds, but we could see the capsule and the tail burning—way cool!"

"Someday, maybe your dad and I will see one of those."

"I hope so, it was amazing! Only six more sleeps and I'll see you guys, gotta run, we're going to the movies tonight!"

> 10:08 p.m. we are so excited to see you! more work on lakedale - it seems it's all i do! i've signed up for an online hotel/restaurant management class at the junior college to get a better handle on the industry. feel like i'm you - going back to school. thought we'd go to the new addition at Denver Art Museum when you arrive, it's supposed to be great. are you up for that? only five more sleeps til you're back! lots of love, mom

December 11

I am working non-stop on the plans for the Lakedale washroom remodel. I think I'm obsessed. I draft plan after plan on my computer, I research countless washroom fixtures, I pour over design magazines to determine what emotion I want those happy campers to experience as they shower off the campfire smoke. It has morphed from "cabin cute" to "prison chic" as I came to the realization that we needed a washroom that will remain indestructible to drunk rugby players from Canada. When I returned from lunch, Kelly's voice rang out from the answering machine, "I'm really ready to come home, Mom, I can't wait to see you guys!" I think she's actually missing us.

December 12

> 11:34 p.m. yay, i can't wait to come home!! yesterday we had the afternoon off, so we went to south beach. it was cool. we walked through the Hotel Delano. very chic! not nearly as scary as i remember when we went there in fourth grade. went shopping and then we saw james bond. he is quite the hunk, you were right. very nice eyes...this morning our coach had me row with the lightweight boys because they don't have enough people. it was interesting and i am not really sure why i was with them, cause usually they borrow a heavy. hmmm. anyways. cant wait to see you!! love you!!! Kelly

> 11:39 p.m. got my grades...i am happy with them, math was to be expected...it was the best i literally could do...i will just tell you now if you want to know, since you will find out any way!!
>
> anthro-b
>
> bio-b
>
> math-c
>
> life goes on!! love you!! Kelly
>
> 5:04 p.m. hi hon! don't worry about your grades. as long as you did your best, which i'm sure you did, that's all that matters. the first term is a huge adjustment. i'm off to a lecture tonight with a local gallery owner about how to market your art work and approach galleries. then only three more sleeps and you're here! have you been able to get more sleep? and make sure you take more $$$ than you need for the cab ride, sometimes cabbies charge more than they should - be aware! love and kisses, mumsy

December 13

The December meeting of the gourmet group was a traditional English Christmas lunch; everyone was busy with holiday parties in the evenings. We drank too much champagne while eating prime rib with Yorkshire pudding, roasted winter vegetables, creamy scalloped potatoes, and finished with homemade English puddings slathered in hard sauce. After we exchanged culinary gifts, everyone went home to nap for the rest of the afternoon.

December 14

> 8:44 p.m. hi sweets! we are leaving for Denver, and my laptop just died, so i am out of email touch. looks like i may have to get an apple computer too. will talk with you tonight. only 1 more sleep - yippee! love ya and see you tomorrow, mom

December 15

I have either turned a new leaf, or the excitement of having Kelly home is too much for me. We got to Denver the day before Kelly's arrival at Denver International; we wanted no excuses to be late. We arrived at the airport early. When Kelly first emerged from the plane and I saw her, tears streamed down my cheeks.

I put my arms around the Big Green sweatshirt she wore that screamed "College Student Coming Home for Christmas." A fraction of the Thanksgiving awkwardness was still apparent, but I didn't care, she was home. I sat in the backseat with Kelly, like I used to do when she came home from summer camp as a kid. With John as our chauffeur, we drove to the recently opened addition to the Denver Art Museum.

The art inside the structure was thought provoking, but the expensive new building was an architectural disaster. The roof leaked under the tonnage of Colorado snow. Patrons, distracted by the art, collided with the museum's interior walls, which jutted into corridors like the prows of sailing ships gone astray.

After lunch, Kelly and I went shopping at the Cherry Creek Mall, just like the old days...three months ago. Kelly couldn't stop talking about how glad she was to be back in Colorado; the clear blue sky, the wide-open spaces you could see out of, and the mountains. Real mountains. As was our annual custom, we dressed up for dinner and a traditional walk down the elegant stairway of the Brown Palace Hotel for a drink in the lobby. Kelly eyed something stronger than a Shirley Temple.

We ate dinner at an Italian restaurant recommended by the hotel concierge. Every surface was hard; the concrete floors, dropped ceilings covered in drywall, walls of stone, and no tablecloths on the maple tables all combined to create an atmosphere in which none of us could hear a word the other said. I also couldn't remember what we had eaten half an hour later, a certain indicator of a restaurant doomed to fail.

December 16

John and I did some power-Christmas shopping while Kelly slept, no doubt alleviating her recent sleep deprivation, then we drove back to Aspen. Warm glows have replaced my hot flashes, and I donned a glittery black cocktail dress, which I could still wiggle into and wear without its sweat-soaked black beads popping off into the champagne (and gin) at Bo and Cheryl's annual holiday party. Cheryl cooked and served the entire meal for seventy-five people and still looked ravishing in her gold taffeta skirt and sheer voile blouse.

December 17

I woke up early aware that Kelly was still dreaming in her bedroom next to ours. Kelso snoozed on his overstuffed pillow in the family room. Every head was in every bed exactly where every head was supposed to be. I felt at peace for the first time since Kelly left.

December 18

Kelly wanted to drive to Glenwood Springs at three in the afternoon to do some Christmas shopping. I wasn't in favor of the plan, pointing out that it was the darkest day of the year and there would be rush-hour traffic, mostly down-valley workers, with no car insurance, six people squeezed into a 1980 Honda sedan with no snow tires, plus roads could be icy....

John and Kelly looked at me like I was mad.

"Don't you see the danger in this plan?" I said.

"Shelley," John always used my given name when he wanted to get his point across, instead of his usual "honey." "Kelly is eighteen years old, she's a responsible driver, she's thought this through, and we have to trust her." Kelly nodded in accord. What was I to do?

In the first days with Kelly at home, it seemed as if we were sloshing around in a teapot full of changing roles, tiptoeing about new realities with awkward moments sporadically dripping out the spout. Learning not to ask what the brew was, and letting the tea pour out on its own when it was fully steeped. Adding the sweetness of motherly advice when it was asked for, after the tea was poured. Trusting that the mixture would be good. And if it wasn't perfect, you could always add some honey, or make another pot until you got it right.

December 19

One of our treasured traditions is the expedition to cut down the Christmas tree. The three of us, sometimes with another family or kid in tow, pack thermoses of hot chocolate, along with saws, ropes, bungee cords and a White River National Forest permit, and head into the backcountry to cut down a tree. We had waited to start our Christmas preparations until Kelly's return, so with only six days to go until Christmas, we were running late. John woke with a robust case of the flu and announced he couldn't trudge up a mountain so, with no other free days on the calendar, Kelly and I set off on the annual trek.

Sandy had told me about a new tree-cutting area. Every local who participates in this tradition has a secret spot that is divulged with great hesitation, and only to the closest of friends. Instead of our customary location in the mountains behind the coal ovens near Redstone, we drove twenty-five miles past the town of Basalt, up along the shore of the Frying Pan River and turned left onto a road past the hamlet of Thomasville. A bar there was the site of a murder a few years ago and the suspect was now on trial; a classic case of too little to do, too much whiskey, and one cute waitress leading on two gunslingers.

The new tree-cutting location was so secluded we passed it twice before realizing we were there. We clambered straight up the hillside, following the tracks of previous tree hunters whose footprints hadn't been eradicated by the recent snowfalls. Kelly and I like really fat trees, but John goes for skinnier versions, his reasoning being that you can see the ornaments better. The trees in this area were all a skinny variety of fir tree. Kelly and I learned our tree species the last time we attempted a solo tree-cutting expedition, after John had undergone knee surgery. We accidentally cut down a Colorado blue spruce, completely forbidden, as it was the state tree, but it was the most magnificent tree we had ever had. Vowing not to repeat our mistake, we checked the branches of every tree we were unsure of. Firs are friendly to the touch and spruces are spiky and dangerous, even with gloves on.

Wading through snow two feet deep, we climbed higher and higher, searching for that elusive, perfect tree. We identified a few potentials, but not the perfect one. None were fat enough for us.

"There it is Mom!" Kelly pointed to a tree halfway up the hill, hidden behind a skinnier model. "I'll take a look, you stay here." In a few moments she called down to me that it was perfect. "Come on up!" Plodding up the hill after her, I agreed and we pulled out the saws. The tree was ten feet tall with a huge wingspan and widely spaced branches perfect for hanging ornaments. It looked like a blue spruce, but had not a hint of blue color; it was completely green. We had a lengthy discussion about whether or not it could be a blue spruce, and in John's educated absence, determined it most definitely was not. It had to be a green spruce. For a tall tree it had a surprisingly thin trunk, so the sawing and chopping took only a few minutes, but hauling the whole tree with its massive branches down the hill wore us out. We reached the car half an hour later, slipping and sliding, snow inside our boots and up our backs, arms aching, laughing like crazy fools.

John was sound asleep when we returned. By the time he woke up, we had erected the tree in its stand in the corner of the living room and were admiring our handiwork, eggnogs in hand. Now all we had left to do was decorate the house, bake ten kinds of Christmas cookies, wrap presents, and sing, "Deck the Halls." No problem.

December 20

Kelly's goal over the Christmas break was to use as many days of her twenty-day college ski pass as she could. She was determined to ski, blizzard or shine, and in the absence of a friend, I was her designated ski partner. To be with Kelly, I disregarded my aversion to flat light and frigid weather and had some of the best skiing I've had in years.

The mountains were barely visible across the valley. We pulled on our ski pants (mine still fit despite the absence of weigh-ins) and drove to Tiehack Mountain. A colossal storm had blanketed Denver with three feet of snow and all incoming flights to Aspen were cancelled. There were no cars at the base of the ski hill and no skiers on the mountain. Just me, Kelly, and knee-high powder with a groomed base underneath. It was like floating through a sea of whipped cream—cool, silent, non-caloric magic.

After skiing, I met my doctor for my annual female check-up and to discuss my current hormone levels. He was a gentle man, formal in an old-school doctor way and he asked me the same questions every year.

"How is the Northwest these days?"

"Just great, thanks!"

"And your daughter, what year is she in school?"

"She's a freshman in college."

"And where is she going?" I proudly dragged out the answer. "D-a-r-t m-o-u-t-h." I loved hearing it roll off my tongue.

"Impressive," he smiled, elevating me to "parent of Ivy-Leaguer" status. He knew I had nothing to do with it, but allowed me to bask in the glow of my daughter's success. He wrote in my chart, no doubt noting in his tiny cursive handwriting Kelly's college so he would be prepared to ask me next year how she was doing at Dartmouth.

"And after our adjustments, how are you doing with the current level of your medicine?" he asked after the usual uncomfortable exam.

I gushed, "I'm almost back to normal, thank God! I wake up only a few nights, and I have no more hot flashes. I feel like a new woman! But I do have a question for you." He waited patiently. I explained the theory of "gutting it out," and asked him if it had any medical merit. In a three-minute scientific response, he completely debunked the theory, articulating that every body was different and reacted to menopause in completely different ways. A woman didn't have to pay her dues with hot flashes, sleepless nights or erratic behavior to get her "I Survived Menopause" pin. I was vindicated. I could take my bio-identical estrogen free of guilt.

On the way home I stopped to pick up Kelly at her friend Lauren's house and chatted for a few moments with Lauren's dad, Harry, who was a hands-on father to his two daughters and had also been active in school affairs.

"Isn't it great having them back, Harry? I love having the girls home!" I beamed with pride at Kelly and Lauren, in a corner, giggling hysterically about some recent college escapades. We gazed at them adoringly, just as we had probably done when they were three months old and spewing digestive juices all over our shoulders.

Harry, ever a voice of reason, said, "Shelley, they're gone... they're not ours anymore," remorse tinged his voice. "They're only passing through on the way to another life and we have to be happy they stop by to visit once in a while." He saw the dismay on my face as I accepted the truth of his statement, but I tried to bounce back, and gave him a hug on my way out the door, Kelly in tow.

"You're right, Harry, but based on the fact that we live in a premier vacation destination and have checkbooks, I hope they'll be good long visits for the next few years!"

Kelly and I sang "Joy to the World" at the top of our lungs all the way home, then baked a batch of cookies, hauled the decorations out of the storage closet, and basked in the atmosphere of goodwill that settles over the holidays like hot fudge oozing over vanilla ice cream.

December 21

We skied through a foot of new snow on top of Aspen Mountain. The locals call it "hero snow" because you can do no wrong. Due to the incredible amount of snow that had fallen, the Denver airport was officially closed. As a result, no one could fly into Aspen. Driving through town was like driving on top of a thick, white flannel blanket. Main Street's lampposts were encircled with garlands of fir and twinkling lights. Carl's Pharmacy was filled with sick tourists picking up prescriptions and scouring the aisles for cold remedies. Visitors walked the streets in fur coats which concealed leather garments trimmed with fringe and jewels; others paraded through town in $10,000 ski outfits that would never see the top of Aspen Mountain. The closest powder they would see would be the salt-rimmed glass of a margarita in the Little Nell après-ski bar.

December 22

My surprise Christmas present for John and Kelly was tickets to the Jimmy Buffett concert at the Belly-Up Tavern. Since I was too late to get tickets from the box office, I decided to check e-Bay on the off chance that some tickets would appear. Sure enough, a scalper was offering eight tickets at twice their original price. I couldn't bring myself to purchase them, but each day when I checked the website, fewer tickets remained. When I saw only three tickets left, I forced myself to hit the "buy" button and the tickets were mine.

We arrived early to secure a place standing at a bar overlooking the stage. To allow for more concertgoers most of the seating had been removed (except for a few chairs for the really big spenders at $700 a ticket).

Jimmy, a short man with a goofy grin and guitar in hand took the stage precisely at 9:00 p.m. After singing a few songs, his band Fishsticks joined him and played nonstop for three hours while the crowd danced and sang along with every tune. Midway through the concert, Jimmy took off his sandals, explaining that life was too short to have to wear shoes and it was important to keep life simple and enjoy it to the hilt. In agreement, the tall blonde model standing behind us sang in harmony with Jimmy, "Let's all just get drunk and screw!" at the top of her lungs. I thought about covering Kelly's tender ears, but decided she'd certainly heard worse at college. When we returned home, happy and tired, John decided he was going to take Jimmy's words to heart.

Could this mean no shoes in his closet or something more drastic?

December 23

Kelly and I skied Snowmass Mountain, then we came home and baked more cookies. The three of us watched the movie "White Christmas," another holiday tradition. Kelly has been back a week, and it is as if she had never left. Any hints of awkwardness have disappeared, and we are back in easy mode.

December 25

One of the advantages of having a college-aged child is that you can sleep in on Christmas morning. In fact, by 9:30 a.m. we finally had to rouse Kelly so we could get on with the day. After opening our stockings, we ate eggs benedict covered with roasted red pepper hollandaise sauce, which provided the sustenance we needed to open the gifts that were sitting under the tree. Unfortunately for me, most of my presents were menopause-related. They included the *Hot Flash Board Game* (for me to play with my similarly afflicted friends), the *Hot Flash Cook Book*, and last, but not least, my own *Personal Cooling System* sent by my sister Julie. It was a hard plastic horseshoe that, when filled with water, blew cold air down your neck and rendered the wearer human again. Too bad my hot flashes were a thing of the past. We had a raucous Christmas dinner with Jayne, Fred and a few other friends, eating and drinking while the snow fell thickly outside.

December 26

I always feel like entertaining around the holidays. About a week ago I realized I had no parties planned so we decided to have Kelly's high school friends over for a casual evening the Wednesday following Christmas. I spent the day down valley in Glenwood Springs buying party supplies and cooking ingredients. The menu would include George's at the Cove's famous soup and homemade chili. Dessert was easy; we had our tins full of Christmas baking. Kelly and I stayed up past midnight working on our yearly jigsaw puzzle, an immense one of 2,000 pieces which boasted colorful detailed logos from hotels around the world.

December 27

At precisely six o'clock, our first guest arrived. He had been Kelly's date to the senior prom and his punctuality was the result of impeccable breeding from his Irish diplomat father and southern belle mother. Soon after her other high school friends (now college freshmen) arrived, well ahead of their parents. They were thrilled to be back together, and immediately gravitated to the living room, organic sodas (not beer) in hand, talking and laughing, exchanging tales about roommates, professors, frats, and completely ignorant of anything else.

We parents watched from the kitchen, glasses of wine in hand, cameras clicking photos of their babies, a scene eerily reminiscent of the days when we would gather, again with glasses of wine in hand, to admire our offspring in their cribs. In those days, the wine was necessary for our sanity, but now we raised our glasses with a sense of relief, pride, and sadness that our hands-on days of parenting were over.

December 30

Every year after Christmas Kathy hosts a woman's hike and lunch. Thirty women who often never see each other in one place except for this gathering assemble, hike up Snowmass Mountain for two hours, then eat soup and chat for another two hours. This year, since many of us were adjusting to having our offspring in college, the talk turned to our common experiences.

Everyone agreed that when children came home from their first term at college, there was a honeymoon period. Family life was as sweet as a warm cinnamon bun eaten straight from the oven. This was followed by intermittent sniping ("Do I really have to go to bed at three in the morning, Mom? That's so lame!"), resulting in either out-and-out rebellion and demands for independence (boys), or acceptance and understanding that being at home, with its loss of freedom, was a temporary situation which would be quickly rectified once they were back on campus (girls). We all agreed that the great telephone and email relationships we had developed with our children over the past three months didn't always mean great face-to-face communication; sometimes the phone worked better. And then there was the heartbreaking recognition that even though our children were successfully launched, maybe we were not quite ready to be done with mothering.

December 31

John was leaving on Tuesday to meet with Lakedale's contractor and he needed to take the washroom plans with him. I worked all day to finish them while Kelly skied with her buddies. After dinner, I assumed we would all have a quiet evening of board games and movies; maybe a little champagne to welcome in the New Year. After two weeks at home however, Kelly and friends were anxious to escape their parent's clutches. Despite the fact that the police chief had declared a midnight curfew for all citizens eighteen years and under, they were determined to watch the New Year's Eve fireworks and partake in some college-type fun in Aspen. After two hours of intense negotiations, John and I agreed she could go into town and spend the night at an in-town friend's house. His mom would confiscate everyone's car keys upon arrival and the fun would begin.

The irony of this situation is that three weeks ago, Kelly could have been out until five in the morning playing beer pong or streaking the Green, and we wouldn't have given it a second thought. Having your child in the same town while wending her way to adulthood is a completely different affair than when she is doing it ten states away. I slid into bed before midnight next to the already dreaming John, took a sidelong glance at the fireworks fracturing the sky, and fell asleep.

JANUARY

January 2

Five in the morning arrived far too soon as we staggered to the car to drive Kelly to Denver for her flight back to Dartmouth. She was surprisingly alert, a vestige of her fall schedule I assumed, and was eager to return to school. The queue for the security checkpoint zigzagged back and forth, with twenty rows of travelers ahead of us as Kelly and I entered the maze. At each turn in the line, I grew more and more frantic at the thought of her leaving and as we approached the final turn, only one teardrop fell out of my bleary right eye. I had been fully prepared to return to my early Dartmouth era blubbering self, but was pleasantly surprised by my grown-up reaction.

Kelly hugged me, waved to John, who had been more mature than I and hadn't needed to clutch his daughter through twenty twists of the security line, then she disappeared into the depths of the airport.

Ready to get back to work, we stopped at a tile manufacturer close to the airport to research yet more renovation ideas for the Lakedale washrooms. While I was leaving their restroom, my cell phone took an unexpected dive from my pocket into the toilet and in a nanosecond, I was an out of control, sobbing mess. As a result of this, I learned the true meaning of the word "transference:" first, that Kelly's departure had been transferred to the soggy cell phone lying at the bottom of the toilet, and secondarily, the fact that when you go to the cell phone store to request a new battery for your dead mobile phone, don't try to lie and claim you don't know why your phone stopped working. They know immediately that you have dropped your phone into a body of water, either clean or not so, because of a tell-tale red dot shining from the inside of the battery compartment.

The only saving grace to the day was the beef Carpaccio we ate for dinner at a new Italian restaurant across the street from our hotel in downtown Denver. If I had been an operatic diva, I would have sung its praises in a Puccini inspired aria; bass notes of paper-thin beef trilling to shaved Grana Padano cheese with brilliantly-dressed arugula floating like a soprano solo on top. Pavarotti would have been proud.

January 4

In one of my previous art lives, I tried to master the technique of silk screen printing. Layers of colored ink are squeegeed through a silk screen (with resistant images attached) to produce a final print. One technique used frequently is called a "blend" and involves spreading two or three different colors of ink horizontally on the screen and blending them together form a seamlessly graduated color sequence.

At dawn, as I drove John to the airport, the sky was a perfectly executed blend; deep blue on the horizon, melting into cerulean blue in the middle and topped with the pale ghost of a blue about to envelope the morning's yellow sun. Jets flitted like fireflies across the canvas of the sky on their way to land at the airport. Even for a non-morning person like me, it was a sight worth getting up to see.

January 5

For the past several months I had been counseling Kelly that the college years are a great time to be alive, where all she had to do is think of herself, *and isn't that a wonderful thing,* when I had another epiphany. All of the things I had been telling her would be true for me too...for the next two weeks anyway. Kelly was back in college and John was on his way to meet with the Lakedale contractor. My days and nights would be completely mine. No responsibilities (except Kelso, who was utterly pliable). I wasn't sure I liked the idea.

Immediately after my epiphany, the phone rang. Kelly. Evidently my liberty was going to be shorter than anticipated.

She wailed, "Mom, my life sucks...I can't get any classes, I'm rowing on the 'f…ing' (*I have noticed the complete erosion of her carefully cultivated language recently)* Erg machine all the time, I am so lame with boys…."

I could hear her crying over the phone. *Hadn't she signed*

up for her classes months ago? Would I have to go through the same conversation we'd had last term again?

"Now, now, peanut," I said in my sweet, comforting mother voice, "tell me about your classes and then we can work on the other things."

"I just found out about a really cool internship this summer in Washington, D.C., but in order to take it, I have to be in Public Policy this term. But Public Policy conflicts with my writing seminar, which I also have to take in order to take my mandatory Freshman Seminar spring term. And Spanish is too basic, so I think I should switch to French." I unearthed my book of Dartmouth class offerings and we spent the next hour on the phone, solving her schedule dilemma.

January 6

> 1:48 p.m. hi sweetie! in light of the fact that you're having rain, i hesitate to tell you what i did this morning, but it involved sliding downhill through 14 inches of new snow on aspen mountain...wish you were here! also, i've sent you some flannel sheets to aid with the cold...let me know if they fit! is the mini-fridge you got for Christmas working out? am going to work on art and the new years card tomorrow. I'm making progress! hope all is well and that you get some snow soon, love and kisses, mom

> 1:52 a.m. i am very sad about the weather, i even made a facebook group called "skiers for keeping winter white." so far it has 29 members! i am very jealous of your powder experiences. the fridge is good. still trying to get milk for it. have a good week doing anything you want! Kelly

January 7

> 8:11 a.m. am off to meet Jayne to borrow her sewing machine for the New Year's cards, which are under way, hope to have them done today, so I can really concentrate on the art thing, which is not progressing at all. i'll have to stop skiing, but it's so tempting on gorgeous powder days like today! hope the snow gods get to hanover soon! love and kisses, mums

7:56 a.m. why do you need a sewing machine for the cards? interesting. love you! Kelly

11:12 a.m. i'm going to sew pages together to create mini-books (the subject is you going off to college). just got a call from your dad. he's really sick up at the island, so don't call him, he doesn't want to be disturbed by the phone. poor guy, sounds like the flu....

January 9

I have now obliterated at least an entire tree's worth of paper in pursuit of completing my annual New Year's card. Revisions, rewrites and reprints. My printer decided not to print anything that involved black ink, and I couldn't find any black ink cartridges in my office. It finally dawned on me that I should try to clean the print heads, and luckily, that worked. The cards were finally finished.

I left for Denver to attend Gail's official swearing-in ceremony half an hour later than projected. I checked into my hotel, quickly changed clothes, and walked six blocks to attend a party to celebrate her last night as a private citizen—although I'm sure she wasn't looking at it that way.

All the walls in the contemporary home where the party was held were painted a brilliant shade of lime green. Large abstract landscape paintings, reminiscent of Frida Kahlo, hung on the walls, each one incorporating a vivid splash of green. The invitation specified that the party would be over at eight o'clock, so I left at 8:03. Well-fed and invigorated by the walk back to the hotel I had just stepped into the room when the phone rang.

"Mom, I need some advice about classes." *I was positive she was enrolled in her classes, had already gone to the first week's lectures, and probably had done lots of homework already. What sort of advice did she need?*

"I think I need to take chemistry. Everyone else on my floor that's thinking about pre-med is taking it, and it's only available this semester. Plus I already know pretty much everything the professor is talking about in French."

I asked, "Did your advisor mention this?"

"No." *$45,000 a year and no advising?*

"Have you found out if you can get into the class, and what about the add/drop deadline?" I continued.

"I can get in, the max is 130 kids and there are only 83 in it now, so it's not a problem. Let me check...oh, good, the drop deadline is tomorrow, I'm OK. What do you think, should I take it?" I had a lengthy discussion with her about getting an advisor other than me, and to go ahead and take the class.

"Thanks, Mom, just wanted to get your opinion! Talk to you tomorrow!"

January 10

I arrived at the state capitol building precisely at 8:45 a.m. per Gail's instructions, Starbucks cappuccino in hand, feeling very smug for having navigated my way there, parked, and arrived where I was supposed to be on time.

The building was beautiful in an 1890's kind of way. Gleaming brass balustrades spiraled under the huge rotunda overhead, flanked the Grand Staircase's white marble risers. Gail shared a corner office on the third floor with a veteran senator with a view that stretched over the city. I wondered aloud how she had wrangled such a plum office as a freshman senator.

"Oh," she laughed, "they call me the Million-Dollar Baby because that's what the Democrats spent to win my seat. I've already been given the vice-chairmanships of two committees so we have a better chance of keeping my seat in the next election."

Gail's friends and family walked into the senate chambers just before ten. Her immediate family stood on the red-carpeted floor while the rest of us watched from the gallery above. Large stained glass windows with images of Colorado's governors surrounded the room, and old oak desks, interspersed with modern dark blue filing cabinets, were arranged in a semi-circle around the floor. The senators sat in comfortable looking high-backed blue velvet chairs.

The opening ceremony was impressive. The honor guards carried flags, and after long-winded speeches segued into the swearing-in ceremonies, the tears flowed freely at the emotion of it all. It was almost enough to make me want to become a senator too, until an hour later when the excitement had passed, an interminable amount of bills were read, and if I were actually a senator, I would now be dozing in my cushy velvet chair.

> 8:53 p.m. i forgot to tell you that i used my lovely flannel sheets last night and they were super warm and cuddly! i don't know how we didn't discover them in colorado before! thanks, love ya! Kelly
>
> p.s. we're going to maine for our first cross-country ski meet this saturday!

January 11

Thank God I'm married, because I would make a terrible single person. I have managed to remember to feed and walk the dog every day, but beyond that, there is no order in my life. All I eat are the seven varieties of soup and the four salads I purchased from Whole Foods last week. I have so few dirty dishes that I haven't run the dishwasher in two weeks. If I eat before nine at night, very bad for Goal #1 (the diet thing), it is a miracle. I talk to Kelso constantly, whenever he emerges from sleeping in Kelly's closet, reinforcing the rationale for old ladies having sixty cats; there would always be one around to talk to.

January 12

Betty, the brassy blond caterer, was booted off Top Chef today as I peddled my way through a second hour on the exercise bike. She was starting to get on my nerves anyway. Before I delved into the New Year's cards again, I quickly designed the invitations for the February art show, which I had decided to entitle *Seeing...RED*. All ten invited artists would be asked to incorporate the color red into their artwork. The image for the invitation was created by the head of the sculpture department at Anderson Ranch, a local art colony. Given his stature in the art world, I considered it a coup that he would be participating in the show.

I had taken my first sculpture class from him. He once gave me some insights into the art world by defining the making of sculpture as one of two processes, art or craft. Art occurred as a result of an artist's need to express himself; it piqued a viewer's curiosity and evoked a sense of mystery that remained long after the viewer had left the piece. Craft was an art form in which the viewer knew exactly what he had seen; in other words, nothing mysterious about it. Craft was purchased more frequently than art. Obviously art was what I should be striving to create, unless of course, I actually wanted to make some money.

After quickly printing, assembling and sewing fifteen more New Year's cards, I threw all seventy-five into a box, took them to the post office and mailed them. I was completely relieved until it dawned on me that I only had three days to finish making all the art for the show before John arrived back home.

Procrastinating once again, I called the Land Rover dealership about my car. I had left it with them five days ago to have them investigate why the transmission light kept blinking. The Service Manager, explained that they were waiting for a special transmission fluid so they could perform some diagnostics tests. The fluid had to be shipped via ground transportation, as it was an extremely hazardous material. This situation reminded me of our last new car purchase, a Volkswagen EuroVan. In the first two months we owned it, the van spent twenty-nine days in the dealer's shop, one day shy of legally becoming a lemon, until the dealer installed a new transmission. This was not looking good.

8:51 p.m. hi hon! have a great trip tomorrow and ski well! luv and kisses, Mom

11:57 p.m. hi mom. i will call you tomorrow from the wonderful town of rumford, maine. love you too! Kelly

January 13

> 5:22 a.m. mommy, i missed the bus for our first ski race at rumford and i don't know what to do! it was supposed to leave at 7 and i didn't press the alarm's snooze button, so i got there at 7:10 ... and now i can't find anyone ...

When I woke up, late, and checked my email, I found the distraught message from Kelly. I sent her a brief email suggestion to buy a second alarm clock and hoped this would be one of those teachable, albeit painful moments. What else could I do four hours after the fact?

Fourteen inches of new snow had fallen overnight, so I decided to take a few runs before seriously working on the art. Ski jacket on, skis and helmet in the car, but where were my ski boots? I racked my brain, as the powder continued to accumulate, and it dawned on me that they were in the back seat of my car, which was forty miles away in Glenwood Springs at the Land Rover dealership. The best powder day of the year, and I had no ski boots. I went to my studio and started to work.

I dipped three foot-long lengths of string into red rubber tool dip.

I made thin wire orbs and dipped them into Plaster of Paris.

I used red thread to sew pockets along the top edge of paper squares, and then dipped them into hot beeswax.

I cracked eggs in two, and dipped their shells into blue rubber tool dip.

I sculpted wire into sausage-like shapes and suspended buttons inside them.

I stabbed a block of clay with a pencil like a school teacher with murder on her mind. Then I used the pencil to makes holes in the clay and filled them with Plaster of Paris. Lastly, I placed small loops of bent wire in the plaster to hang the jagged shards of clay that I'd created.

All in all, a productive day.

> 9:54 p.m. campus wide snowball fight!

> 10:33 p.m. fun! how was your weekend? did you buy an alarm clock? time to get back to the art world! love, mums

January 15

It has been cold, really cold the last few days. Usually when snow arrives, the temperature hovers at a balmy 32 degrees and it's possible to walk up the driveway in a T-shirt to fetch the paper (despite years of cajoling and hundreds of treats Kelso remains unwilling to do it for me).

Last night the thermometer sank to 26 degrees below zero and didn't rise above 10 degrees all day. When I took Kelso for his afternoon walk, the air was so burdened with cold I could touch it. The setting sun sat low in the sky, surrounded by a halo of frozen pink cotton candy. As we walked up the hill, the tiny hairs inside my nose froze solid and became miniature stalactites that swayed with each breath. And when the sun finally slipped behind the mountains, it sucked all the light from the valley along with it. Kelso and I slid back down the hill in total blackness, feeling lucky to make it back to the house. I rewarded him for his unwavering devotion in the face of my erratic lifestyle by whipping up a batch of his favorite homemade dog biscuits.

Kelso's Favorite Dog Biscuits

Yield: 4 dozen

1 CUP ROLLED OATS
⅓ CUP BUTTER
1 CUP BOILING WATER
¾ CUP CORNMEAL
2 TEASPOONS WHITE SUGAR
2 TEASPOONS CHICKEN BOUILLON GRANULES
½ CUP MILK
1 CUP SHREDDED CHEDDAR CHEESE
1 EGG, BEATEN
3 CUPS WHOLE WHEAT FLOUR

Preheat oven to 325 degrees F. In a large bowl, combine rolled oats, butter, and boiling water. Let stand 10 minutes. Grease cookie sheets.

Thoroughly stir in cornmeal, sugar, bouillon, milk, cheddar cheese, and egg. Mix in flour, 1 cup at a time, until a stiff dough has formed.

Knead dough on a lightly floured surface, mixing in additional flour as necessary until dough is smooth and no longer sticky. Roll or pat out dough to ½-inch thickness. Cut with a bone shaped cookie cutter, and place 1 inch apart onto the prepared cookie sheets.

Bake 35 to 45 minutes until golden brown. Cool before serving. Store in loosely covered container.

7:53 p.m. i ordered a cool "neverlate" alarm clock that has a different alarm for everyday! which will be super useful as i never wake up at the same time every day anymore! the snowball fight was awesome! love ya

10:52 p.m. is there any snow left on the quad after the fight? what a great idea for an alarm clock...perfect! i spent my entire day at doctor's offices, nothing serious, but i have to have a little physical therapy on my shoulder, too much skiing. beautiful sunny day today...if only I had my ski boots - i think i'll have try to get them from the car dealership tomorrow! xox, mom

January 16

Kelly's despair at missing her first ski race had dissipated after her Nordic teammates had returned from the race. She was back in happy Dartmouth-land.

"Mom, I forgot to tell you about my internship! I applied for a program for pre-med kids to see if they really want to be doctors. We had to choose between five different specialties and shadow that doctor throughout the term. Isn't that cool?"

"Incredibly cool," I agreed. "What kind of doctor did you get?"

"My first choice, the cardiovascular surgeon. I already have my official badge, and get to scrub in on a surgery next week...I am so excited! By the way, when was my last tetanus shot? And have I had a Hepatitis B vaccine?" My major concern was that cardiovascular surgery was a somewhat bloody proposition, and my daughter had a hard time picking a zit. In the old days of active parenting, just last year, I would have called the hospital, arranged for a chair for her to sit in during the surgery, and been waiting in the car with smelling salts to rescue her after she fainted. I am now in the brave new world of "letting go," so I bit my tongue.

"Oh, and I've signed up to be a tour guide...you know all the ones we saw on our college tours? The fun part is that they teach you how to walk backwards while you talk. And I'm sending you some photos of our Bikini Ski!"

"Bikini ski?" I asked.

"After the first snowfall of the year, its tradition for all the Nordic girls to put on bikinis and ski around the Green... it was so cold!" I quickly checked my email and there was the Nordic team, ski-caps on, bikinis revealing goose-pimpled bellybuttons, skis attached to quivering legs, and big smiles on every face.

John returned home this afternoon via San Diego, where he had had a growth removed from his ear; it was bandaged into a pointed appendage that made him look like Mr. Spock. We celebrated with lunch at Gusto, our favorite Aspen trattoria. It felt good to be in the outside world again, eating something other than soup. A grilled chicken panini with fresh mozzarella, arugula, and roasted red peppers was the perfect coming-out meal.

January 17

> 12:52 p.m. its 6 degrees, but it feels like -6 ... its soooooooooooooo cold! my nostrils are freezing off! and that alarm needs to get here soon because i almost slept through another class...luckily I made it. until then i was thinking of taping over the button that turns off the alarm so that i can't push it. what do you think? love ya, Kelly

January 18

"Hey Shelley Bogaert, this is the Service Manager from Land Rover." He calls everyone by his or her first and last names. I think he likes the sound of two names clanking together.

"Thank you so much for sending up my ski boots!" I exclaimed. He had delivered them to me yesterday so that I could take advantage of the bounteous powder.

He continued, "I hate to tell you this, but we received the transmission fluid, ran some tests, and the warning light still came on. The factory has authorized us to put in a new transmission, so you'll be without your car for another week. I am really sorry!" What are the odds of two brand-new cars both having their transmissions replaced within the first year? Not a glowing endorsement for the automobile industry.

12:06 hi sweetie! was just thinking about dinner reservations for when we come to Dartmouth...i'm so excited! i got the schedule for the winter carnival and it looks like wednesday night might be good for the canoe club? do you want to invite some friends? lov ya lots, mom

4:20 p.m. am thinking about where to go abroad next year and am looking at barcelona, fez or prague. the more i think about it, the more i would MUCH rather go to somewhere like fez or prague...so much more interesting and you can't just go there all the time. you can do barcelona any time, and i am sure it would be great, but there's no magic to it... wednesday would be fine for dinner, i will ask some people if they want to come, but it might be less awkward if you just met my friends at the dorm rather than at dinner. you will meet them either way.

5:31 p.m. when you said there was no magic to it, that's the key. you want to be excited about what you're doing, and have fun too! i just made reservations at the canoe club for four people on wednesday the 7th - so if you want to add anyone else, let me know! I hate to admit this but i actually watched American Idol last night while i was making a sculpture - weird show! not american culture at its finest, but i'm going to watch next week, because one of our island neighbors' nieces is in it, and may have made it on to the show! XOX, mums

January 19

Another powder day, and another day of work on Lakedale. For the most part, I was enjoying what I was doing and I have to admit, I brought it on myself. I spent hours at the computer researching economical design solutions for the cabins; washable area rugs for $29, curtain panels for $39, wall sconces for $49. I can't imagine designing without the internet now. Gone are the days of reps arriving for scheduled appointments laden with catalogs and fabric samples. It can all be done with click of a mouse.

After a lengthy discussion, John and I finally agreed on the basic furnishings for the cabins and I started ordering sofas and upholstered side chairs. The rest would be easy. On the spur of the moment, we went to see an afternoon movie, *Letters from Iwo Jima,* Clint Eastwood's latest epic and another Academy Award contender. We left the house at 3:30, and as we drove down Cemetery Lane, we passed two school buses, filled with kids on their way home from school. It suddenly occurred me that I was enjoying the freedom of not having to wait at the bottom of the hill for the bus, not worrying about Kelly's after-school activities, and not worrying about when she would arrive home after she could drive herself. We could leave home at three and not come back until midnight, and no one would care, except maybe the hungry dog. It was liberating to be freed from the world of day-to-day education. Stepping off the ever-chugging train of school events. Leaping from the storied towers of academia into...afternoon movies.

January 20

"Hi."

"Uh, hi! ...Who is this?"

"It's me."

"Kelly?"

"Yea."

Her voice was so faint and tired I hardly recognized it. I should probably get iChat going on my new Apple laptop, so I could picture her in moments like this.

"You sound really tired, honey," I said. "How did you do in your Nordic race?"

"OK, considering it's the first time I've been on classic skis in a year, the race was thirty kilometers, and all I had for breakfast was half a bowl of oatmeal." She groaned at the memory.

"Holy shit (pardon my French), that's eighteen miles!" I exclaimed.

"Yah...."

"I can barely hear you, maybe you should take a nap." *Sometimes I just couldn't control myself.* "Sounds like the Neverlate alarm clock worked...you made it to the bus on time?"

"Like a charm! I'm heading down for a nap...love you, bye." Her husky voice faded off and I sensed she was almost asleep before she switched her phone to off.

January 21

I emailed Kelly about the eye surgery Kelso had yesterday to remove a harmless growth from the inside of his eye. The vet who performed the procedure called him a nut, because Kelso happily wagged his tail throughout the entire operation, one in which, the vet said, most dogs would have tried to bite his arm off.

> 4:13 p.m. oh, poor puppy, give him lots of hugs for me! by the way, i auditioned for the dartmouth chamber orchestra today and played terribly but i think the director was desperately in need of clarinetists, since there were none, so i got in! love you!

> 5:22 p.m. you are too much! congratulations! how often do you have to practice? it's snowing here, but am going to take Kelso out for a walk. poor guy, he has to wear a collar so he won't scratch his eye out - he looks like he was in a fight with a pit bull, but seems to be taking it well! he's getting lots of love so is in heaven! love, M

January 22

In the spirit of being a "life-long learner," and because I actually wanted to know something about the hospitality industry in which we are now heavily invested, I signed up for a web-based course called *Hotel Sales and Marketing* through our local junior college. I had dutifully ordered the textbook and was ready to study. Today was the first day of the virtual class. Despite the fact that I already had a college degree and an MBA I was as excited as if I were five years old and walking into my first day of kindergarten. Unfortunately, the klieg lights illuminating the X Games at Buttermilk Mountain across the valley kept me awake all last night, making me a lot less ready to study.

In 2002, the Aspen Ski Company agreed to host the ESPN Winter X Games. The event originated in California as an alternative to the Olympics but had since gone mainstream. In its first year in Aspen, snowboarders with baggy bottom-dwelling pants, shaggy-haired freestyle skiers and cigarette-smoking snowmobile drivers all mingled at the base of Buttermilk. It was a crazy quilt of music, freebies, and local high-school kids ditching school to hang out on the slopes. And there were no lights at night.

In the second year of the X Games, ESPN arrived a few weeks earlier and added a single brilliant light that burned all night, not enough to rob me of sleep, but an annoyance all the same. This year there would be over 75,000 attendees, and ESPN had arrived for the setup a month ahead of the event. They started preparations with one small, but brilliant light. A few days later, as the 150-foot long half-pipe was being groomed, more intense spotlights higher up the mountain were added. Then colored lights arrived, defining the performance areas, the snowmobile course, the half-pipe, and the slope-style course. Next, five immense television screens were placed on the lower portion of the ski hill, so the event that was in progress, or its rerun, could be replayed for those attendees who had missed it while talking on their cell phones to their friends back in LA. After all the lights were installed, they were then kept illuminated all night ...for the rest of the month. And in an ironic twist, the Aspen Ski Company was just awarded the "Green Ski Company of the Year" award.

I had to wonder why, after I had finally returned to a normal pattern of sleep, was I forced to wake up again at all hours of the night? At least I wasn't covered in sweat this time, but this was certainly going to affect my studies.

> 1:22 pm hi Kelly! how's your day going? it is so gorgeous here; sunny day, blue skies, your dad and i blew off our work this a.m. and went skiing for a few hours. we had about six inches last night! any thoughts about spring break? xoxoxoxoxoxox, mom

January 23

Lakedale...sculpture...Lakedale...sculpture...Lakedale... sculpture...Lakedale...sculpture...Lakedale...sculpture... Lakedale...sculpture...Lakedale...sculpture...Lakedale... sculpture...Lakedale...sculpture...Lakedale...sculpture... Lakedale...sculpture...Lakedale...sculpture...Lakedale... sculpture...Lakedale...sculpture....Lakedale...sculpture... Lakedale...sculpture...Lakedale...sculpture...Lakedale... sculpture...Lakedale...sculpture...Lakedale...sculpture...

Lunch

Lakedale...sculpture....Lakedale...sculpture...Lakedale... sculpture...Lakedale...sculpture...Lakedale...sculpture... Lakedale...sculpture...Lakedale...sculpture...Lakedale... sculpture...Lakedale...sculpture...Lakedale...sculpture... Lakedale...sculpture...Lakedale...sculpture...Lakedale... sculpture...hermit...Lakedale...sculpture...hermit... Lakedale...hermit...hermit...sculpture...hermit...hermit... Lakedale...hermit...hermit...hermit...sculpture...hermit... hermit...going nuts...hermit......

4:34 a.m. hi peanut! sorry i missed your call today. I've made reservations for Kathy and Bill and us (including you if you can) for dinner on the friday night we're in hanover - let me know! let's talk tomorrow - i miss hearing your cheery little voice! by the way, what's that big white thing in the middle of the green? (i'm doing my voyeur-thing watching the Dartmouth webcam) love ya lots! mums

5:03 p.m. they are building the snow sculpture

5:32 p.m. it looks huge - what is it going to be?

6:15 p.m. i think it's a rabbit, the mad hatter going off a ski jump

7:02 p.m. productive art day today. probably will have six pieces done before we leave, no last minute rush this time! yippee - hope all is well with you - is everything OK with us? I think I might have been grouchy on the phone last night. must be my hospitality studies getting on my nerves. let's talk tomorrow!

January 25

Seven of the art show's ten artists gathered at the chapel gallery to attach address labels and stamps to the invitations for the upcoming show. Discussions about art dominated the conversation; what techniques the artists were using, what the theme for the food would be for the opening reception, and more importantly, what the cocktail of the evening would be. This was a crucial decision as it has been proven that the more people drink, the more art they will buy. We decided on pomegranate cosmopolitans as they were vibrant, red, and were made with lots of alcohol. A perfect drink for *seeing... RED*. Say what you will about the esoteric merits of a piece of art or the motivation behind the artist's creative process, an artist gains credibility when his pieces are purchased. And if a patron has enough to drink, he will buy.

Pomegranate Cosmopolitan

Yield: 6 cocktails

- 2 CUPS (16 OUNCES) GOOD QUALITY VODKA
- 1 CUP (8 OUNCES) GRAND MARNIER
- 1 CUP (8 OUNCES) POMEGRANATE JUICE
- ½ CUP FRESHLY SQUEEZED LIME JUICE (3 LIMES)
- LIME PEEL STRIPS FOR GARNISH
- POMEGRANATE SEEDS FOR GARNISH

Combine the vodka, Grand Marnier, pomegranate juice, and lime juice in a pitcher and refrigerate until ready to use. Pour the mixture into frozen martini glasses with a twist of lime peel and a few pomegranate seeds and serve immediately.

January 26

I completed six pieces of sculpture, which will be enough for the show, and I have three pieces still in process that I can complete when we return from our trip to Dartmouth. I am over the hump. I can return to the land of guilt-free skiing and dinner parties. The Service Manager from Land Rover called to say that my car was repaired. It has a new transmission, a new battery, and the dealership would deliver it this afternoon with profuse apologies and a huge thanks for my incredible patience. Apparently not all Aspen clients are quite so understanding.

I am not so understanding about my new on-line web course. I still have not heard from my "professor" and have no idea what my assignments are. I've decided to start reading the book in anticipation of the homework I know will soon arrive. And, on my stint on the exercise bike today, Ilan won the title of Top Chef, besting Marcel, he of the hair that sprouted like a noncompliant cat's after a bath and who insisted every dish be slathered in flavored foam. He lost only because he wasn't able to perfect a vinaigrette encased in a sugar bubble for his salad.

January 27

My phone rang as we were walking down the ramp to board a plane to Seattle.

"Hi Mom! I am so excited, you won't believe what I did yesterday!"

I asked Kelly if it was her day to shadow the cardiologist.

"Yes...it was unbelievable. I scrubbed in, had to wear surgical clothes, and they sat me on a stool at the head of the patient with the anesthesiologist...he was so hot!" she was squealing with excitement.

"Honey, I'm sorry but we're about to take off, I'll call you as soon as we get to Seattle!"

"OK, love you, Mom!"

I called Kelly when we landed, but her little buddy had just arrived for an afternoon of sledding and movie watching, so Kelly said she'd call later.

"Hi, Mom...what are you doing?"

"We've just finished walking through nine art galleries in two hours, it was great...and now we're going to the Seattle boat show. We're in the parking lot, and there are a lot of compensator boats." (Compensator is a term we use to describe gigantic boats with three hundred horse power engines, fifty-foot bows, and three-foot sterns, commonly seen on *Miami Vice* and not so commonly seen in the Pacific Northwest, boats that short men with Napoleonic complexes drive to compensate for whatever else they are missing in their lives.) "Tell me about the surgery!"

"It was unbelievable. The patient was an older man who had evidently smoked four packs of cigarettes a day. The amazing part was when they put his heart on a bypass machine and then replaced two valves and did a quadruple bypass. When the heart was bypassed, it shrank to about a quarter of its previous size...unreal!"

"How long was the operation?"

"Four and a half hours. I'm glad the doctor told me to eat a hearty breakfast!"

I asked her if she had felt at all queasy during the operation.

"A little at the beginning, but after that, it was so interesting, I didn't even think about it. They sewed up all the arteries, reattached the heart, and it worked. If I were doing it, blood would have been squirting out all over. It was so exciting! Oh, and I went to the freshman formal last night...everyone dressed up, loads of fun!"

I pinched myself at the opportunities Kelly was being offered at Dartmouth, and the fact that she was jumping in with both feet, despite the fact that she still hadn't mastered the intricacies of her new Neverlate alarm clock. She sheepishly explained that she had missed the bus to go downhill skiing because she had set her alarm clock to 8:00 a.m. but failed to press the "Set" button. She woke up, saw the alarm which read 8:00 o'clock and felt quite smug that she had woken up on her own, and on time...until she ran into some of her floor mates, and discovered it was 11:30 a.m. Time for lunch, and the bus was long gone.

I ate the best sea bass I've ever eaten in my life tonight at Wild Ginger, a nouvelle Asian restaurant in Seattle. Freshly caught sea bass was roasted to quivering perfection then lovingly enveloped with a fish stock reduction mixed with fresh lime juice, chili, herbs and peanuts. Alongside were spicy, perfectly cooked green beans. It was a combination of flavors almost too good to swallow. John and I were in such food nirvana that we devoured scoops of lush house made toasted coconut and fresh ginger ice creams for dessert, proving that with truly exceptional food, you shouldn't stop eating.

Wild Ginger's Sea Bass with Peanuts and Herbs

Yeild: 1 serving

1 8-OUNCE FRESH CHILEAN SEA BASS FILET OR HALIBUT FILET
4 TABLESPOONS OIL
1 GARLIC CLOVE (FINELY MINCED)
1 WHOLE SHALLOT (SLICED)
1 GREEN ONION, WHITE PART ONLY (FINELY SLICED)
1 TABLESPOON THAI BASIL (ROUGH CHOPPED)
1 TABLESPOON VIETNAMESE MINT (ROUGH CHOPPED)
½ INCH FRESH GINGER (PEELED AND FINELY JULIENNED)
1 TABLESPOON CHOPPED PEANUTS
1 SMALL GREEN CHILI (FINELY SLICED)
1 TABLESPOON FISH SAUCE
1 TABLESPOON WATER
2 TEASPOONS LIME JUICE
PINCH OF SUGAR
1 TABLESPOON CHOPPED DILL AS GARNISH

Prepare garlic, ginger, shallot and green onion. Mix the basil and mint together. Prepare the peanuts and chili. Have all these items lined up on a plate ready to cook. In a small bowl mix together fish sauce, water, lime juice and sugar.

In a hot pan put in half the oil and fry sea bass until golden color. When fish is 80% cooked remove fish and place on a serving platter to rest and finish cooking. Take the reminder of the oil and heat in a fry pan until hot. Add shallot, ginger and onion. Cook until just starting to change color then add minced garlic. Cook mixture until it is golden brown, then quickly add fish sauce mixture and cook a few moments until slightly reduced. Add basil, mint and peanuts. Remove from heat, toss quickly, and place mixture over top of fish. Garnish with fresh chopped dill.

Wild Ginger's Sichuan Green Beans

Yeild: 4 servings

- 1 POUND TENDER GREEN BEANS
- 1 TABLESPOON SICHUAN PRESERVED VEGETABLES: PICKLED TURNIP, AVAILABLE AT ASIAN SPECIALTY STORES (CHOPPED AS FINE AS YOU CAN)
- 1 TEASPOON SESAME OIL
- 2 TABLESPOONS SOY SAUCE
- 2 TEASPOONS RICE WINE VINEGAR
- 1 TEASPOON SUGAR
- 4 CUPS PLUS 1 TABLESPOON PEANUT OIL
- 2 TABLESPOONS. MINCED PORK FINELY CHOPPED (THE EYE OF A CHOP WILL WORK NICELY)
- 1 TEASPOON HOT RED CHILI FLAKES

Wash beans and snap off ends. Rinse the pickled vegetable thoroughly under cold water to wash off the salt in which it was packed. Mix sesame oil, soy sauce, rice wine vinegar and sugar in small bowl and set aside.

Heat 4 cups peanut oil to 400 degrees F in a wok or deep fryer (oil begins to smoke when ready). Fry beans for 60 to 90 seconds (until they begin to wrinkle). Remove and drain.

Pre-heat a clean wok to 400 degrees. Add peanut oil, heat till it starts to smoke. Add pork, pickled vegetables and chili flakes to hot oil and stir fry for 10 seconds. Add sesame sauce mixture and heat for 15 seconds (be careful not to burn sugar).

Add beans, toss for 30 seconds or until most of the liquid is reduced or absorbed by the beans, serve and enjoy!!!

January 28

In my relentless internet foraging for furniture for the Lakedale cabins, I had discovered that the yearly Seattle Gift Show would correspond exactly with our stay in the city. I was ecstatic: over 1,200 booths filled with furniture, jewelry, gift items, clothing, Northwest specialties, handicrafts, and antiques. John was not quite as ecstatic, especially when at booth #749 our stomachs told us we had missed lunch. Fortunately, the gourmet food section of the show started at around booth #923. We chomped our way through samples of beef jerky made by a local Indian tribe, chocolates, soups, and a glut of dips and home-made chips, all packaged and ready to sell to the lucky campers at the Lakedale General Store. We left the Convention Center laden with heavy bags full of samples as night fell and then stopped for an early dinner of tapas at the bar in a new restaurant called Purple. The two-story space encircled a round caged wine cellar that was flush with wine bottles from floor-to-ceiling. According to our waitress, servers could climb up the exterior of the structure to retrieve bottles of wine. We ordered a bottle in anticipation of some aerial excitement, but our bottle of Spanish Albarino arrived on a tray from somewhere in the depths, not the heights, of the restaurant. Depths or not, it was just what the doctor ordered.

January 29

We woke at the crack of eight, threw on yesterday's clothes, and took a brisk walk to the newly opened Olympic Sculpture Park on Seattle's downtown waterfront. Despite the opening ceremonies, there were signs of construction evident all over the park; freshly strewn bark chips on the walkways were white and slippery with frost, yellow tape cordoned off a sculpture yet to be secured to the frozen ground, and boxed chairs were strewn helter-skelter across the terraced entry pavilion. Below the pavilion, five Goliath-sized weathered steel sculptures by Richard Serra undulated through a man-made valley. Walking in the spaces between their powerful curves, it felt as if the prows of massive freighters were churning through the gravelly sea, pushing us aside as easily as pieces of seaweed.

The other site of the Seattle Gift show was the Pacific Market Center, which was my destination today. John opted for another day at the Boat Show, not willing to face a day with more booths and no real food. As an interior designer for most of my adult life, I've visited design centers all over the country; in Chicago, New York, Los Angeles, San Francisco, Denver and points between. The difference between interior design centers and the two merchandise marts I've recently visited is palpable. Design showrooms are staffed with young men with attitudes and snooty middle-aged women who wanted to be interior designers. They always seemed to give me the overwhelming feeling that I was very lucky they were selling to me, and if I didn't behave appropriately, I would be tossed out with last year's fabric samples.

Merchandise marts, which are wholesale sources for the retail trade, are a completely different universe. Their motto is "Buy, buy, buy." As I entered each showroom, I was asked if I'd like food, what no food? How about some wine? OK, maybe a sample of our new chocolate-mint martini mix? The helpful staff-member stood patiently by my side armed with an order pad to jot down anything my little heart decided to order, and in general, they had a wonderful time helping me spend money. Except for "minimum purchases" of between $100 and $500 per showroom, there were no restrictions on what I could buy, no credentials to produce, and no questions about who I worked for. It made me vow I'd never pay retail prices again.

Burdened by even more bags of samples, I caught the gift show shuttle bus and met John for a very late afternoon lunch at the Oceanaire, one of our favorite Seattle seafood restaurants. The Pacific Northwest produces an abundance of oysters, so we shared a dozen sweet Kumamotos topped with a champagne mignonette, glasses of sauvignon blanc, and soon the world was right again. To add another entry to my personal chowder contest I ordered a bowl. It proved a little thicker than I normally like, but had finely diced potatoes, bacon and excellent seasoning. It was tied for third place on my chowder scale, just behind my Northwest chowder recipe and the Lime Kiln Café, and on even par with Legal Sea Foods' and the Ocean Crest restaurant's soups.

When Kelly called late in the day, she wondered aloud if she should come home for spring break or attend the rowing crew's spring training camp in Tennessee. She had decided not to row again next year anyway, so I tried to sway her into coming home by telling her about the huge mosquitoes in Tennessee, something I knew nothing about, but at least sounded plausible. John rolled his eyes and gave her a more logical approach to assist in her decision-making process, mentioning that the cost for her return flight had gone down $150 since we first checked on airfares.

> 10:33 p.m. i don't know what to do, dad did have a point, but Miami was fun, but not that fun and all the rowers hate Tennessee...and i want to come home...but i still want to be part of the team...is it ok if i order another alarm clock from your account and send the other one back? it doesn't wake me up, so this new one has three separate alarms, with different sounds so you can have nature and then music and then a buzzer, which is perfect!! love you! Kelly

January 30

John and I had nothing work-related on our agenda, so we donned our walking shoes and hiked two miles to the boat show on Lake Union. We tromped in and out of powerboats, sailboats, mega-yachts, and tug boats, each time removing our shoes so as not to ruin the shiny teak and holly soles on the freshly detailed boats.

Missing lunch was now becoming habitual and we settled for another late afternoon snack/lunch/dinner in the bar of Chandler's, a seafood house on the water adjacent to the boat show. Another day and a new clam chowder winner. This time it was light, full of clams and shrimp, with some corn thrown in for sweetness. I rated it #2 and moved the other contestants down a notch.

"Hey Mom!" The tone of Kelly's "Hello" was usually a clear indicator of her state of mind; did she have something exciting to tell me? did she need some motherly love? was she desperate for dollars? or did she just want to check in to make sure we were still alive. Tonight was an excited "Guess what I have to tell you!" call.

"What's up honey?" I asked.

"Well, I've just joined the College Democrats, and I'm volunteering for an event tomorrow."

"Let me guess, who's coming to Hanover, New Hampshire?"

"John Edwards...I'm an usher, and we all get to sit in reserved seats in the front row and meet him after he speaks! How cool is that?" *Pretty darn cool.*

"So I guess if you're in this group, you'll be meeting more presidential candidates as they come through?"

"Yup!" How in the heck did she become this proactive, self-sufficient young being?

January 31

As we left our room on the eleventh floor, we encountered four people in the elevator on the vertical journey down to breakfast.

"John, have you ever noticed how everyone in a hotel elevator smells exactly the same in the morning?" I asked my husband at the breakfast table. He looked at me quizzically. Had he never thought about this important fact? How often do you smell exactly like everyone else?

In this case, we all exuded Molton Brown's Thai Vert shampoo, conditioner, and shower gel. I suppose it's much more noticeable in a small enclosed space. When the amenities smell so good it makes you want to engage in a group hug with everyone in the elevator.

We flew to the island for a short week's worth of on-site work at Lakedale, and some mid-trip dieting opportunities, before continuing to the East Coast to visit Kelly. The air was clear, the sun high in the sky, there wasn't a cloud nor a raindrop in sight. This drove John crazy, as the past few times he has been here without me, the skies spewed torrents of rain, the wind howled, and the dinghy ride to Brown Island was miserable. We happily shopped for groceries and ignored our work to take in a screening of *The Queen,* another Oscar contender. Surprisingly, the ancient movie theater in Friday Harbor receives more first run movies than the Aspen five-screen theater, and it had three movies we wanted to see before February 25, the night of the Academy Awards.

FEBRUARY

February 1

Our twenty-first wedding anniversary dawned bright and sunny. The weather on the East coast, as evidenced by the Dartmouth webcam, was sunny too, but bitter cold. The construction of the monolithic Winter Carnival sculpture was well under way. Winter Carnival was our excuse for visiting Kelly, despite her thinly disguised attempt to dissuade us from coming.

"Wouldn't you rather come at another time when there isn't as much going on and you could see more of me?" was her lament. It was the biggest party weekend of the year and her parents would be there. She was somewhat placated when she learned Kathy and Bill were accompanying us and that we would only officially see her on Wednesday and Thursday. We had agreed we would entertain ourselves on Friday and Saturday even though we'd still be in the vicinity.

I worked at the resort all morning and then John and I joined the VP assigned to Lakedale by our management firm and our recently hired general manager for dinner at the Friday Harbor House.

Our GM was a tall man. His ruddy cheeks and even ruddier nose were sheltered by a pair of salt-and-pepper eyebrows, which erupted over his face like a flock of ducks scattered by buckshot. Extra-sturdy black suspenders supported the pants covering his girth. In the course of the dinner conversation, the fact emerged that he was a former Catholic priest who had given up the religious life. When I asked him why he had left the priesthood he said, "It was complicated," but that the decision had been made while he was in Israel on the shores of the Sea of Galilee, while sharing the Eucharist with a Jewish rabbi. *Interesting.*

After thoroughly grilling them about the financial performance of our little resort, i.e. why can't we get more "heads in the beds?" a phrase I had learned in my recent online studies, we ate our way through five delicious courses, accompanied by champagne, a lovely Viognier, and Vin Santo for dessert, all furnished by Friday Harbor House's new chef. Goal #1 may now be utterly unattainable, but I rationalized that it was our anniversary, after all, and when twenty-one pink roses appeared at the table at the end of the meal, I gave up worrying about Goal #1. It was also very apparent that our new GM was a wine connoisseur who might have really enjoyed his sacramental wine.

> 12:03 p.m. mom, it's warming up here, don't worry about bringing winter clothes, its about 60 degrees, and I think they're going to have to move the Carnival races to Vermont! there's no snow at Dartmouth.

February 2

"Hey, honey, only five more days until we see you. I'm so excited!" I said when I called Kelly.

"Me too!" Kelly replied, and it sounded as if she really wanted to see us too. "I am so ready to be done with midterms."

"How did they go?"

"Chemistry will be OK if the professor curves it, I might get a B, and I think Public Policy was all right. But I did really well on my paper, so I think it will even out. But get this, the Dartmouth ski team won last week's Carnival in Vermont. I am on an unbelievably amazing team!"

"Are you going to ski this weekend?"

"Yep, we're going to Massachusetts and Maine, the courses are twenty minutes apart, one in each state. But I have a dilemma." *Couldn't wait to hear this one.*

"What's the problem?"

"I think I have an over-commitment issue."

I asked what that might be.

"I'm going to the ski meet, and we don't get back until late in the afternoon on Sunday, but the conductor has scheduled a rehearsal for the Chamber Orchestra, and I missed the last rehearsal because I didn't have an A clarinet, so I have to go, but I don't think I'll be back on time."

"Well, what is more important to you?"

"Skiing, of course, but I really want to play in the orchestra, and I don't know what to tell him. What should I do?"

An interesting phenomenon was occurring. My normal response:

fix the problem…

find a solution…

give advice…

make things better...

…was gone. This was not my problem. This was Kelly's problem and she needed to deal with it. I was aghast. Am I giving up motherhood? No, I decided, it's about helping her to grow up. Learning to make her own decisions. I was concerned, but out of the loop. It was refreshing. I gave her a few helpful pointers about how to make decisions and left it at that. And I was almost guilt-free.

February 3

It was early evening and the dinghy was sluggish as we set out for Lakedale to attend our new GM's first wine tasting evening in the great room of the Lodge. The boat wouldn't steer to the left, barely to the right, and there was no reverse action.

"Grab the paddles, honey!" John said.

We were close enough to quickly paddle to the dock and find the million-watt dinghy flashlight. Scanning the engine, John burst into laughter. Just in front of the propeller was a ten-foot long log, sitting horizontally underneath the boat. We were riding a log. We managed to dislodge it, dashing John's hopes of not having to attend the event, and arrived at the wine tasting only half-an-hour late. The GM had assembled a disparate group, locals he had known before his new job with Lakedale, newcomers to the island, and strays.

One of his friends, a firefighter who loved wine, had donated seven bottles of Zinfandel for a blind tasting (the winner was BV's Coastal Estates Zinfandel, at an affordable ten dollars a bottle). After the tasting, one of our front desk clerks, who had just won a scholarship to the prestigious American Music and Drama Academy in New York, serenaded the group with a melancholy rendition of *Lonely House*, and then sang an impromptu love song to celebrate our anniversary.

According to the first chapter in my Hotel Sales and Marketing textbook, relationship marketing was what one had to do in order to be truly successful in the hospitality industry. Our new GM was a natural.

February 4

I stood at the kitchen window, watching the ever-changing water, while seagulls swarmed above the water's surface searching for the cache of fish below, when Brown Island's eagle and his young son flew by. Soaring and free, with no responsibilities except the need to find nourishment, and in them I saw myself. My only responsibility was to prepare dinner, preferably by 7:00 p.m. if John prevailed, and it helped if the dinner was fish, like the eagle's. I was getting used to not having Kelly around. Her not being here was now more usual than her being here. I was still sad...but achingly sad, not raw, flesh-eating sad. Could I actually be learning to soar again?

February 5

> 8:15 a.m. mom, forget that message I sent yesterday...it's freezing here now…bring all the warm clothes you can…. luv you!

Our flight was scheduled to depart at 1:10 p.m. Fog clung to the islands like peanut butter to jelly. We needed 550 feet of visibility to leave the San Juan Airport, but the heavy sky insisted on hovering at 200 feet. We had a leisurely lunch in town, and gave up at four o'clock. Luggage dragging behind us, we walked onto the ferry bound for Anacortes. The Kenmore Airlines shuttle driver, who would drive us to Seattle, met us outside the Anacortes ferry terminal. She was five feet two, both ways, with long black hair and dark sparkling eyes. Her multi-colored dragon-lady fingernails furiously tapped the steering wheel of the van while she verbally herded all six passengers from the missed Kenmore flight inside.

She revved the engine. The van sounded like a wounded wart hog on its way to the slaughterhouse. Our driver asked where we all needed to be dropped off, with one passenger asking to be dropped off first for an 8:00 p.m. flight. It was now 6:20 p.m., and we would need divine intervention to get to the airport by eight.

"Hey, you guys want some music?" the driver yelled. She scanned through seventeen music stations, all struggling to be heard over the grunting engine, but none succeeded. The passengers finally persuaded her to turn off the radio. And the interior lights.

Her cell phone rang. After overhearing her conversation, she then told all of us about her date that evening with a fellow employee who had just been released from the hospital. She was as anxious to get back to the city as a breeding mare was to get back to the barn. She increased the van's speed and was soon averaging seventy-five miles an hour, well past the 60 mph speed limit. Fog oozed over the freeway, and the taillights of cars ahead of us were luminous red orbs. The closer to Seattle we got, the faster she went; at times she was driving in the HOV lane. When we encountered a slow driver, she swerved sharply into the adjacent lane, passed the sluggish offender without using turn signals, and swiftly moved back into the fast lane. Every ten minutes, she grabbed her cell phone, dialed a number and talked to someone, usually someone from Kenmore Airlines, then swerved wildly all over the road and hung up. The only bright spot about the drive was the comprehension that I had worn my knee-length down jacket for the entire journey with no hint of menopausal heat. Just nervous sweat.

By the time we were twenty-six miles from Seattle, I felt as if Emeril Lagasse had whipped up a spicy jambalaya using my intestines as the main ingredient. We passed the Lake Union turnoff for the hotel, completely enraging the honeymooning couple in the back of the van who had already endured three hours without sex, and proceeded on to SeaTac to drop off the passenger on the 8:00 flight. The driver then deposited us at our nearby hotel, all the better to get herself to Seattle for date night. We celebrated surviving our near-death encounter with drinks at the bar and room service.

February 7

Driving up the main street of Hanover to the Hanover Inn, Dartmouth's Baker Library loomed straight ahead, its ivory tower topped with a domed copper roof silhouetted against the blue sky, not exactly Aspen cerulean but better than grey. I felt an immediate rush of bonhomie. I loved this place! I wanted to live here! Become a Dartmouth student, wear green all the time, exist in a constant state of euphoria. This was college paradise!

Students were atop a giant scaffold in the middle of the Green, chipping away at a thirty-foot square block of ice that would become the Winter Carnival sculpture, a white rabbit vaulting onto the Green from a giant ski jump. Kelly had remarked that at this point, all it looked like was someone's mammoth bum launching into space.

We arrived at our room overlooking the Green and watched a pair of giant red drops made of fake fur, wearing blue tights and over-sized tennis shoes, walk into the inn. Apparently it was blood-donor week, and these were students dressed as symbolic drops of blood. They waved their arms, danced and gesticulated, encouraging students to donate the essence of life.

"John, it just doesn't get much better than this!" I beamed. Kelly was at Nordic practice all afternoon, so we agreed to meet her at her dorm room before dinner to check out her digs. On the way, as the freezing air stung our cheeks scarlet, we passed Occum Pond. Graceful ice skaters slid past a game of ice hockey, while kids sledded through an immense ice gate onto the frozen pond.

When we knocked on Kelly's door, she flew out in a fury of energy, closely flowed by a friend, whose cell phone camera was trained on our faces to catch the moment we first saw Kelly's new hairstyle. Bright pink, glow-in-the-dark, fluorescent PINK hair. She actually looked great, like a healthy version of Lindsay Lohan. Her hair almost matched her burgundy t-shirt. She and the rest of the freshman Nordic team had dyed their hair the previous night as part of Winter Carnival tradition, and she was hyped about it. If you couldn't do it in college, when could you? I was almost tempted to do it myself.

After we finished dinner at the Canoe Club, Kelly dashed off with the rest of the team to design raunchy Valentine's Day cards for all of the men on the Northeast Nordic circuit. She was in her element, just as it should be. Even if her head was pink, three blocks away and not quite in bed yet, I felt a serenity being in her world and knowing she was happy.

February 8

We woke up late again and met Kelly for brunch at Lou's, where all three of us downed huge plates of corned beef hash. After I finish the Clam Chowder Contest, I may have to start the Corned Beef Hash Competition, since, like well-prepared clam chowder, there is nothing better than a well-prepared plate of hash for breakfast, topped with perfectly poached eggs.

Our little pink-head escorted us to Rocky (alias the Nelson A. Rockefeller Center for the Social Sciences) where we attended her class on Public Policy, basically a course on how to become a lobbyist and influence public opinion in Washington, DC. As we left, she stopped at one of the thousands of computers placed strategically around the campus and in two minutes selected her classes for next term (a freshman seminar on EcoPsychology, Economics, and Chemistry 6), then rushed off to another class. We browsed the latest exhibit at the college's art museum which featured wall-sized metal blankets fabricated from discarded liquor bottle tops created by an African artist. The highlight of the afternoon was watching the Human Dog Sled Races on the Green. We glimpsed Kelly and friends giggling like mad at the antics of the "dog" students pulling home-made sleds in the fourteen-degree weather.

Winter Carnival officially opened with the lighting of the obscene rabbit, followed by a speech by the college's president and one from the head of the carnival, a senior, who was in tears when she spoke to the freshmen. "I would give anything to be back in your shoes right now and have four more years at this wonderful place!" I was in tears when I realized I would only have four more years here myself, unless I managed to get accepted as an undergrad. Did they have an age limit on incoming freshmen? Maybe I'd qualify as a minority...are senior citizens minorities? Kelly joined us for an hour of *Grey's Anatomy* on TV and a family cuddle before she headed off to parts unknown, and eight feet of snow fell in upstate New York.

February 9

There was no luxury of a late departure today, as we had to drive to Stowe, Vermont for the Dartmouth Winter Carnival Nordic races. Despite the fact that every state around us was engaged in an epic winter storm, Hanover didn't have enough snow to set Nordic tracks. Vermont did, along with temperatures of one below zero and winds raging at forty miles an hour. This was the coldest I could ever remember being, and I wore every piece of clothing in my suitcase, a good ten layers worth.

We met up with Kathy and Bill who, much to Kelly's chagrin, had decided to stay in Stowe instead of Hanover for the carnival, since that was where Elissa would be racing. Kelly was on Dartmouth's development team and wouldn't be competing, but would lend moral support to her teammates. When Kathy and I finally found Kelly, she was attempting to look stylish while shivering in a pair of jeans, tennis shoes, skimpy wool mittens, and a short down jacket, all of minimal use in the Arctic conditions. "But Mom, I have long underwear on underneath!" I encouraged her to raid our duffel bag of extra clothes, but she was having no part of my mothering.

I had volunteered to help with the races and while I was out on the course, throwing wayward spectators off the tracks, I met another freshman girl's mother. Between the wretched gusts of wind we launched into the inevitable "What do you do?" discussion. I stopped dead in my tracks and had to completely shift from my normal response of "school volunteer, mom, artist" to...what *do* I do? I thought about the mothers (and some fathers, I suppose) who had left the work force to raise their children, and how much easier it must be for people like her to say, "I'm an attorney" and keep on working at their jobs, as if nothing monumental had just rocked their worlds. There was a sameness to their lives; they still had the same job, the same workplace, the same commute every day, the same everything. Their everyday work world did not involve walking by the Chasm *(OK, it had now shrunk to the size of a major ravine)* down the hall in the middle of the day. A quandary. I would have to invent a new stock answer to the dreaded question, "What do you do?"

February 10

Kelly had decided to stay overnight in Stowe with her team, so after our drive back to Hanover, we watched the women's basketball team annihilate the University of Pennsylvania. Come morning, we were on the road back to Stowe. My official volunteer duties had ended, but I chatted again with the other freshman skier's mom. Our conversation today was less threatening to my psyche. It involved an in-depth analysis about how the young Nordic men protected their family jewels in the extreme cold.

Kelly had the preliminary symptoms of a wicked cold, not a huge surprise. I resisted all my mothering instincts and let her make her own, really bad, clothing decisions. She gave us periodic hugs, interspersed with avoidance, and John and I left just after noon, with a stop for lunch at Mr. Pickwick's British Pub in Stowe. There were hundreds of beer selections

(John downed a Young's double chocolate stout) and great food: pastrami sandwiches, spinach salads, and mulligatawny soup. We had a leisurely drive back while another three feet of snow blanketed New York, the most ever recorded.

February 11

Kelly's eyes were red, her nose was red and her cold was raging as we met for a late breakfast. She sat next to me on the bench seat, snuggling, occasionally dispensing spontaneous hugs, and whether they were due to her cold or our imminent departure, I didn't care. We wandered back to her dorm room, passing the site of my miserable September meltdown, without a trace of emotion from me. I was going to be fine, I thought, although I had made a similar assumption a mere four months ago, and had clearly been incorrect.

Kelly's room was piled high with sweaty clothes, some of which I had lent her at Stowe. She scrumbled through the clothes, searching for my things, which were already smelling musty. She and the Nordic team had used the clothes as swimsuits while jumping into a fifty-person Jacuzzi set up on the Green after they returned from the races.

In the foyer of Bildner Hall we had a dry-eyed family hug. Kelly was the hot dog between her parental buns. I was surprised, and a little disappointed, expecting more emotion from myself. Was it because we had just seen her at Christmas, or the fact that she may be home for spring break? Either way, while I might not yet be embracing empty- nesterdom, I was certainly starting to adjust.

As we arrived in Boston at the Boston Harbor Hotel, we met up with our friends Ron and Jane, who greeted us in the lobby. Jane was thirsty for champagne after their drive from Connecticut, so we adjourned to the Wharf Bar to catch up on recent events.

We had met Ron and Jane in Geneva, after Kelly and their eldest daughter became friends, and we enjoyed discovering new Swiss restaurants together. Jane was the breadwinner in the family, a hard-charging human resources executive, holding jobs at major corporations all over the world, with salaries to match. Ron was a good-looking, loveable, stay-at-home dad, mothering their two girls. He was the "trailing spouse" and not permitted to work, so he made the most of his time in Geneva, biking with John, working out, searching out new wines, and eating.

Lucca, an Italian restaurant in the North End, was our dinner destination. We laughed our way through a bottle of an exquisite 2002 Rosso de Montalcino, while mangia-ing a rustic tart filled with tender duck confit, spinach, and leeks, encased in a flaky crust. John tore through a perfectly seasoned steak tartar of finely diced beef tenderloin with cherry peppers, capers and arugula, while Ron and Jane sensibly ate salads garnished with roasted beets and goat cheese. Thinking that life couldn't get any better, we ordered another bottle of red wine with our entrees. My house-made linguine with lobster meat had the barest whisper of lemon sauce, and I knew it was high on the list of things no dieter should ever eat *(oh, right, that's me!)*. Ron consumed a pork chop stuffed with Gorgonzola, Jane devoured beef tenderloin, and John stuffed himself with rigatoni in a wild boar sauce, decadent enough for dessert.

Our Italian-American waiter, having already steered us in the direction of culinary glory, could now sell us anything he felt inclined to, so we proceeded to down a flourless chocolate cake with vanilla bean gelato and a unique carrot cake topped with some sort of nutty heart-attack-inducing icing. We agreed we could always order a cheese course later. When the waiter asked if we wanted some dessert wine, we raised our almost empty red glasses in mutual, idiotic agreement, and ordered a bottle of sparkling Italian rose dessert wine *(after all, it was less expensive to get a bottle than four individual glasses, wasn't it?)*. We laughed all the way back to the hotel, all happily expecting out-of-control hangovers in the morning but knowing they would be worth every drop of Montalcino that had passed our lips.

February 12

Morning light glanced off the north-facing window. John read the paper. I opened my eyes and groped for the Advil, drug of preference for the hungover over forty crowd. But I felt...nothing. My head was fine. My mid-section had probably gained five pounds, but the pulsing, throbbing headache I expected was missing. I had discovered the cure for a hangover: drink expensive Italian red wine, chased with copious amounts of sparkling water at fifteen dollars a pop. How could I patent this discovery? On the other hand, (referring back to Goal # 1) instead of losing weight on this trip, John and I had both gained. He informed me that this was the most he had weighed in our twenty years of marriage, not a good omen for the scale back home, the scale upon which I now could not possibly get back on, not at least until we had eaten nothing but lettuce for three weeks.

On the positive side, being a glass-half-full kind of gal, my foot fungus was clearing up (Goal #9). I had achieved this miraculous breakthrough by spraying a mixture of hydrogen peroxide and water on my toes every day. John recently read about another concoction, a fifty/fifty mix of Listerine mouthwash and vinegar, which you also sprayed on your toes. I may have to alternate that with my current potion and speed up the process.

Fortunately for my clam chowder competition, our flight was delayed so we retested Legal Sea Food's clam chowder at the airport. I moved it up to the number three position and had to move Chandler's and Oceanaire each down a notch. It was that good.

Just before we departed, Kelly called, sounding terrible.

"Mom, I think I have an ear infection...what should I do? What are the symptoms? I woke up at three in the morning and couldn't get back to sleep...." She called again as we landed in Aspen, having gone to the health center, where she couldn't see a doctor until Monday. She sounded so sick and helpless that I was seriously worried. I could hardly sleep; traveling all day, jet lag, and an almost hangover did me in.

February 13

> 4:20 p.m. hi sweets - hope you're feeling better! i think you need some better shoes, maybe that's why you're sick...take a look at these:
>
> Merrell - Primo Chill Slides
>
> Columbia - Maatu
>
> Rockport - Candlen Place
>
> Easy Spirit - Time Travelers
>
> Propet - Nordic Walkers
>
> Uggs has lots of options
>
> you'd feel so much better if you had warm feet – it's a mom thing.
>
> 7:56 p.m. my ears are feeling a little bit better. and there is supposed to be an epic snow storm tomorrow. the president even blitzed the campus about it! love ya!

February 14

Kelly sounded slightly better as she called to wish us a Happy Valentine's Day. The health center had confirmed the ear infection diagnosis and given her antibiotics. Dartmouth's president blitzed the entire college community a second time to let them know that everything other than essential services would be shut down in anticipation of the upcoming blizzard. Kelly wanted my advice on whether she should go on a Nordic team "adventure" skiing across the campus. *What? Had the antibiotics caused brain damage? She needed to be studying in bed with warm compresses over her tender little ears, drinking warm lemonade for the sore throat she would most certainly get if she went on that hare-brained adventure!*

"Well, honey," I said, delivering my now too familiar refrain to her aching ears, before proceeding to give her more advice. John got on the phone just to say hello, and made the mistake of asking if she needed any more advice.

"NO! Bye Dad!"

February 15

Just as I was about to get out of the car and meet Sandy for an Artist's Breakfast at the Aspen Art Museum, Kelly called. We chatted as she walked across the campus; this was one of her favorite multi-tasking tricks. I could tell by the huffs and puffs and occasional greetings she called out to friends.

The call started out innocuously enough. She was not having a very good day. Yesterday was Valentine's Day, and as she had walked back to her dorm, the dining hall was decorated with cute little candles, red tablecloths, flowers on the tables and gooey-eyed couples holding hands as they ate a romantic dining hall dinner. And she was without a boyfriend.

"And I had just had dinner with some friends, including an especially cute skier from the Nordic team, and my ear was so clogged up I couldn't hear out of it. I said "Pardon?" and "What?" so much that people started ignoring me. So I went back to the dorm to write up my chemistry lab, and the boys next door were making so much noise, I had to leave and go to the library." *This wasn't all that bad, just a question of learning how to deal with a little adversity, which, after all, was what college was all about.*

She continued on, talking and walking faster, through the frigid air back to her dorm. "So it took me twice as long to write up the lab as it should have, partly because I didn't understand it, and I have my midterm in seven hours, and I'm so up a creek.... I have no idea what I'm supposed to be studying, and I ran out of time last night and I have a public policy paper due tomorrow which I haven't even started, and I don't even know what topic I'm going to write about!" *She can handle this. It's all part of the process.*

"And then, just three minutes ago," the tears were falling fast and furious now, and I envisioned teardrops freezing like sparkling Swarovski crystals flowing down her cheeks, "I went in to have a little chat with my crew coach about going to camp…augh...aughhhhhhhh...augh...." She was starting to sound like me a few months ago.

"It's OK honey, let it all out," I said, all I could utter were the usual platitudes at that point. "It will all work out."

"And she was sooooooooo mean…aughhhh…she," gulp, swallow, sob. "She said 'No camp – no crew. We've invested a lot of time and money in your training and if you want to stay on the team, you have to go to the camp.'"

At this point I had already missed the best part of the Artist's Breakfast, the sweet rolls, so I stayed on the phone and tried to help assuage the emotional beasts roaring inside her cute, red-headed body.

"Sweetie, I have some great advice.... I know this works. Go take a shower, and just cry until nothing else comes out. You can tell your friends your cold has been acting up and you needed to steam it out!"

After a few more sobs and aughhhs, she agreed my plan might have some merit. She said she'd try it after she figured out her paper's topic and what the heck her chemistry test was all about.

"Thanks, Mom. You're the best...I'll talk to you later."

I walked into the Art Museum drained. Luckily for me, Sandy had saved me a sweet roll and some coffee. We walked up to the second floor gallery and listened while the guest artist explained his work, a giant sandbox filled with glitter you walked through in bare feet. It was placed underneath a row of silver chains hanging from the ceiling that spelled the word Avalanche. The third component was a wall covered with paint that, when scratched off by participating museumgoers, revealed a secret painting underneath. Understanding Kelly was infinitely easier than understanding contemporary art.

After a mentally and emotionally exhausting day, I was ready for my book club meeting. When we first started the club, we drank tea and non-fat cappuccinos and had intellectual discussions. We now drank wine and had much more raucous, lengthy discussions, which didn't always involve literature. *Marie Antoinette*, though I'm sure a fascinating creature, rated a twenty-minute chat, which evolved into a dissection of one of our member's newly single status, a two-hour analysis of men, and then a heated debate about what our next book selection should be. We settled on *The Female Brain*, a book about how the female brain functions, as opposed to the male brain, which doesn't always. It would have the added benefit of providing us with insights into the erratic psyches of our female collegiate offspring.

February 16

The tile installer for Lakedale called after having determined that the 3" x 6"tiles I had specified would cost twice as much to install as 12" x 12" tiles. This meant I would have to redo the entire layout, and find new tile. Again.

I ignored the tile dilemma and worked on another sculpture instead.

> 2:38 p.m. how did the paper go?
>
> 3:11 p.m. i think it was a good paper, didn't get to sleep until four though...
>
> 3:32 p.m. yikes! what's up with the cold/ears? hopefully you can fully recuperate this weekend! we are supposed to get two feet of snow tonight - very windy out so no skiing today! and more work on the lakedale restrooms - will it ever end? xox, mums
>
> 4:47 p.m. oh my gosh, did you see grey's anatomy? ahhhhhhh.
>
> 5:41 p.m. yes, i'm on pins and needles... but she's the star of the show so she can't die. also, what was your paper on? i'm finishing a few more bathroom elevations, then heading to the hot tub. its windy and feels as cold as stowe!
>
> 9:17 p.m. it was on the CLEAN energy act of 2007
>
> 10:08 p.m. excellent. email me a copy so i can learn something. am off to bed early, as i need to finish all my sculpture this weekend for the show hanging on monday! you're not racing this weekend are you? xox, m

February 17

Kelly reported that she skied in a five-kilometer race even though she was still sick, and then came back to the dorm and napped for three hours.

"But Mom, I'm feeling a lot better!" She still hadn't decided whether to come home for spring break or go to the crew camp in Tennessee. Having read a few chapters of the *Female Brain,* I suggested she make a decision, live with it for a few days, and then change her mind if it didn't feel right. As John often said, "You make a decision so that you can have something to change from," and she decided this could be a good plan.

When asked about the results of the Nordic race, she said she was really terrible.

"Grandmothers were beating me! I'll prove it to you, here...I'm checking the results on the computer...yep, I'm dead last. Sixtieth place. Can you believe it?" Before I could jump into my usual warm, smother-mother mode, she started laughing.

"I can't believe they let me stay on the team when everyone else is so good!"

"Are you worried you might get booted off?"

"Mom, this is Dartmouth, they're very egalitarian. Everyone gets to be on the team." *Egalitarian? Must be an Ivy League thing.*

The art show opened in four days and I finally finished my last piece.

February 18

A perfect winter's day...sunshine, blue skies, and fresh powder. John and I headed to Aspen Highlands and strapped on our skis. We'd forgotten it was the middle of a holiday weekend. The mountain was jammed with fair weather skiers, resulting in ten minute lift lines, usually unheard of on Aspen area mountains. I spent the afternoon assembling clear acrylic shelves and drilling them with tiny holes to accept the tinier metal feet of my sculptures. I was ready to hang.

February 19

All nine other artists arrived on time, including one who was notorious for never doing anything on time. As a result, we were able to spread all of the work on the floor, arrange where it would be placed on the walls, and hang it in just under four hours. A record-setting pace.

February 20

3:22 p.m. i asked an online magic eight ball if i should row and it said "no chance" hahaha

6:53 p.m. feel good about your decision?

8:10 p.m. i had a moment of doubt, but then i went to a Dartmouth Ends Hunger meeting and stopped doubting again. i will tell you how i feel in the morning. heads up, i think I failed my chemistry exam...

10:29 p.m. have just finished the very oriental arrangements for the flowers for the show's opening tomorrow night - your dad is in bed with a cold. love and kisses and sweet dreams! m

February 21

The show's opening was scheduled from 5:00 until 7:00 p.m. The artists arrived an hour early carrying plates of homemade appetizers (all in various shades of red) to feed the large crowds who usually attended. Not all of the attendees were art lovers, many came just to schmooze, eat and drink, so each artist brought enough food to feed eighty people.

From an artist's viewpoint, an opening is an energizing event, ripe with the promise of potential sales, an opportunity to receive accolades (truthful or not) from friends, and a welcome emergence from the studio's enveloping egg into the scrambled reality of life. Ten minutes before show time, the artists buzzed around like baby chicks.

The art patrons arrived before five o'clock did. John and Peter, Sandy's husband, manned the bar, pouring stiff pomegranate cosmopolitans to facilitate sales. Carol, one of the gallery's directors, handled any sales that occurred, so when a patron wanted to make a purchase they found Carol and she placed a sought-after red "sold" dot on the piece's label. Each artist stood adjacent to his or her work to explain the process used to produce it and its abstruse significance.

Six o'clock arrived and the gallery was full. The chatter was so loud that the Bach being played by the pianist couldn't be heard. Sales were being rung up at a steady pace. I hadn't sold anything yet, but I was patient.

Six-thirty p.m. and I still had no sales. Even though I really liked the pieces I had produced, and was hopeful something would sell, I realized it might not happen.

Six forty-five p.m. Only fifteen minutes left to go. A tiny white-haired lady I had chatted with early in the evening approached me once again and said she'd like to purchase one of my pieces, *Litany*, a tall bell-shape made of rusted metal, which provided the framework to hang hundreds of the plaster shards I had made. I rushed over to Carol to ask her to help with the purchase. She told me she had someone who wanted to purchase *Litany*. At first, I assumed it was the same tiny white-haired woman. But when we both arrived back at my piece, there was another tiny white-haired lady standing next to the first. At 5'2", I am not a tall person, but these ladies were so short, I was looking down at the tops of their pink scalps through their gorgeous white hair.

Evidently both women, who were friends, wanted the same piece. Carol and I were in a quandary. They were still arguing with each other when another short, white-haired woman arrived. She pulled me aside and said she'd like to purchase a piece entitled *Glass House*. As I turned to Carol to tell her this, the first two septuagenarians announced they had come to a conclusion. One would take *Litany* and the other would take *Glass House*. Since they were friends, they could visit the pieces at each other's homes.

The third woman overheard the conversation and insisted that she had the rights to *Glass House*. I was beginning to wish seven o'clock had rolled around and I hadn't sold anything. After half an hour of negotiations between themselves (evidently all three women were friends), they hammered out a deal whereby they would each buy a piece and rotate them between their houses. I was beginning to see the value of having a gallery as an intermediary and I was ready for a glass of wine.... Vow: Work really hard on Goal# 5 so I am not in this pickle next year.

10:52 a.m. i just went and talked to my chemistry professor and he gave me ten extra points on the test! there are bennies in getting to know your profs! so now i didn't fail! i got a D! yay! he told me to stop concentrating on skiing though...and i haven't been, which is the sad part, so rowing is probably not a grand idea, although i am still hesitant just because its such a fun sport and i may never be able to do it like this again!

11:33 a.m. there are now rowing clubs all over the country, so don't think it's your only chance. remember, you can have it all, just not all at the same time! and remember why you're at dartmouth - education, education, education!

February 24

7:02 p.m. oh man! my friend Katie and i just went and looked at all the dorm rooms for next year, and we are so spoiled in mclaughlin! there is a lottery for rooms, so we have to decide who we're rooming with and where we want to be. they are all so icky!!

10:29 p.m. are you going to room with Katie? she seemed really nice when we met her, and yes, you have been spoiled with dorm rooms forever, but what fun going into a new situation. you'll have a good time! really good decision not to ski on sunday - getting your studies under control is a huge positive!

February 26

5:25 p.m. do you think i should blitz the crew coach and ask for a meeting, or ask for a meeting and tell her it's because i am not going to tennessee? i think that might be easier especially since i don't want to get nervous and back away from my decision...

8:38 p.m. you should probably blitz, ask for a meeting, but maybe give her a heads up on not going to Tennessee. and i think you've made a good decision, so don't worry about that. xox, mums

February 27

2:09 p.m. i feel a lot better about my decision because today was a beautiful day skiing and the ski team is great and funny and completely nice and i love it!! wahooooo! and i love you too and can't wait to come home and relax and i am in such a free happy mood that i know this was the right decision! have a good aspen day! Here's what I sent to my crew coach and her reply:

Hi Coach,

I was wondering if I could set up another meeting with you because I have decided not to go to Tennessee, so I wanted to discuss what that meant to my commitment to the team and rowing with you.

Thanks! Kelly

Kelly,

If you are not coming to Tennessee then you will not be able to race with us this spring. I don't think that there is much else to talk about so there's no need for you to come in. I am obviously disappointed that this is the decision you have made. I would imagine that being committed to two teams is a challenge but it was one that you signed on for and it is unfortunate that you will not be seeing it through to the end of the year. I will let the team know about your decision. Good luck with skiing.

4:04 p.m. i had a really long conversation with Lacy today about her summer plans, she can't decide between two things, so i know what that's like! and yes, i will physically miss rowing but i will get over that in about four hours or so! love you! kelly

4:55 p.m. forgot to ask if you had gone to career services yet? just talked with Jayne, and we've set up a raclette dinner when you and Lacy are here together over spring break!

7:11 p.m. sounds good, i asked Lacy about the weekend thing too and there is a west side story production in boulder the first weekend i am home, might be fun for a girl's weekend if we bring Jayne! saw senator joe biden today. he was pretty good. yeah, love ya!

February 28

8:02 a.m. you're going to have to be our guru about who to vote for in the next election, since you'll have seen every candidate! did you like biden better than edwards? we had a ton of snow last night, so am going to catch a few turns on tiehack before i do more lakedale work - wish you were here, but soon!

10:44 a.m. biden was pretty good, i had to leave early for a chemistry tutorial, but he was very well-spoken. edwards was definitely more charismatic and kennedy-like. chemistry test tonight, wish me lots of luck!!

10:22 p.m. hi sweets, just wanted you to know i saw Leif today at Jayne and Fred's and he said the best part of spring break would be having you home! m

MARCH

March 2

> 8:35 a.m. i'm off to mexico! in case you can't get hold of me on my cell - i'll be staying at the La Posada de la Aldea. will talk later - am off to get some pesos! xox, mums

March 3 to 11

I have known Sue since the fifth grade. She was the first friend I had in the United States after my family emigrated from Canada. We stayed friends through moves to San Diego and Iowa, college and grad school, jobs and careers, boyfriends and husbands. We sang *Maggie May* along with Rod Stewart at the top of our lungs driving across the bridge to Balboa Island in college; I recall some pilfered beverages from her parent's liquor cabinet being involved. We sent each other outrageously creative letters in the mail in high school and made hand-stitched leather sandals together. In more recent years, we have been spa buddies. Our spa trips have at times included our mothers and our infant daughters, and as spa dilettantes, we always cheat with some wine before or after the dry, but healthy, spa cuisine dinners. Everyone knows a little red wine is good for the heart, so why give up important health benefits just because you are going to the spa?

A few months ago when I was buried in sculpture, I knew I was going to need a break and our last spa trip had been two years ago.

"Sue! It's me...." And of course she knew who it was. When you have been friends as long as we have, names aren't necessary. The sound of your old friend's voice is like the freckle on the back of your hand; it is imprinted forever.

"We need a spa trip, when can you go?"

"Let me check my work schedule," she said. Sue was a tax attorney for a large nationwide CPA firm. "I'll let you know tomorrow." After a few days of scouting our usual spa getaways, Canyon Ranch in Tucson, and a couple of spas in Utah, we were astounded at the prices they were now charging. We must have always gone in the off-season.

Sue phoned, "I have an idea...what do you think about taking a photography class? I found a National Geographic Photo Expedition to San Miguel de Allende in Mexico. It's half the price of the spa!" And with that, our photographic careers were born.

A famous National Geographic photographer whom neither of us had ever heard of, was teaching the class. On the first day he asked each of the twenty-five participants why they had chosen to take the course. Sue explained, in her best lawyer/CPA voice, the cost benefits of the photo expedition vs. the spa, and the fact that both of us thought it would be pretty cool to be able to use a setting other than Automatic on our entry-level digital SLR cameras. He was not impressed.

In addition to being a world renowned photojournalist he loved women, and his latest projects all featured them, even when they were supposed to be about, say, men with tattoos. He had recently been on assignment in Spain to photograph a fiesta and was sent back to retake the photos when his editors saw the image proofs. There were no men, no children, no buildings or colorful pieces of pottery in the photos. Only women. He had also recently discovered blogging, and so he spent inordinate amounts of time in the lobby of our two-star hotel instead of at his deluxe National Geographic-provided condo, because we had wi-fi and he didn't. When he wasn't asking women to pose for him, he was posting items to his blog.

He was assisted by another National Geographic photographer who didn't have as much charisma, but who did know how to use the manual settings on his camera. He handled the nuts and bolts of the expedition. He also had no patience for the novice photographers in the class, but made plenty of time for single women and people who actually knew what the knobs on their equipment were for.

The third instructor was very talented and very patient so he was the person we usually turned to for advice. In addition there were two pretty female assistants, who were of course always available to model. Our schedule for the week went as follows:

8:00 a.m. Arrive for breakfast in the hotel's dining room, and chitchat with the other participants about camera disasters from the previous day.

9:00 a.m. Short lecture by one of the instructors about interesting topics like resolution, exposure, lens and gear selection, (Sue and I didn't have much interest in this topic since neither of our cameras had removable lenses, and the only gear either of us had purchased was a tripod, which we didn't use the entire week) and a lot more sophisticated subjects which we may understand in a few years after some additional classes. I wasn't as nervous about taking the course as Sue was because I had deduced that I could bluff my way out of the terrible photographs I was sure to take by doctoring them with Adobe Photoshop. I promised to spend the first night teaching Sue some Photoshop basics so she could use that technique as well.

At the end of the first short lecture, as an aside, the second instructor said, "Oh, by the way, you *will not* be using Photoshop for anything except minor adjustments in levels. You need to learn to take *real* photographs, and Photoshop is just a crutch!" *Great.*

10:00 a.m. Edit photos from the previous day. Select twenty-five of our best shots, and with the help of the instructors, who rotated between class members, narrow these down to five.

11:00 a.m. Critique. Everyone's five best photos (or more if the instructors happened to like you and/or you were a drop-dead gorgeous female under the age of thirty) were shown on a large screen at the end of the classroom. This was always entertaining.

12:00 p.m. Lunch in the hotel's dining room. Chitchat with other participants about who had the most amazing photographs in spite of the previous day's disasters.

1:00 p.m. Depart for afternoon excursions on the group bus. I had a hunch the famous photographer might not like me when, on the first day (after the lecture on punctuality and an announcement that if you weren't on time for the bus, they would leave you behind) he looked directly at me and said, "And I think you could be the worst offender." I mean, how could he actually know? And, worse, how could he be so right about me? I made a vow not to be late just to prove him wrong.

The excursions were fantastic, like what I imagined a real National Geographic photo assignment would be: attending a local bullfight, going to Guanajuato (a non-touristy town an hour away from San Miguel), traveling to a local Don's hacienda to see another bullfight and have his relatives pose for us in native costumes, watching pre-Hispanic dancers dress and dance in the ruins of Posos, investigate an old silver mine, and in our free time, photographing on the streets of San Miguel de Allende.

7:00 p.m. - 8:00 p.m. Return exhausted from excursions.

8:00 p.m. - 10:00 p.m. Dinner with members of the class or the whole group at organized events or restaurants around town. Most of the dinners involved one or more margaritas. As the group's photo-neophytes, Sue and I became more abstinent when we grasped what was in store. After dinner on the first night, we casually walked back to our room to edit our day's photographs down to the requisite twenty-five. We'd each taken over 400 photos. Bleary-eyed, we turned off the lights at 2:00 a.m., having narrowed our selections to one hundred.

Sue woke up first the next morning.

"Do you know we could be having massages right now if we were at the spa?" she groaned.

"You take the first shower," I muttered, thinking I could squeeze in a few more minutes of sleep, until I realized being late wasn't an option.

"OK...but you do realize that this is no expedition, it's boot camp with a camera!" she said as she trundled off to the shower. I didn't remind her that it had been her idea to come.

By the end of the week, we had taken some astonishing photographs. The most sincere validation I received was from a fellow participant who owned a $15,000 camera. He couldn't figure out how I had managed to capture such great images with such a "cheap piece of crap." I felt vindicated. It was about "seeing" after all.

And in a total victory for both empty nesterhood and photography, I had completely forgotten to call both John and Kelly all week.

March 12 to 24

Kelly returned home from Dartmouth for spring break. Her finals had been uneventful, and she was ecstatic to be home. When Kelly was two, our world was easy to navigate; she was a sunny, dancing, happy child. Then a few months later, it felt like we were living in World War Three. Our daughter was screaming, crying, and throwing tantrums for no reason. It was after one of these manic periods that I decided to wait until she calmed down before we baptized her, to avoid an embarrassing scene at church. She was finally baptized when she was eight years old.

I pored through scores of child-rearing books to find the cause of this erratic behavior, and finally discovered a book about the stages of development. Its basic premise was that children go through phases of either equilibrium or disequilibrium, each of which usually lasts about six months, depending on the child. The disequilibrium stage occurred when the child was learning new skills, followed by the relative calm of the equilibrium stage, which happened after they had mastered those skills. Once I started paying attention to the timing of her behavior, the theory worked like a charm. It didn't cure the learning phase, but it did make it much easier to understand.

We were in equilibrium during spring break. We spent our days skiing, shopping, eating, taking overnight trips to Boulder, Denver, Colorado Springs and enjoying each other's company. I can only assume that in her first six months at college she had been in a disequilibrium phase, which I was happy not to witness firsthand after having already gone through it a few times. Instead, we were now enjoying the fruits of her expensive education. My personal moment of equilibrium emerged when I realized I felt great when Kelly was home, but I remained on firm emotional footing when she was away. A revelation.

One afternoon while Kelly was skiing the Aspen Highlands Bowl with Lacy and Leif, while I was in the midst of having all of these personal revelations and simultaneously trying to finish all of my Lakedale projects, John climbed the stairs to my studio.

"How about another project?" *I love him to death, but what is he thinking?* I was overwhelmed with Kelly being at home (equilibrium or not), my existing Lakedale projects weren't completed, and we were leaving on a three-week driving trip when Kelly departed. Nevertheless, my creative instincts were piqued.

"We need the interiors of the new tent cabins designed, purchased and installed by mid-May." Long pause...*how would I have the time to do this? but who else would do it besides me? if someone else did do it, we'd have to pay them...I like doing this...why let someone else have all the fun?*

"OK. Sign me up."

March 25

Kelly sauntered into the kitchen, wrapped her arms around me, and gave me a huge smooch on the cheek.

"I love being home, but I'm not so excited to go back to school," she whispered in my ear. Could this be real, or could it be the smell of the oatmeal pancakes I was whipping up that had her in such a mellow mood? Or was it the thought of returning to the dregs of the East Coast winter? And more studying? Whatever the reason, she had missed her house, her town and her friends. And the three of us in our comfortable new reality. After the pancakes were devoured, John and I discussed a proposed trip to a Caribbean beach resort

"Wait...we can't go to the Caribbean in April," John moaned. The Aspen winter and Lakedale had been too much for him. "Sometime this spring we have to pick up the boat in Canada and take it back to the island. When is that going to happen?" A lengthy discussion ensued about what we should do. After all, weren't we empty nesters and didn't they take trips whenever they felt the urge? To the far ends of the earth? Although Dartmouth probably didn't count as an end of the earth, unless you lived in Zimbabwe. And especially when the trip was to visit the reason for the empty-nesterness.

Finally John said, "Why don't we just sell the boat, then we don't have to worry about picking it up?"

I thought it was a rather drastic solution to a simple logistical problem, but the more I mulled it over, the more I began to see his logic. No more *Bull...Beast...Boat* problems and no more marital docking discord. That afternoon, John called our boat builder and listed the boat-bull for sale. And I made reservations to go to the Caribbean.

Kelly was far less comfortable with the new reality when it sunk in that the Caribbean trip didn't include her. Like a slot machine, I could see the dials spinning in her smart little brain, and then the *Jackpot!* moment when she realized that because of school, she wouldn't be traveling everywhere we went. After nineteen years of life revolving around her, her parents had spun off into a separate orbit that wouldn't always include her. No doubt it was a shock to her well-ordered world, but given the rest of the year's massive changes, I figured it was nothing a few nights back at the frat houses wouldn't cure. I was more concerned about which bathing suits to take and how I could jumpstart Goal #1, once again.

March 26

We drove Kelly to the Aspen airport for her morning flight to Boston. Our eyes were dry as we hugged her good-bye and watched her confidently navigate airport security. John and I waited for a last wave while she placed her backpack and shoes on the conveyor belt and re-donned her clothing. We waited while she gathered her belongings and without a look back, she boarded the plane. I was getting a little tired of revelations at this point, but another one struck me as we watched her plane disappear into the sky. Kelly's freshman year was two-thirds of the way over. She had one more term, and then she would be a college sophomore. She had matured, we had grown up...and we were all on new paths.

It was a good thing I had some menial labor to do to avoid further soul searching. We swung through town to get a coffee before heading home to finish packing for a trip to California.

My mom was spending a week in Hilton Head with a friend and my sister Lea to play golf and attend a practice round of the Masters Golf Tournament. She had been applying for tickets via a lottery for five years. The practice rounds were the only reasonably priced tickets available to the general public, as tickets to the actual tournament itself were considered heirlooms, and were passed down from one generation to the next like Great Uncle Will's silver spittoon. John and I had agreed to come west to spend time with my dad while mom was on her excursion.

Leaving at noon, with no hotel reservations, we stopped at the Sorrel River Ranch near Moab, Utah to check the facilities for a future stay. It was a three-star Western-themed resort on the banks of the Colorado River where the waters were swollen with the muddy brown spring run-off. Towering above the resort on the other side of the river was an immense red stone butte. It was too early to stop, but there was a room available and it came complete with a rugged log bed, and horseshoe door handles. Who could resist?

March 27

Not in a huge hurry to start the day's driving, we took an early walk by the river. Strong winds swirled its currents into chocolate eddies. From the looming red cliffs above, the wind stole fine streaks of sand and threw them onto the canvas of the sky, like a mobile, crimson abstract painting.

When we stopped for lunch in Monticello at the Peace Tree Café, the wind followed us. It whipped the desert into dust storms that obscured the view. Hazy mesas and pinnacles appeared with no warning out of the studded landscape and tumbleweeds sped by at thirty-five miles an hour. There was a constant cloud of sand in the air swirling around us, as if we were tiny particles in a vast dust blender. It careened up high enough to meet the white clouds overhead, and at one point so low that the road beneath us completely evaporated. The usually inescapable enormity of nearby Monument Valley was invisible.

March 28

We awoke to two inches of fresh snow on the Ponderosa pine-covered grounds of the Little America hotel in Flagstaff, Arizona. And to the phone ringing.

"Hi Mom, how are you?" It was Kelly's cheery college voice.

"Fine, hon, how was your day?"

"Really fun, I was a little bummed on Monday, I wasn't sure I wanted to be back at school, but now everyone's in the dorms again, classes are going, and...I still love it. A friend from Aspen came with her mom to look at Dartmouth, and my friend Katie and I talked with them for two and a half hours, so we missed the school play. But that was OK because we went back to the dorm and played Catch Phrase for three hours."

Wheewww! She was back in the saddle again. "How are your classes?"

"Well, I had all four classes today...." she said.

"Wait, you're only supposed to be taking three classes. Wasn't that the point of giving up crew, so you'd have some stress-free time?"

"I know, I know, but I have this statistics research class I have to take if I want to get into the public policy internship in D.C. this summer, and I didn't drop Econ yet, and I still have my freshman seminar on EcoPsychology, and Chemistry, which I really love, by the way. The professor is soooooo funny!"

"O.K. then."

"So what I want to know is, do you think I should buy the Econ books?" I questioned her decision to buy the books if she didn't know if she'd be taking the class.

"Here's what I was thinking...I could take all four classes, and then if I don't get into the internship, I can drop the statistics class, and if I do get in, I can drop the Econ class."

"Do you know when you can drop the classes, and when do you find out about getting accepted for the internship?"

"No, but I think they're both sometime in May."

"Well, the timing should probably have some bearing on your decision. What does your advisor say about it?"

"He doesn't know anything."

"How about the first year advisor?" I asked resignedly.

"I guess I could talk to her."

"Kelly, remember, all that tuition should get you a heck of a lot of advising." Pause. I heard the clanking of her mind's doors closing on the fingers of my carefully reasoned arguments.

"Right, right…but should I buy the books? They're kind of expensive and the professor sounds really boring." I asked if she could return them and she replied in the affirmative.

"Well, talk to your advisor and then you decide." I could hear the excited hum of voices and a cash register clanging in the background.

"OK, gotta go, I'm at the front of the line at the bookstore. Talk to you later!" I realized that the first week of every term would probably consist of the same scenario: questions asked, answers given, answers ignored, apron strings loosened and retied, and ultimately, left dangling in the breeze.

March 29

Your fifty-fourth birthday, as long as you are still alive, is a fairly innocuous event. It sounds a lot better than fifty-three because it's an even number and yet you realize you are closer to fifty-five, at which point sixty is on the horizon. That is a scary thought, especially when you wake up on the morning of your fifty-fourth birthday in a Marriott Springhill Suite in the midst of a busy freeway intersection engulfed by chain restaurants in Yuma, Arizona. But on the positive side, the weather was warm and it would only take three hours to drive to La Jolla.

After arriving at my parent's house late in the day, I opted to have my birthday dinner at George's at the Cove, which had recently reopened after a two and a half million dollar remodel. The restaurant was also sporting a new name, George's California Modern, and a new menu. So the four of us ate very, very well on:

California Avocado Halibut Ceviche, which tasted like Thailand on a plate

Ricotta Raviolis with fresh Cove's Nest asparagus and lemon sauce

Roasted bone-in halibut served over clam chowder and wilted pea shoots (without a doubt, this was *my* choice)

Lemon pudding cake with strawberry mint sauce

Warm chocolate tart

Beignets with raspberry sauce

An auspicious start to my next year.

March 30

After Mom departed on her golf getaway, and in between bike rides, sailing, eating out and drinking appletini's on a friend's rooftop deck with my dad in tow, I tried to finalize the design for the tent cabins. John's mental image of the interiors was a pseudo-safari look; Paul Bunyan meets Jungle Book. My eyes were glazed after tedious hours hunched over my computer searching for inexpensive log bed frames and teak campaign chairs, trying to satisfy John's vision. Not my favorite pastime when the sun was shining and there wasn't any snow on the ground.

California Avocado Halibut Ceviche

Yeild: 3 servings

3 CUPS FRESH HALIBUT FILET, DICED
1 CUP FRESH LIME JUICE
1 TABLESPOON SALT
1 CAN (14 OZ.) UNSWEETENED COCONUT MILK
¼ CUP FRESH LIME JUICE
1 LEMONGRASS STALK
2 TABLESPOONS FRESH GINGER, PEELED AND MINCED
¼ RED ONION, SHAVED THIN
½ RED BELL PEPPER, SEEDED AND JULIENNED
½ YELLOW BELL PEPPER, SEEDED AND JULIENNED
1 JALAPENO, SEEDED AND JULIENNED
¼ CUP FRESH CILANTRO LEAVES
3 CALIFORNIA AVOCADOS
CUT IN HALF WITH PITS AND SKIN REMOVED

Combine the diced filet, lime juice and salt together and let sit in the refrigerator until cured, approximately 45 minutes, drain well and reserve.

Combine the coconut milk and lime juice in a small sauce pot. Smash the lemongrass with the back of your knife and add to the coconut milk with the ginger and bring to a simmer. Simmer for 20 minutes or until reduced slightly and thickened. Remove from the heat and let sit for 30 minutes to infuse, strain and chill.

Combine the halibut, the coconut dressing, the onion, peppers and cilantro in a bowl and mix well. Season and place in the cut California avocados and serve.

APRIL

April 1

John left for a quick working trip to Lakedale to finalize the locations of the four new tent cabins, leaving Dad and I to fend for ourselves. Because of his rather prickly exterior and explosive temper, I've always been semi-scared of my father. His forceful personality had served him well in business, but not as well living in a household with four women. When I was growing up, he socialized more with his golf buddies and our beagle Butch than with his family. He was a disciple of the "children are to be seen and not heard" school of childrearing, popular in the eighteenth century. It was either that or he felt we probably wouldn't have anything interesting to say until we reached the age of forty.

He has become more relaxed in recent years. I am convinced that either his testosterone is non-existent or his recent diagnosis of Alzheimer's disease has caused him to forget his previous persona, but either way, the change is not all bad. He insisted that we go to dinner at Restaurant Nine-Ten in La Jolla's village so I wouldn't have to cook. We shared a mustard-dressed salad of white asparagus with a perfectly poached quail egg. My entrée of sautéed scallops were nestled in a creamy cauliflower custard. Dad had duck breast sliced over sautéed English pea shoots with truffle foam. We laughed, talked and enjoyed each other's company. I guess I should have started talking to him before I was fifty-four.

April 2

Once again, I worked on Lakedale, ordering more furniture for the lobby. Dad and I decided to go to the local IKEA store to research inexpensive furniture options for the tent cabins. Afterwards we stopped at Costco to see if they had any furniture and strayed into the food section, where we found mountains of fat, green, spring asparagus along with just-off-the-boat Alaskan King Crab legs. I had read that Julia Child used to buy all her meat from Costco, so I didn't have any qualms about the freshness of the crustaceans. Add a little Chablis from Dad's wine cellar and we would have another flawless dinner.

A large cedar gazebo blocked our way to the checkout counter. *This could be a great project. Keep Dad busy in his twilight years.*

"Dad, it's a bargain! Only $1600, and there's just a little assembly involved!"

"Shell," (he was one of the few people who called me this) "you've been working on your little resort too long. I don't need a gazebo...did your mother put you up to this?"

April 4

Midway through spring break, Kelly had mentioned that having a bike at school might be a good idea. It would be great exercise and a way to get to class quickly when her schedule was tight. We had explored shipping an old bike from Aspen to Dartmouth, but she managed to find a great deal online, a brand new ten-speed from Wal-Mart delivered to the Hanover post office for only $47. She ordered it before she went back to school, so it was waiting for her when she arrived. She tackled the "some assembly required" part with help from a friend then registered the bike with Safety and Security in the unlikely event it would be stolen.

Soon after it arrived, Kelly called. "Guess what Mom?"

By now I was accustomed to these early morning phone calls and was prepared for whatever catastrophe the night had brought—I would will it into a minor event with my Herculean powers of positive thinking. *Positive energy... positive energy...pos...* "Mom...are you there?"

"Of course, sweets! Love ya, how are you doing?" *Positive energy...positive...*

"Great, how about you?" *Positive energy...positive energy...positive energy...*

"Mom, are you OK? You seem a little spacey this morning."

"I'm super, what's up with you?" *Here it comes, I am ready, strong and positive...I can take the worst...positive energy....*

"You won't believe this, it's snowing here!" she screamed.

I am strong, this is nothing, positive energy.... Snowing? She chattered away, while I congratulated myself on the astounding mental feat I had accomplished. Keeping evil at bay with only my positive thoughts.

"Oh, and by the way," she said casually, as she was about to hang up, "my new bike was stolen last night. It was outside my dorm room, and it was locked too, can you believe it?" *I had let my guard down too soon, what was I thinking? Positive shmositive....*

What the heck, it was only a $47 bike.... It's all relative.

Mom was due back tonight, and John had driven to Orange County for a hasty business meeting. I sat hunched over my computer at the kitchen counter, slogging over more furniture options for the tent cabins, too immersed to remember to take a shower, when Dad emerged from his office.

"Shell, let's go." He could be abrupt. He wouldn't tell me where we were going, but we ended up at his favorite jewelry store. In appreciation for my staying with him, he wanted to buy me a pair of earrings. I got a little teary-eyed as we chose a beautiful pair of silver loops with diamonds, until I realized I hadn't showered, had smelly armpits and greasy hair. Fortunately the smell of the dim sum lunch at Emerald's Chinese Seafood Restaurant overpowered the smell of me, and we had a great afternoon...eating again.

Later that evening, as John and I were retrieving Mom and her friend from the airport, my cell phone rang. It was Kelly, distraught, in tears, sobbing. She had applied to four Dartmouth overseas programs for the next academic year; Barcelona, Italy, Fez, and Prague. She had been turned down for the Barcelona trip, and was on the waitlist for Prague and Italy. She would have to wait until next week, after an interview with the professor of the Anthropology of Islam course, to determine if she was accepted to go to Fez.

"Everything I've ever applied for at Dartmouth, I've been rejected," she moaned. "I'm a failure, I can't get into anything! I think it was a huge mistake that I was even let in here, pretty soon they're going to catch on and kick me out..."

Trying to put a positive spin on the situation, I gently asked how many students applied to these programs.

"I don't know, maybe a thousand?"

"And how many positions are available?" I questioned. "I don't know, maybe fifteen in each...." The sobbing eased.

"And besides, what about the Dartmouth Chamber Orchestra? You got into that!"

"I forgot to tell you, I got kicked out...the two regular clarinetists came back and the conductor told me he didn't need me anymore. And this means I probably won't get into the Public Policy Fellowship in DC this summer...."

Eventually, I neutralized Kelly's melancholy with questions about her weekend's activities, her kayak class and the club tennis team she was going to join. I brought her around to thinking that maybe Dartmouth wasn't that bad after all. However the bike was still missing, and I had missed all the details of the ladies eating egg salad sandwiches on the lawn at the Masters.

April 6

John packed the car, while I handed the house keys and the wifely duties back to Mom, feeling a sense of loss that my time with my father was over. Staying with him had rekindled my need to take care of someone, even if it just meant hanging out watching TV with him; just being there. I realized that even though I was starting to relish being my own person again, with the ability to do what I wanted to do when I wanted to do it, the years of motherhood clung to me like a fabric softener sheet to a towel. It was still good to be needed.

April 7

The feeling vanished as quickly as a stack of steaming blueberry pancakes as we arrived at the Mission Hills Country Club in Palm Desert to begin two days of golf lessons. With my new mental acuity (stemming from sculpture, photography, Lakedale, golf...it didn't matter which) I would be totally in the present, conquering each new task like an Olympian track star on steroids.

We had played golf sporadically for six years, having taken up the miserable game just before we went to live in Switzerland. I was so impassioned I insisted we ship our golf clubs all the way to Europe. In the sixteen months we were there, I played a total of nine holes of golf, my only round played on a course situated in the midst of a former apple orchard. Since it was autumn, I alternated shots between rotten apples and the golf ball.

The first year of my golf obsession, I took a series of golf lessons, which allowed me to play an adequate game with a friend who immediately became serious about the game. In one of the few rounds I played with her recently, she shot an 86. This was more than discouraging, since my average score hovers around 120. When I played for the first time last summer, my score shot up to a really embarrassing 128. Yes, something had to be done, so I jumped at the opportunity when John suggested that we tag the lessons on to the end of our trip.

Our instructor was the head of the golf school and was a low-key, likeable fellow. He was named PGA Teacher of the Year in 2003 (this fact was imprinted on our golf cart's windshield). He started us off with a review of putting, then chipping, and then on to a full swing. I've always been able to hit a golf ball straight down the fairway, but, like millions of other people whose name is not Tiger, the short game gets me every time. I arrive to within thirty yards of the green, then launch a vicious whiplash of golf balls careening from one side of the green to the other, sometimes close to the pin, sometimes fifty yards away. I hit my putts confidently, but they swerve around the pin into the nearest pond. It is not pretty.

As he packed us off to eat lunch before our 12:30 tee-time, I was convinced the pro had me on the right track. After eighteen holes in stifling 90-degree heat, I managed to score 103. OK, if you counted a few mulligans it was actually 106, but I was ecstatic. It was the best score I had ever recorded.

April 8

I was so excited I woke up two hours before our lesson. When John and I arrived I enthusiastically hugged our instructor, thanking him profusely for the miraculous cure for my lousy golf game. We worked on pitching, full swings, sand trap shots and fairway sand trap shots, in addition to having our swings video-taped. I could barely contain myself as we hopped into the golf cart for our 12:30 tee time. This could actually be the day I broke 100!

After four grueling hours in the searing heat, I had landed in every sand trap on the course, lost four balls in water hazards, used every specialty shot I had learned and had the amazing score of 116. The minor adjustments I had made to my swing obviously weren't working...back to the drawing board.

April 9

To make matters worse, the final day of the Masters golf tournament was on TV, and in my new state of golfoholism, I hounded John to drive like a madman to reach our next destination, the Furnace Creek Inn in Death Valley, in order to watch the last hour of the tournament. We drove north into rivers of smog (even on an Easter Sunday) that flowed through the break in the mountains from Los Angeles to the desert. At the mouth of the notch, fueled by the same wind that carried the smoggy air, acres of massive white wind generators twirled like toy whirl-a-gigs.

The drive took six hours instead of four and we missed the tournament. Fortunately when the highlights were shown that night, the golf professionals were hitting shots back and forth across the frigid Augusta greens and into ponds, exactly the same way I did. Somehow they still managed to score in the seventies. I would have to keep practicing.

When we called Kelly for Easter Sunday, she had just returned from attending her first high Catholic Mass with a friend, and was giggling about the whole episode. Throughout her childhood Kelly had accompanied me to church at the non-denominational Aspen Chapel.

"There were so many prayers they knew by heart, the only one I knew was the Lord's Prayer, and then they crossed themselves a zillion times with holy water, and I never knew when to kneel or stand up, or sit down. It felt like our church is a touchy-feely hippie love-in church after this. I miss it!" Her years of religious training were obviously well spent.

April 10

I dragged John to the driving range to work on my errant swing. I felt better after hitting two buckets of balls, and we spent the rest of the day lounging at the pool.

When I got Kelly's call at poolside she was ebullient. "Mom, guess what?"

"What, honey?" I asked.

She answered that she had found her wayward bike.

"No way, where was it?"

"I was coming out of a Dartmouth Aids Bangladesh meeting in Baker Hall, and it was parked in the bike racks in front of the building.

I was shocked and said, "I'm amazed. I was sure you'd never find it. You should have waited around to see if the perp tried to retrieve it."

"Mom, did you actually say perp? You have been watching way too much TV. Anyway, I looked in every bike rack on campus since it was stolen, and I think it was there for a while since it was covered in snow. I know it was mine since I memorized the Safety and Security identity number."

"Good work! Say, how are your classes doing? I haven't heard much about them recently."

"Really good, " she replied. "My chemistry prof is extremely funny and interesting...I went in to see him the other day about a question. It's kind of spooky though, because since the first day of class he has known a lot of the kid's names. I thought he might have had some of them in class before, but yesterday, he called on someone by name who was in chemistry last term with me who said he had never met him before. So when I went in for office hours, he looked at me and said, 'Hi there, you must be Kelly.' I freaked out, but then someone told me that professors receive photos of every student in their classes. He obviously studies them to learn who's who, but it's still kind of creepy, he's like a stalker professor."

"You would have to have a somewhat eclectic mind to understand those periodic tables," I concurred.

"And even though the economics teacher is fairly boring, I'm enjoying the material. But statistics is horrible, I hate it, and the teacher is truly monotonous, so if I don't make it into the Public Policy Fellowship, the upside is that I can drop it. The downside is that if I get the fellowship, I have to stick with statistics. So I'm kind of torn...."

"Is it the old 'grass is always greener' scenario rearing its ugly head again?"

"Guess so, and speaking of that, my EcoPsychology course is phenomenal...I love the professor, he's amazing. He had all of us come in to meet with him and talk about ourselves. I'm sending you a paper I just wrote for the class. It had to be autobiographical, and about how we relate to the environment. Tell me what you think!"

After I read it, I found it to be one of the most heart-felt, personal papers she had written, and she said she had written it in an hour. Must be like a golf swing, if you think too much, it doesn't work.

KELLY'S ECO-PSYCHOLOGY PAPER

Kelly Bogaert
EcoPsychology
4 April 2007

The Grass is Greener

People are always saying that the grass is greener on the other side. The side you came from, started at and must have left. It goes along with what people have been telling me my whole life, the fact that you can't always get what you want or you can have it all but not all at the same time. All those clichés of life. But they have to be clichés for some reason and I have found out why. They are true. They are true for me at least. Because the grass is actually greener on the other side sometimes and I am getting some of what I want, but not everything right now.

I discovered the grass cliché initially on a plane from Denver, Colorado to Geneva, Switzerland at the youthful age of twelve. At the time I was only concerned with getting there and, of course, what movies were playing on the plane and the fact that they gave me chocolate and a red pin for being an unaccompanied minor. And when I got to Europe things did change. I was astonished by the fact that the toilets flushed differently and that people around me were speaking French and driving tiny Smart cars. The wonder of the new experience took me away from the place I was from and the grass on the other side that I never believed I would long for. I had to leave it to realize it was a part of me that I had taken for granted, which is all a great cliché in itself. Where was I leaving? The small, beautiful, ritzy town of Aspen, Colorado that I had called home for most of my life. Known for its fine skiing and glamorous residents, Aspen meant something completely different than this stereotypical image to me.

Aspen was the place I went sledding down the mountains in piles of crisp winter snow, where I hiked up to lakes, following closely behind the yellow blur of my lab, Kelso. It was where I drove over mountain passes with my parents with my mom constantly commenting on the "glowing" aspen leaves quaking peacefully on the mountains as fall came. Where my school had taken me as a first grader into the wilderness to roast marshmallows around the campfire, as a sixth grader to ski to a tenth Mountain Division Hut and run from the sauna into the snow piles, and later as an eighth grader to hike over 12,000 foot passes and endure a solo experience in the woods with no food for twenty-four hours. This was my Aspen. The place I belong to this day. And to think I took it all for granted only to partially realize it on a plane to a foreign country for a year.

It became more evident as I looked out at the rainy gray skies of Geneva that I was missing more than my friends, my dog, and my school at home, but that I was actually missing the place and regretting I hadn't taken advantage of it when I was there. It was all right though, because who wouldn't want to live abroad for a year and still be able to go right back to where you came from, hoping nothing had changed? I learned so much in Europe that it became my second grass turf. A home away from home. A place where I could still ski or go biking through the dense woods outside my house to buy baguettes from the local bakery. Life was good there. It just wasn't connected to the natural world like Aspen was; the world I hadn't really appreciated as much as I should have. It had always been there and wasn't going anywhere in my mind. So what if the grass did seem a little greener there, I enjoyed being twelve years old in Geneva; it was fun, and I missed home but I knew I would go back. And it was no surprise then that when I returned, Aspen was just as I had left it. It also shouldn't have been a surprise that after a few months I appreciated it just as much as I had before I left. Nothing had substantially changed in that relationship, except of course, me.

I returned to Aspen for eighth grade, where I knew I belonged. For our eighth-grade outdoor education trip, our teachers had us hike over mountain passes, stay outside alone for twenty-four hours without food, and experience Outward Bound activities, doing everything possible to have us engage with our beautiful surroundings. I appreciated the tall mountains after I had worked so hard to get to their peaks, lugging a heavy pack on my back. I appreciated the trees and the views and the scenery that were now becoming more like friends than the foreign people of Geneva. But then something happened, something that took all of our thirteen-year-old minds away from the paradise we were discovering. September 11 happened while I was in the woods, miles away from civilization, finding myself and my relationship to the natural world. The incomprehensible shock of September 11 immediately disconnected us from that world, brought us back to the reality of an America that was far, far away from anything nature offered. I now realize that nature provided everything to combat a situation like September 11; peace, solitude, a place for discovery, connection and appreciation. Nature brought my class closer to each other as we waited, in the woods, for the enormity of the event to set in, the sheer magnitude of it. For a while, nature sheltered us from that terrifying world. But driving home the chaos flooded our minds, removing us too quickly from our experience with the natural. This was the first time I really appreciated the mountains for all they were, all they gave me, and all they took me away from. I didn't know it, but I was now deeply and integrally connected to the Rocky Mountains.

Yet, I still went back to my usual ways. I appreciated Aspen for its natural beauty, or at least I thought I did. I wanted to. But the truth is, although I was constantly in it, interacting with it on the Nordic ski team, hiking, downhill skiing and sitting outside just to enjoy it, I am not sure if I was ever truly aware of my connection to it. There always seemed to be more important issues on my mind, like my grades in school, where I was going to college and how it could under no circumstances be in Colorado. I applied to East coast, West coast and Midwest schools, but there was only one school in Colorado that I visited, let alone applied to. I chose Dartmouth partially because of its location out of the city. At least I knew that part of my connection to nature; I knew whatever it was, I wouldn't do well in an urban setting. And so for the second time in my life, I took a defining plane ride, this time to Boston, Massachusetts, and in my first week, I ended up hiking through the New Hampshire Mountains with the Dartmouth Outing Club. I loved it, it made me feel at home to be hiking through the chaos of my new college life, and although it was one of the most fun experiences I had ever had, something wasn't right. I couldn't see out, I couldn't see my mountains and I knew I wasn't in Colorado. For the time being that was OK.

I have found some connection to the land around Hanover, skiing through it, walking through every season's weather in it, and even rowing on the river in it. But it's not the same. My connection to nature has dissipated. I receive blitzes from Cabin and Trail and read the hiking descriptions, they sound exciting, and I want to go. But I never have. I had ski practices all winter and knew that I loved being outdoors, yet it always seemed to be a hassle to go, a drag even. It took me a while but I have now realized that I miss Colorado almost more than my parents and my friends. I miss my mountains and the grass has once again become greener on the other side. I had taken Colorado for granted, but I understand that now. Don't get me wrong, I love Dartmouth and wouldn't have gone elsewhere, but I often wonder what was stirring deep down inside that made me want to get out of the mountains of Colorado so badly. I don't know, maybe it was my adventurous spirit or the fact that I might have known that the only way for me to leave a place I love was to force it on myself and then be able to appreciate it so much more. And going back home, I have. I have appreciated that home in nature for all it is worth. I have gone home on my college breaks and sat among the trees on the ski slopes, put my head back in the snow, looked up among the piney branches and felt at home and in the exact right place. Maybe all along I knew that only by seeing that grassy patch of Aspen from far away again would it look so much greener and maybe even stay that green forever no matter where life leads me. But it pains me to realize that it is changing, that its nature is slowly being eaten up by the new developments that crop up in the middle of my view of the mountains. It confuses me to see fresh scratch marks from tractors tearing up the earth to develop affordable housing, so that the homeowners of Aspen can have housekeepers. It seems I may have to find a connection with nature elsewhere and that really scares me. Maybe that is why I haven't gone hiking with Cabins and Trails or appreciated nature in Hanover. Because in doing so I would have to acknowledge my home has changed and when I return next, it may not be the way I left it.

So maybe all I can do right now is make a grassy green patch for myself in the middle of these New Hampshire woods. All I have to do is get out there and find a place that works for me. Maybe it will have to seem like Colorado for my plan to work, but I know that somewhere out here that grass is waiting for me. And when I find it, I will go back to Colorado and realize that I have found most everything I want from nature, but that I can't have it all at the same time.

April 11

My attempts to lure John into a round of golf at the Furnace Creek Ranch golf course, the course with the lowest elevation in the entire United States, were futile, so we spent the day poolside. I finally finished reading *The Female Brain,* which was probably more important than scoring well in golf anyway.

April 12

Highway 50, known as "The Loneliest Road in America," winds its way across the barren Nevada desert from Carson City to the edge of western Utah. It closely parallels the old Pony Express Trail. We joined the now-paved route just north of Death Valley. Fortunately for us, we didn't have to meet the hiring requirements to become a rider in 1860. We were definitely not what the 19th century ads were looking for, "young, skinny and wiry fellows under the age of eighteen." And, except for the hazards of the modern highway, we were not "willing to risk death daily." We were also not orphans.

Dirty sand punctuated with abandoned plastic grocery store bags stretched for hundreds of miles into the blue mountains in the distance. Brothels, whose names must have been inspired by the natural world around them (Cottontail Ranch, Kit-Kat Ranch, Chicken Ranch, Shady Lady Ranch), competed with the sagebrush for roadside privileges and from what I had read, somewhere out there was a nuclear waste dump. Since the loneliest road was 300 miles long, we had hours to kill. I played DJ on my iPod, we high-fived truckers burdened with tons of travertine in their truck beds, and we ate mediocre Mexican food in Ely, halfway through the route. We stopped for the night at an outdated Rodeway Inn in Salida, Utah. The lobby reeked of take-out food and cigarette smoke, and the towels were as thin as tissue paper. The only salvation was the delicious pizza delivered by the local video-rental joint.

April 13

In keeping with the whole "Loneliest Road/Awful Hotel" aspect of the trip, we decided to eat breakfast at a Denny's in Salida. I have only eaten at Denny's once before in my life. John took the advice of the redneck trucker in the booth behind us and ordered the Meat-Lover's Special. It arrived on three groaning plates; bacon, sausage, ham, eggs, pancakes, biscuits. An obscene amount of food for one person.

When we arrived back in Aspen there wasn't a trace of snow in our yard, chives had sprouted in my herb garden, and Kelso romped in the yard, happy to have spring back.

April 14

"Hi Mom!" Happy Kelly was on the phone. "How's Aspen?"

"Really, really green. The green in springtime is a completely different green than the rest of summer, it's...fresher," I enthused.

"Cool." She sounded cheerful, so I assumed she had good news about one of her summer options. Instead, she said, "I didn't get into the Public Policy fellowship."

I reached for my grief-counselor's hat, but before I could put it on, she said, "I'm actually relieved because now I can drop statistics! Yahoo! And I don't think the internship was really my cup of tea anyway, living in DC for the summer would be too hot and muggy, so now I can check out other options." I was still puzzled by her reaction, yet relieved at her new maturity. I was almost starting to expect it now. She said she was exploring an internship at a non-profit group called Invisible Children in San Diego, had just taken a hip-hop aerobics dance class and had played club tennis earlier in the day. After Kelly's call, John and I played eighteen holes of golf; I shot 113, John shot 109. I didn't judge myself too harshly since I knew why my chip shot had gone astray, and with my extensive notes, I thought I knew how to fix the problem.

April 15

I made an appearance at the hippie love-in church...to pray for more endurance with Kelly and the energy to complete the tent cabins. The advantage of going to an anything-goes church is that you can ask for anything.

> 2:51 p.m. eeeek! look at the Dartmouth webcam. welcome to new hampshire during a nor'easter!
>
> 3:35 p.m. wow, that looks like it really sucks, pardon my French!
>
> 6:51 p.m. can you take a look at this paper?? gracias! love ya!
>
> 7:11 p.m. hi sweets! here it is with a few modifications. good luck on your test tomorrow! love and kisses! m

April 17

The Lakedale tent cabins had to be up and running by mid-May when we had guest reservations already on the books, which left me precious little time to get furniture ordered, delivered and installed. I also had to finish the project before our upcoming trip back East to visit Kelly for Freshman Family Weekend at Dartmouth, an event I wasn't about to miss. At the end of the day, I gathered up my latest concepts for the design and brought them to our bedroom where John was engrossed in the weather report, a source of constant entertainment for him, and one, I'll admit, I could really care less about, unless it was rain that was predicted to threaten my golf game.

"OK, honey," I said, as I carefully spread more than fifty images of bed frames, fabric colors, and accessories across our bed. "Take a look at these so we can make some final decisions and I can order everything tomorrow."

Whether it was because his weather was being interrupted or that I had wiped out another few trees with my excessive paper usage, John's response resembled a lion ready to pounce upon a baby water buffalo.

Empty Nester Insight: Never take work to bed.

April 18

In a last ditch attempt to finalize the plans, I decided to take a more methodical approach to the problem. Eight hours later, I had produced seven new design options, ranging from a cabin with rustic wood furniture and rag rugs, to a fully developed cabin with an African Queen theme, complete with photos of Humphrey Bogaert and Katharine Hepburn hanging from the canvas walls. Long before the news and weather came on, I placed a large glass of red wine in front of John, anticipating a fruitful conversation. "Seven options? You have to be kidding!" the lion roared.

> 11:11 a.m. guess what? i got accepted to Fez!! wahoo, i think everyone did, but c'est la vie! it's something!
>
> 11:42 a.m. EXCELLENT! I think everything is on the up and up now. why don't you start applying to more things?

April 19

I had started to believe that by getting my emotions stabilized after Kelly's departure, in discovering my new career as a hospitality professional, and by successfully becoming an empty nester role model for next year's crop of newly adrift parents, my life would be under control. But the Lakedale project almost sent me plunging into the depths of mental illness. Never had the phrase *Back to the drawing board!* resounded so clearly. After a few more hours of tedious work, John and I hunkered down over lunch, and pulled the pieces together. I would start ordering the furniture tomorrow for the "Northwest Safari" look we had agreed upon: dark wood headboards and futon frames, forest green flannel duvet covers with green, cream and red accent pillows, and wrought iron accessories that would provide a glamorous camping experience for our guests. We would call it "glamping" for short.

To celebrate the design's miraculous completion, I cooked a Canadian Maple Leaf duck on the barbecue. A friend at the hippie-love-in-church had shared the recipe with me and was adamant that if I cooked the bird over low heat on the rotisserie for two hours, it would be the most amazingly tender duck I had ever eaten.

The work on the Canvas Cabins, our sexy new moniker for the tent cabins consumed most of the day. I decided the duck wasn't cooking quickly enough, so I ignored the instructions and turned the rotisserie heat up to medium. When I returned twenty minutes later, the duck was pitch black and smoking. It looked like a charred carcass from one of the forensic murder shows which we were far too fond of. I attempted to salvage the duck by pulling off its blackened skin, praying that we might have a few shreds of meat left for dinner. Astonishingly, the meat was only slightly overdone. When slathered with a few spoonfuls of the clove-scented orange sauce from the packet that came enclosed with it, the duck was delicious. John liked it so much he suggested we give the ducks to the guests in the new Canvas Cabins to roast over their campfires. Instructions included.

April 20

> 6:22 a.m. a bunch of us went streaking across the green last night – it's a tradition!
>
> luv ya lots, Kelly
>
> 7:31 a.m. sounds like fun... looks like it's a beautiful day at Dartmouth! i'll check the webcam again this afternoon to see if you're out there playing Frisbee, hopefully with your clothes on. mom

April 21

I spent all day ordering furniture and accessories, all of which were scheduled to arrive with ample time before our first Canvas Cabin guests arrived.

> 1:41 p.m. the weather has been so amazing, i have been chilling on the green all day! With my clothes on.
>
> 1:58 p.m. where are you on the green? i'm watching it now, I even sent your grandma a link so she could watch you!
>
> 1:59 p.m. i just left, but i was right outside baker library, not

actually on the green because of the woodsmen.

2:21 p.m. who, pray tell, are the woodsmen?

2:23 p.m. teams from colleges all over come here to compete...log rolling, climbing up poles, throwing axes, the usual lumberjack stuff. lots of plaid flannel roaming around. gotta go to dinner, ciao!

April 22

It was another sunny day in Hanover. Students lounged on the Green, some threw Frisbees, some practiced their fencing skills, and some were even studying. When she called, our freshman sounded happy, her mood had improved with the coming of spring and the warm sun overhead.

"Hey, Mom, I'm one of thirty kids getting an interview to be a campus tour guide, I think I may actually get it this time!" I was relieved that something she had applied for might come to fruition. I asked when the interview was.

"Tomorrow. And did I tell you I'm applying for jobs at Roche Harbor for the summer in case the internships don't work out?"

Roche Harbor was a quintessential summer resort at the north end of San Juan Island. In the 1880s it was the site of a major lime production company, and now the focal point of the resort is the aging Hotel de Haro, decorated with sagging decks and white gingerbread trim. Bountiful flower gardens border the hotel and extend to the large marina where mega-yachts dock on their circuits of the San Juan Islands. Every evening at sundown, six members of the dock crew march in time to tinny old recordings of *Taps*, the *Star-Spangled Banner* and *O Canada* and lower the flags. During the ceremony, all activities at the resort stop, even service in the restaurants, and guests squint into the setting sun to watch the event.

"Great. What do they have available?" I said, secretly hoping this option would work out so we could have her with us at the island all summer, but I didn't want to sound too excited.

"I'm going to apply to be a dock girl, and a hostess at the

restaurant, but I have to ask you something...the application asks whether you want to work part-time or full-time. What does that mean?"

We must have completely missed the chapter on *Work* in our Dr. Spock book. Kelly was a freshman at Dartmouth College but she didn't know what a forty hour workweek was. Without a doubt, it was time she had a job.

April 23

"Hi Mom! How are the Canvas Cabins going?"

I replied that all was going well and that all the furniture was ordered and scheduled to arrive in time for the guests.

"Did I tell you I figured out the roommate situation? Katie and I are going to room together next year. She has a really good priority number, so we should get a great room." She sounded so mature and focused, especially when she transitioned to the next topic, the fact that she thought one of her friends had an eating disorder.

"I brought it up to him in a matter of fact way, and asked if there was anything I could do to help, and then I went to the Peer Eating Disorder counselor to make sure I had done it correctly. After that I went to lunch with Nicholas Kristoff, an author and expert on Darfur."

"How did you manage to snag that lunch date?"

"I won a spot because I'm in the Pre-Med Society. He was fascinating in a morbidly depressing way with the genocide and all. Oh, and I had my tour guide interview today. It was with a guy from the admissions office who was just filling in, so I'm not sure how it went. He asked a lot of questions, but I had some great answers for him, I'm sure he was just glad to get out from under his stacks of applications...I'll find out next week when you and dad are here." *Great. I could console her in person.*

Kelly was talking a mile a minute so I let her ramble on. "I think I might have been a little depressed over the winter, but now that spring's here, there is so much to do." *Note to self: Buy Kelly one of those indoor lights next winter to stave off sunlight deficiency disease.*

"I just love spring...I also went to a Cabins and Trails Meeting where the highlight of the evening was someone streaking in the Dartmouth newspaper's room next to us, and then we ate hot chili peppers. But I also need some boy advice from you."

"Sure, what would you like to know?"

"How do you tell when something is something, or when it isn't?" I think I got the essence of what she was trying to ask, and tried to quickly think of what Kathy, expert advice-giver, would say.

"Tell me about what happened." The query could buy me a little more thinking time.

"Well, it was late, we'd all had a few cervezas, and most of the people on my floor were walking arm-in arm and singing together on our way back to the dorms...and this kid and I started holding hands. And he remembered my name the next day, so I think that's a good sign, don't you?"

Depending on how many beers they had consumed, it was probably a good sign, and so I launched into some motherly advice about men, the dangers of alcohol, and flirting. After all, it had been a long time since I had been in her shoes, but I recalled all too well those emotions...*does he like me, is he just a flirt, will he call, what happens next?*

"Why don't we talk about it when I get to Dartmouth?" I asked.

"OK, Moo (her childhood nickname for me), gotta go to another meeting...love ya!"

April 26

"Hi guys! Are you here yet?" Her perky voice chirped from my phone. We had just checked into the Hanover Inn and were deciding where to meet Kelly. "It looks so cute with all the families walking across the Green! Everybody has their Family Weekend nametags on and they're carrying their green Dartmouth bags. Why don't you meet me at my dorm room so we can walk across campus and look like everyone else?" Kelly has a very sentimental streak and bows to tradition whenever possible. We were glad to oblige since it also seemed that she was thrilled to have us back at Dartmouth. "Remember to wear your badges!" she reminded me.

The weekend passed in a mélange of activities designed for parents and their soon-to-be sophomore students: lectures by favorite faculty members, tours of campus facilities like the Baker Bell Tower and the Rauner Special Collections Library (which, we discovered, included a first folio of Shakespeare's works and the original sculpture of Rudolph the Red-Nosed Reindeer), concerts by a cappella groups, sporting events, and of course, dinners with Kelly at the Canoe Club.

On Saturday morning, we walked to a private breakfast hosted by the college president and his wife, held at their home on campus. Since we didn't exactly know what to wear for an eight o'clock breakfast on the East Coast, we dressed casually. As we mingled with the sixty other parents, we found that most of the men were sockless in their leather loafers; showing off perfectly tanned ankles that emerged from perfectly creased khaki pants. Most of the women wore strands of pearls over their tasteful Chanel sweater sets. Everyone chatted politely and sipped coffee but no one ate much from the buffet, obviously worried about stray green flecks from the spinach crepes lodging in their teeth. We had no idea why we'd been invited to this get-together, but I finally realized that we would soon be asked to contribute to the college's endowment fund, and John admitted I probably had a point.

Midway through that evening's performance by The Aires, Dartmouth's most popular a cappella group, Kelly looked queasy and whispered to me that she felt sick. I ran with her back to her dorm room, in a state of panic that she was having another allergic reaction. She hurriedly swallowed some Benadryl and we chatted on her bed until she felt better. As she walked me back to the hotel across the Green, she greeted friends, arranged study dates, and basked in the glow of her new life, into which we had just interjected ourselves. We were like the filling in a jelly donut, a familiar and comforting element, but not really necessary if the donut was good...and Dartmouth was a really good donut.

A giant wave of separation anxiety washed over me. Whether it was the realization that she had only five weeks left until the end of her freshman year, or that we were leaving in the morning, I said to John after we dropped her off, "To hell with Goal #1, John, take me to Dunkin' Donuts!"

As I was licking the grape jelly off my fingers, the phone rang.

"Mom, Mom, you won't believe it! I made it as a tour guide! And I just found out I'm going to be a leader for an Outing Club trip this summer! I am so excited!" I should really eat donuts more often.

April 29

When we had at first planned our trip to Dartmouth, John mentioned that the Eastern seaboard boasted some serious vacation destinations. It was time to start acting like real empty nesters and take a beach vacation—enough work, we deserved some fun.

I scoured the internet and found seats on the last non-stop flight of the season from Boston to Providenciales in the Turks and Caicos Islands, then booked a reasonably priced partial ocean-view room at the Grace Bay Club.

When we arrived, we hauled our bags up three flights of stairs to a room that was the lock-off bedroom to a larger suite, and whose balcony was smashed into a sidewall of the hotel. If you dangled yourself sideways off the balcony and peered through the lower limb of the palm tree on the right, you could see the ocean. We would have to switch rooms.

As I've mentioned, wherever we travel, we search for the perfect room, in the perfect location, with the best view. We call this the "Bogaert Shuffle." This time the shuffle resulted in a room that was three times the size of our original room and cost three times as much, completely obliterating any cost savings from my hours on the internet. But the new room was a stunner. Its third floor balcony spanned fifty feet and overlooked the glittering white sand and clear waters of the twelve-mile long Grace Bay Beach, a beach as perfect as the alabaster bosom of a Botticelli maiden rising from her crystalline aquamarine gown. The grand living room boasted a well-equipped kitchen (pretty much unnecessary as far as my idea of a vacation went) that was over 1,000 square feet and the deluxe bedroom and bath area were a similar size.

Since our room was so spectacular, we decided to try the hotel's restaurant, Anaconda, for dinner. No disappointment here. In fact, it was one of the most exciting restaurants we had ever dined in—or out, since every table was outside and open to the sky. Yet each table was completely private, surrounded by three-foot tall green hedges that created individual dining areas. Adjourning to the al fresco bar after dinner, we discovered built-in white plaster banquettes with mounds of pillows. We could lose ourselves atop plush sofas, beneath the white sails overhead that glowed by the light of Moroccan lanterns. Empty nesters paradise.

Within a day, our vacation routine was organized.

> Morning: Walk five miles of Grace Bay Beach in either direction (on the sand, or through the water, depending on how many calories we had to remove after the previous nights' dinner). Gawk at the new construction along the beach. The classic beach hotels were one or two stories of colorful Caribbean gingerbread; the new timeshares were seven stories of pink faux-Italian columns and French mansard roofs.
>
> Ask Carlos, the beach concierge, to position an umbrella and beach chairs on the beautiful white sand beach.
>
> Read fast-paced summer novels, including the latest John Grisham legal thriller.
>
> Swim in the beautiful aquamarine water
>
> Lunch: At hotel's beach bar restaurant, usually inclusive of rum punch or mojito, Caesar salad (to control vacation weight gain), conch salad or panini. Maybe two rum punches.
>
> Afternoon: Back to beach. Swim. Read. Swim.

Read. Nap.

Late Afternoon: Watch destination weddings on the beach below us from our sinfully long balcony.

We saw at least four of these events; the most amusing occurred when the best man dropped the bride's five-carat band of diamonds in the sand five minutes before the ceremony. The groomsmen searched frantically through the sand for half-an-hour, stalling the bride (and her eighty seated guests) with liquid refreshments.

To save the day, the maid of honor gave her similar band of diamonds to the minister. The bride finally proceeded barefoot up the sandy aisle and was married (at the time unbeknownst to her) with her maid of honor's ring. While the happy couple celebrated in the Anaconda bar, the enterprising wedding planner called a friend with a metal detector who finally found the ring buried in the sand.

Eat dinner: At Anaconda in the outdoor dining room.

After five days, we needed some variety in our dining regime, so we walked to a highly recommended restaurant down the beach. Grace's Cottage was a quaint yellow and white bungalow surrounded by a lush tropical garden. I nearly gagged when I saw the menu's prices, but we were already seated outside and enjoying a glass of champagne, so I stifled my urge to escape to the local conch chowder joint.

The restaurant's stated culinary mission was to blend authentic Caribbean cooking styles with a contemporary flair, delivered without compromising the uniqueness of the cuisine. I began with fried hearts of palm on a bed of hummus and drizzled with mint oil, followed by Caribbean Fish and Chips. The dish consisted of a piece of ridiculously fresh grouper the size of a hangnail, arranged atop a bed of avocado and mango, with plantain chips placed vertically around it, looking much like a culinary version of Stonehenge. The presentation was engulfed with frothy lemon foam.

After John had eaten his appetizer, foie gras mounted on a thin slab of chocolate cake with a berry sauce drizzled over it (which I suggested he should have for dessert), he moved on to a slow-cooked duck breast fanned across seasonal beans napped with a sugar cane demi-glaze. We shared a made-to-order chocolate soufflé for dessert; it bled gooey dark chocolate under vanilla bean ice cream.

It may be hard to believe, but we were sick and tired of eating and drinking. Waddling back to our suite, we counted the number of gourmet meals we would have to consume before the trip ended, and determined that we couldn't handle many more. Even with five-mile walks in the morning. I was sure I hadn't lost a pound, and my abs were looking like rows of Mounds candy bars. But I had a month left until Kelly finished her first collegiate year. There was still hope.

MAY

May 4

This was the first beach vacation we had taken without Kelly in thirteen years and it felt strange not having her beside us, reading books and snorkeling. Just last year at this time, we were at Little Dix Bay on Virgin Gorda, running to the business center every few hours to check on college acceptances and learning she had been accepted to Dartmouth.

May 6

After a travel day from hell (twenty hours to get from the Caribbean to Colorado) and while eating dinner with Fred and Jayne, Kelly called. We hadn't made contact with her in a week; we had no cell phone service or internet in the Turks and Caicos and couldn't reach her during our travels yesterday. Once we heard her cheerful little chirp, she informed us that she had been on an overnight camp-out with the outing club for trip leaders. Sleep came easy for me that night.

> 8:06 p.m. san juan safaris outfitters have all the employees they need. any other outdoor ideas for summer jobs?
>
> 9:07 p.m. is that the company that Captain Pete works for?

might be fun to work on the whale-watching boats! what about the university of washington marine labs? how about going to the San Juan Island chamber of commerce site – they may have some ideas...

10:04 p.m. the chamber of commerce doesn't know anything about jobs. and yes Pete works for san juan safaris, but they said they were full, ...and I don't know what to do....and yeah, guess I will be working at Lakedale.....or something....

May 5

11:15 a.m. don't despair - there's lots of time to find a job and avoid the dreaded Lakedale forced work program! getting a job is just like applying for college - the squeaky wheel gets the job. first off, call the places where you want to work, don't email. If they say they are full, ask if you can be put on a waitlist, as you'll be living in the islands and will be available on the spot. Ask when you can call them back to see how things are going. At Roche Harbor, ask to speak with the person in charge of hiring for the docks or the restaurant and see if there is anything you can do–phone interview, send photos, experience, etc. you have to sound really EAGER AND EXCITED for the job even if you're not...AND even if you get a better offer somewhere else, they don't have to know that, and you can always call them back later and say you won't be able to take the job, etc., etc. Another good thing is to make up your own job or internship - very few people will turn down free labor!

May 7

I woke up early, jet lag kicked in, and I discovered that in addition to having no cell phone messages, my land line hadn't forwarded any calls, so I had twenty-five urgent messages, all of them relating to problems with the Canvas Cabin furniture, the furniture plan I had spent weeks making sure was bullet-proof.

The futon company had shipped the futons and bed frames via a freight company who had lost the entire shipment.

Pottery Barn had delayed shipment of the tables and chairs until June 19, a month past our deadline.

I had tried for a week to make contact with Roost, a company supplying accessories and doormats for the tent cabins. Still no contact.

The lodge's sofa table, due to be delivered two weeks ago, was sitting at an obscure freight loading dock in Seattle.

Seat cushions for the outside patio chairs at the lodge hadn't arrived and the supplier couldn't find a record of the order anywhere.

Two eight-foot silk palm trees designated for our house in Aspen had ended up at a post office box in Escondido, California.

This must be why I retired from the interior design business. I spent the entire week tracking down furniture, trying to find new tables and chairs, ordering last minute items, and getting ready to go back to Lakedale to install the lobby and Canvas Cabins.

> 12:23 p.m. i think i lost my drivers license...is that bad? luv ya, Kelly

> 12:43 p.m. not that bad, except that you need it as an ID to fly. best bet is to search for it - where do you think you lost it? check with the Colorado DMV - I thought I lost mine once, and got a replacement without having to go in person. here's the address for the lost license application - you should do it quickly as you'll need it to fly home!

May 8

"Hi Mom, how are you doing?"

"Great, sweetie. Working away as usual. What are you doing?"

"I have a question, should I go to my kayak class today?" *What?* I thought we had grown beyond this sort of question in our parent/child college-era decision-making process. But I would remain calm.

"Why not?"

"Well, I have a Chemistry final in six hours." I resisted my urge to scream. *Be a calm mother. A really calm mother.*

"Do you feel you've studied enough?" I calmly queried.

She answered with a very vague "Maybe." *I'm 2,000 miles away, how the heck am I supposed to give advice about this? I think I need to get out of the advice business. I'll try to teach her about time management instead, better late than never.*

"How long is your kayak class?"

"Four hours, plus the time it will take to walk there and back, so four and a half."

"Well, what do you think you should do?" A long pause ensued. I didn't say a word.

"Mom…mom…are you still there?"

"Sure, hon."

"Guess I should study...right?"

"Right." Bravo, it worked.

May 9

When we talked the next day, Kelly informed me that she had not gone kayaking and that after taking her chemistry final, had pulled an all-nighter to write the first draft of an eco-psychology paper. She watched the sun rise and went to bed at 7 a.m.

Kelly and Katie had received their dorm assignment for next year in the room draw the previous night; They would share a third floor corner room in the mid-Fay-Fay's, short (as everything in college life is abbreviated) for the Mid-Fayerweathers. The room was much older than the McClaughlin complex where she was currently living, but it overlooked the Green and was situated immediately behind historic Dartmouth Hall, in the center of all of the campus action. She was thrilled.

May 10

Kelly and I talked again this morning. She was only up until 3:00 a.m. last night, but wasn't as efficient in her studies as she could have been because other people on her floor had been out for the Wednesday night parties and she had been frequently interrupted. I was no longer in shock at the hours she kept, I totally accepted her erratic schedule, and I wasn't even psychologically tired when she told me about it. She was still pounding the pavement for a summer job. She had received a call from Roche Harbor requesting she come in for an interview, but she informed them that she couldn't, without explaining the fact that she was still at college. I have concluded that

1. she really doesn't want a job,
2. she secretly wants to work at Lakedale, or
3. she doesn't have a clue about what fun a summer job can be.

May 11

Kelly emailed me about a new program she was really excited about for the summer. In the program, students worked in a third-world country, were at risk of getting a communicable, possibly fatal disease—or worst case scenario, of getting shot—all in the name of "helping local people raise international awareness of the economic challenges in developing countries and supporting cross-cultural communities in finding more effective solutions to development issues." For which their parents paid $3,000 for them to work for eight weeks. Airfare not included. I mentioned that a real, boring JOB might be a better life/earning experience for her than traveling to Uganda and living in a mud hut.

My mood changed 180 degrees when the guard from the Starwood gate called to say that a bouquet of flowers had arrived for me...from Kelly for Mother's Day. They were organically grown roses, and 10% of the profits would go to the charity of my choice, and my charity of choice would be, of course, the third-world summer program. I decided see if I could smuggle them through the TSA checkpoint when we traveled to the Northwest tomorrow, hoping there was less than three ounces of illicit liquid in the beautiful peach-colored blossoms.

May 12

After savoring our traditional first-day-on-the-island lunch of salmon tacos at Downrigger's Restaurant, we drove to Lakedale to see the results of months of hard labor. We noticed more cars than usual in the lodge parking lot and upon walking through the lobby doors, found ourselves in the midst of a wedding reception, eight round dining tables occupying the space where my brand-new sofas were supposed to be. Partygoers were swilling champagne and munching nibblies on top of the intended location of my new lounge chairs. A designer's nightmare.

I craved some visual satisfaction so I said to John, "Let's walk to the campground and see what the Canvas Cabins and the new washroom look like." We were both pleasantly surprised when we arrived at the new washroom. It still needed some finishing touches, but the tile was beautiful and the showers worked. It was the Taj Mahal of campground washrooms. At the Canvas Cabins site, the foundations were in place to accept the floorboards, gravel had been trucked in for the patio areas and it appeared that we would be ready for the erection of the wood supports and canvas membranes in a few days.

May 13

I woke up depressed that this would be my first Mother's Day without Kelly at home, so it was a good thing our friends Kevin and Debbie were arriving from Calgary today. It occurred to me that this empty nester business resembled the death of someone close to you. Death wasn't a subject I was chummy with, but it was similar in that you had to experience all of the occasions you had always shared together...without that special person. Especially that person who brought you breakfast in bed on Mother's Day, on a tray with a handmade card, signed with a touching personal greeting, a fresh cappuccino...slight sob...and your favorite book to read while you wiled away the morning...sob, sob....

John drove the dinghy to the floatplane dock to pick up Kevin and Debbie. They were the parents of three daughters between the ages of ten and sixteen, so they hadn't experienced any empty nester trauma yet, but Debbie was managing splendidly sans daughters on this trip, so I knew I had to shape up. It had been eight months since Kelly's departure, for God's sakes!

We sauntered into town, where Kevin, a beer aficionado, quaffed a few ales at Friday's Crab House. Instead of beer, I quaffed a cup of smoked salmon chowder, but it didn't rate a mention in my Clam Chowder Competition.

Later in the day we stopped by Steps Restaurant for their "Second Anniversary Open House" and noshed complimentary appetizers and champagne. Eating and drinking seemed to be the main activity when we got together with Kevin and Deb. Between the four of us, we won homemade chocolates, a champagne bucket, a $75 dinner coupon, two jars of jam, and a free plant. And then Kelly called, and the day was as perfect as it could be...without her.

May 14

I drove to Lakedale and finally saw the lobby with its new decor. A few crucial items were still missing, like the waylaid sofa table and some wicker chairs, but it looked bright and comfortable compared to the black leather sofas and grey tapestry-covered arm chairs that had recently lived there. I was so thrilled with the new look, I proceeded to "de-fishify" the lobby of all the kitschy fish paintings, fishing tackle, and other old fishing lodge memorabilia that were still hanging on the walls. The staff rolled their eyes, wondering when I'd stop, and weren't surprised when I grabbed the keys to the log cabins and stripped them bare of all of the fishing nets, duck decoys, and garage sale décor accumulated during the previous owner's lackluster design tenure.

May 15

John had warned Kevin and Deb that we would be working during their visit, so while they slept we went to Lakedale to install more furniture. The sofa table had arrived the day before, as had the silk orchids and plants, and the wicker chairs. I inventoried all of the items in the storage building to make sure I knew where I stood in this furniture mayhem, and discovered a double shipment of chairs for the Canvas Cabins, *and* that our general manager had given the fire department all of the furniture taken out of the log cabins; furniture I was going to recycle for other parts of the resort. I was furious. Could this possibly have something to do with his wine buddy/firefighter?

As John and I left for the night, we discovered him (not Number One on my General Manager hit parade at the moment) in the beautiful new lobby talking with a band of hillbillies. A very, very large hillbilly woman, her hillbilly husband, and two other related hillbillies, all missing teeth and in desperate need of showers. Our GM was sweetly saying he'd be happy to COMP them one of our newly redecorated cabins...for two nights! *Who are these people and why are they staying in our cabins for free? I will have to get to the bottom of this tomorrow! On second thought, maybe I'm not cut out for the hospitality industry after all.*

I turned my frustration into a cooking extravaganza for Kevin's fiftieth birthday. Since he was such a beer nut, Debbie and I cooked every course with beer...scallop fritters in beer batter, Westcott Bay mussels and clams stewed in white ale, beer-marinated chicken, and a beer infused chocolate cake, all paired with exotic beers to go with each course. Kelly called mid-way through in the feast to wish Kevin a happy birthday, and was in hysterics that we were cooking an all-beer meal. She insisted on knowing the details of each and every item, a testimony to her newfound fondness for hops.

Chocolate Stout Cake

Yield: 12 servings

2 cups stout (such as Guinness)
2 cups (4 sticks) unsalted butter
1½ cups unsweetened cocoa powder (preferably Dutch-process)
4 cups all-purpose flour
4 cups sugar
1 tablespoon baking soda
1½ teaspoons salt
4 large eggs
1⅓ cups sour cream

ICING:

2 cups whipping cream
1 pound bittersweet (not unsweetened) or semisweet chocolate, chopped

Preheat oven to 350°F. Butter three 8-inch round cake pans with 2-inch-high sides. Line with parchment paper. Butter paper. Bring 2 cups stout and 2 cups butter to simmer in large heavy saucepan over medium heat. Add cocoa powder and whisk until mixture is smooth. Cool slightly.

Whisk flour, sugar, baking soda, and salt in large bowl to blend. Using electric mixer, beat eggs and sour cream in another large bowl to blend. Add stout-chocolate mixture to egg mixture and beat just to combine. Add flour mixture and beat briefly on slow speed. Using rubber spatula, fold batter until completely combined. Divide batter equally among prepared pans. Bake cakes until tester inserted into center of cakes comes out clean, about 35 minutes. Transfer cakes to rack; cool 10 minutes. Turn cakes out onto rack and cool completely.

Chocolate Stout Cake Icing

Bring cream to simmer in heavy medium saucepan. Remove from heat. Add chopped chocolate and whisk until melted and smooth. Refrigerate until icing is spreadable, stirring frequently, about 2 hours.

Place 1 cake layer on plate. Spread two-thirds cup icing over. Top with second cake layer. Spread two-thirds cup icing over. Top with third cake layer. Spread remaining icing over top and sides of cake.

May 16

Debbie and Kevin left on the early ferry to Canada and once again, John and I went to Lakedale to try to finish the innumerable projects underway. I hung the historical photos I had framed, tried to sort out a double shipment of pillows from Pottery Barn, hung extra pictures from the breakfast room in the Lake House, and distributed all the silk flowers. But the biggest thrill was the installation of the frames and canvas for the first new Canvas Cabin. John worked all day alongside the contractor and the representative from Rainier Industries who had built the units, nailing wooden beams overhead, attaching the canvas sides and roof and laying the fly on top of the finished product to protect it from rain, tree debris and the occasional wayward camper. I could only pray the interiors would live up to the standard of the Canvas Cabin structure. Weary, we dragged ourselves into town for another dinner out, barely staying awake long enough to drive the boat home across the pond.

May 17

In a welcome change of pace, meaning not going to Lakedale and working from dawn until dusk, we caught an early ferry to Anacortes and dropped off Peaches to get her convertible top repaired. The dealer had searched eBay and found a part that would cost $100 to repair, not $8,000. Afterwards, we drove north to the Canadian border.

As I was giving John directions on how to get through the Nexus lane, Kelly called. “Mom, what classes should I take next fall? I thought I had to register in the summer for the fall, but I have to do it now!”

“When, honey?” It was becoming a familiar refrain. I was calm, cool, unruffled.

“At four this afternoon!”

“Let’s see,” I made an on-the-spot decision to record a series of questions to play next term when she called me with the exact same questions, “have you talked to your advisor?”

A sheepish “…no.”

“OK, what’s the dilemma?”

“I have to take all the prerequisites for the foreign study programs that I’m waitlisted for, *and* the one I’ve already been accepted to in Fez. So that’s Italian, Asian studies, and Human Geography 11…and then I can’t decide whether I want to go pre-Med, so I don’t know if I should take orgo (*oh right, organic chemistry*) or not.” She called out to someone walking down the hall, “Hey Travis, is it easy to crash orgo?”

“Mom, he says it’s easy to add and I have to decide in the next five minutes because I have a chem lab to go to.”

Meanwhile, John was getting nervous and at the wheel of a car, never a good combination. “Honey, we’re five minutes from the border, where do I turn off? Tell Kelly you’ll call her back!”

“Kelly, don’t do anything yet, I’ll call you right back!” We found the lane marked Nexus, whizzed past hundreds of other cars waiting in the regular line, flashed our card at the tollbooth, and we were across the border. Ten minutes later I called Kelly.

"Kelly, we're in Canada now, where are you with the classes?"

"No worries, Mom, I'm already signed up."

"Wait, what in the heck are you taking?" I asked.

"I decided to take all the prerequisites, and I'll add on organic chemistry when I determine what abroad program I'm going on."

"That was far too easy...how about going to see your advisor to make sure it will work?"

"Mom, my advisor sucks, but fine, fine...I'll go see my UGA." I asked her if a UGA was officially an advisor.

"Sort of." I would accept any sort of quasi-official figure at this point, so I sighed and said, "Good enough for me."

"OK, Mom, say Hi! to Dad, I've gotta go—I'm going to be late for chem, love ya, bye!"

We had a smooth ferry ride to Gibson's, where the boat-bull had wintered with our boat builder. We spent the afternoon removing our gear, a tricky task given that the boat was ten feet high in the air in dry dock. Our rational for this elevated exercise was that the boat would look fresher to would-be buyers with none of our boating possessions aboard. After we finished the move-out the production manager asked us if we'd like to see one of the new forty-two foot trawlers they were now building. It was decked out with state-of-the art electronics, new Volvo engines that used a joystick as the steering mechanism (Gameboy grown up, which might actually take all the fear and pain out of the boating experience), a flat-screen TV that hydraulically lowered from the ceiling, a summer kitchen on the fly bridge, a lower state room and more. John's eyes got wider with each new feature he saw, and despite some initial reticence about selling our boat, he had now convinced himself that if we were to be serious boaters, we couldn't live without a boat with these new features, and selling boat-bull was a brilliant move.

"Honey," I said, "do you have any idea how much the new boat would cost!?"

"I'm worth it aren't I?" he chuckled. A difficult argument to rebut.

I had recently read about a lodge just north of Gibson's that had added some tent cabins to their lodging inventory, so we drove north in our now jam-packed van and checked into a Tenthouse Suite at the Rockwater Secret Cove Resort. The suites were connected by an elevated 1200-foot long wooden walkway that snaked through an arbutus forest and overlooked a protected waterfront cove on Malaspina Strait. Unlike Lakedale's more modest tent cabins, our unit was complete with heated slate floors, a free-standing bath tub, shoji screens dividing the shower and bath, and a clerestory window overhead; all the luxuries of home, minus the internet and a flat-screen TV. The zippered canvas windows were the only details our cabins had in common with these accommodations.

The resort's intimate restaurant was excellent as well. We feasted on ginger and apple gazpacho, mussels three-ways, crab cakes served with a hint of smoked bacon, and then to end the gluttony, lemon crème brûlée and banana bread pudding for dessert. In the spirit of achieving Goal #1, my current philosophy was to only eat one, possibly two bites of dessert, and then only if the dinner was exceptional. Ordering two desserts didn't exactly aid the plan, but John's birthday was tomorrow, so he had decided to splurge. On the way back to the suite, I was lucky to safely navigate the wooden walkway and not end up swinging from a tree after John ordered me a B-52 coffee, in honor of Kelly recently telling him that she had just tried one.

May 18

The drive down the Sunshine Coast was spectacular, cool and clear, the green sea glittered like a Christmas tree strewn with tinsel. After another successful Nexus border crossing, we detoured to Anthony's Restaurant in Bellingham for lunch and discovered another Clam Chowder Contest aspirant; this chowder had chunks of bacon, and not too many potatoes. It was a solid B+ contender, surprisingly good for a large chain restaurant.

May 20

A typical island Sunday; a trip to town for coffee and the newspapers, where both of us behaved well by abstaining from muffins and John's favorite cinnamon bun at the Doctor's Office. There had been no word from Kelly for a few days, so after reading the Sunday newspaper cover-to-cover in true empty nester style, I called her.

The past few days had been Green Key Weekend, the spring term equivalent of Homecoming and Winter Carnival, and one of the three notorious party weekends at Dartmouth. As her parents, we were unequivocally banned from attending these events for the rest of Kelly's college career. When she called, Kelly was slightly giddy during the whole conversation, not revealing much, but revealing enough for me to know her Green Key weekend had involved a member of the opposite sex. I casually mentioned that I just wanted her to be safe, and somehow found the words "birth control" spewing out of my mouth. She was shocked and astounded that I would say such a thing. She gave me what could only be described as a serious daughter/mother lecture about the fact that she would never do something like that until she had been in a committed relationship for at least...three, maybe even four months! There were still no breakthroughs regarding her summer work prospects.

May 26

The week hurtled by as quickly as a TGV train on the tracks from Paris to Marseilles, but instead of great French food to ease our palates, we ate kosher hot dogs on the sunny Lakedale lodge deck, in between:

Finalizing the "defishification" process

Removing all of the extra furniture from the log cabins

Ordering new futon covers for the ones that had arrived in the wrong color for the Canvas Cabins

Completely rearranging the new lobby furniture after the delayed wicker chairs finally arrived

Conference calling for hours with the management company team in Seattle about their latest marketing strategies to increase our occupancy, and other unexpected tasks that resort owners have thrust upon them

The highlight of the week was an invitation from one of our Brown Island neighbors to join her and the other islanders for cocktails, freshly-caught spot prawns (a shellfish that looks like shrimp, but is more tender and sweeter in flavor) and to watch her niece as she competed in the finals of *American Idol.*

Unfortunately, after two hours of the contestants singing every Beatles song ever written, they didn't announce the winner. So the next evening, our entire group, now completely sucked in, reconvened at our house over margaritas and chicken enchiladas with mole sauce to see if our neighbor's niece would prevail over her lackluster male opponent. By the time the drum rolls hailed her as the winner, we all felt as if she was our new favorite relative.

May 27

After an uneventful flight back to Colorado we were driving through Vail when an excited Kelly called, expounding on the fact that she had just seen Barack Obama at a rally on campus.

"I waited an hour and a half in line, and it was excruciatingly hot!" I wondered aloud how many people had attended the rally.

"I think about five hundred," she answered, "but I'm not that good at estimating crowds...let me look it up...no way, there were five thousand people there...cool! And he was an incredible speaker; mostly talked about how he had gotten to where is today and not so much about policy, but I loved him!" Another advantage of an Ivy-league Dartmouth education, one we had been oblivious to in the college planning process, was the fact that Dartmouth was located in New Hampshire. By state law, New Hampshire was required to hold the earliest presidential primary and as a result, every candidate from both parties pays numerous visits to the campus in an election year.

"Have you seen many other candidates yet?"

"Quite a few," she said as she rattled off the names of the mostly Democratic candidates she had been able to see. My initial assumption was that the Republicans had decided not to visit this year, but after further questioning, it became apparent that she wasn't interested in listening to any of them. Although she had seen John McCain from a distance, she hadn't been impressed.

Her last set of freshman finals started this weekend, but she didn't appear too worried as she had just received a great review from her ecopsych professor on her oral presentation about eco-tourism. She and a group of fourteen other friends were leaving momentarily to spend the weekend at a lakeside cabin owned by the college.

"But don't worry, Mom, we're all going to be back at eight in the morning to start studying. Safe travels, love ya, bye!"

With John calmly at the wheel of the car, it dawned on me that I had four years (in reality now only three, since the dreaded freshman year was almost at an end) to forge a new identity for myself. An identity not as Kelly's mom, not as a volunteer for the Aspen Public School District, and not as the mother of a Dartmouth student. It would have to involve some serious thinking about who I was, and who I really wanted to be. General Manager of Lakedale? National Geographic photo-journalist? The next Picasso? This was far too heavy a train of thought for me to dwell on for long. Recognizing that my identity would not involve that of New Age Philosopher, I yelled at John to pull the car over at the next freeway off ramp. "Honey, there's Costco…let's go shopping and get a hot dog."

May 29

1:25 p.m. hey hon, any news on your driver's license? do i need to send your passport?

1:30 p.m. i just called the DMV and it was sent a few days ago and should be here soon, so wait on the passport for a few days. oh, and i was asking my prof when our paper was due and he wrote back "BTW, I thought you did a great job explaining the issues of ecotourism today." yay!! hope the rest of your day is good. i want to go back to the cabin! so much fun, such cool kids.

2:59 p.m. okey dokey! say, do you want me to fax you an employment application for Pelindaba, the local lavender farm... they're hiring. luv ya lots!

May 30

11:16 a.m. i got my license so no worries about the passport. i think one of my wisdom teeth might be coming in...ow. how's aspen? its so hard to study because its so warm outside and loverly. but it must be done. i will call you later. Lyl

5:39 p.m. oh-oh! mine came in when i was 20. how painful is it? and do you have time to do the application or should i do it for you? i could ask you the pertinent questions that I might not know, it's a fairly basic application.

5:47 p.m. haha, if you really want to you could, i will have time on saturday. i dont actually know if its my tooth, sinus or ear... hmmm. i need a haircut. we should go get pedicures. girls day at the spa?

7:51 p.m. we are definitely due for a spa day! I'll fill out the application and email it to you for review. maybe you should get checked for a sinus infection? how's the studying going? your dad and i think that we should fly to the island with kelso so i can get the house ready for summer, instead of spending three days sitting in a car. sound good?

10:36 p.m. great, summer is definitely sounding good. i can get my first job, lose 20 lbs, figure out my life in terms of organic chemistry, and keep up my non-profit. good plan. lyl

May 31

> 11:28 a.m. mommy! i'm really nervous for chem. what do i do if i fail? i have studied so much and i still have no idea what is going on!

I quickly emailed Kelly with sage words of advice to see her advisor and study some more, then John and I biked from Basalt to Carbondale with Jayne and Fred, part of the never-ending pursuit of and, dare I admit, never achieved Goals #1 and #2. My best intentions were negated by the delicious Mexican food we ate at the Village Smithy restaurant at the end of the ride.

JUNE

June 1

> 7:39 a.m. how's the studying? remember, relax, stay calm, all is well! love ya lots!

> 2:11 p.m. going good, i think I survived chem...here's my eco-tourism research paper! enjoy.

> 3:51 p.m. hey, the paper is really good! I actually learned a lot! and i will try to be a more sensitive traveler in the future. this may include swimming across the atlantic on future european trips to avoid using so much fuel! what a relief to have that over with. How much sleep did you get? so now only econ left?

June 2

> 5:22 p.m. hi hon! good thing you aren't trying to study here, it was a gorgeous day so your dad and I hiked up sunnyside trail with kelso. Jayne just dropped off their new dog who is staying with us for a few days before we pick you up in denver. kelso is barely enduring her presence. hope the econ is going well. just think - you're almost done! i can't believe your first year is almost over...

5:45 p.m. here's a picture for you of my activities at the cabin! i don't ever want to graduate! how sad.

7:27 p.m. i loved the photo, can't believe you can get that many kids laying on a dock without it sinking...and as far as graduating, in three more years, you'll probably be a little more ready, but based on the great experiences you're having, i think it will be tough!

June 3

For weeks I had been looking forward to a charity dinner we'd been invited to by Peter and Sandy to benefit an organization called Bring-Me-A-Book, which provided books to children in the African country of Malawi. John raised his eyebrows when I told him it was completely free, no admission charge, and no silent auction items to have to bid on.

"Honey, I will make you a bet that this event won't be free," he said, as he gazed lovingly at me and hid his checkbook. At a local restaurant, five well-respected local chefs volunteered their culinary expertise to create a five-course meal. Each chef had prepared an appetizer, which was passed around during the cocktail hour, and then cooked one course of the meal. The menu:

> Appetizers: Chicken liver pâté on crostini with homemade jam, fresh chèvre and pea sprouts, "deviled eggs," Taos Farm's quail with a port reduction, lobster salad profiterole.
>
> Entrées: Finocchiona salad (fennel and Chianti cured salume), julienne salad of celery, apples, walnuts and herb leaves with a grape juice reduction, truffle potato agnolotti with morels, asparagus and oregano brown butter, sea scallop and crispy rillettes with watercress, corn emulsion and cherry vinegar glaze, piñon-smoked elk filet and foie gras with scarlet potato flan, organic sweet pea and cosentino wine and peppercorn sauce.
>
> Trio of Desserts: Twinkie, Devil Dog and Strawberry Milkshake.

Each course elicited ooh's! and aah's! from the four of us and it seemed as if every one outdid the previous in both taste and presentation. Sandy and I agreed that if we were ever on death row, the truffle potato agnolotti would be an item on our final menus. What was there not to love about silky smooth potato puree wrapped tenderly in fresh pasta topped with a generous shaving of freshly sliced truffles?

After dinner, Sandy gave a heartwarming speech about the children and their books. We left the restaurant a few pounds heavier, and predictably, with John's checkbook a few dollars lighter.

> 1:08 p.m. still studying econ...it's so sad, people are leaving/ gone already and i am still stuck in the library which is emptying out and becoming lonely. tear. i don't want to be a sophomore yet! Ahhh

June 4

Kelly's last final occurred as I was in the process of wrapping up the remaining pieces of the Lakedale/all-consuming mission/life-changing saga, which did not include the retail sales area for the lobby, which may or may not happen.

I was ordering new tables for the deck outside the breakfast room (to replace hideous faux mosaic round tables which clashed with my newly installed blue and green "Lakeside Stripe" cushions) when John trooped up the stairs to my studio. We proceeded to have an in-depth discussion about the nature of the lodge's main deck, all 800 square feet of it. I had preciously placed twelve rocking chairs across its front edge adjacent to the lake, to evoke memories of past eras when people actually rocked together and talked about life. I had personally never participated in this activity, but having read numerous books about the South, I thought it would be a nice tradition to add to the Lakedale experience. However, I failed to recognize the effects of the summer's heat bouncing off the lake, and the fact that couples may want to sit together, so John and I added one last furniture project to my "To Do" list. Before we left on Wednesday to retrieve Kelly from the Denver airport I would order new deck furniture and umbrellas.

Once more I sequestered myself in my studio; cleaning up piles of accumulated fabric samples, sculpture supplies, furniture catalogs, and Christmas cards, while simultaneously visiting dozens of websites to look for outdoor furniture. Between frantic calls to vendors, the deck furniture was ordered, and would arrive in time to accommodate a full house of July Fourth guests.

> 3:45 p.m. holy cow! what's that big cloud of smoke behind the Hanover Inn? mums

> 5:35 p.m. ummm, the campus steam power plant is back there, sometimes there's a cloud...today was so much fun. we went to the river and played frisbak, aka ultimate frisbee in kayaks!!! so much fun. and then we ran through the rain. god i love this place. lyl, Kelly

June 5

Kelly called at mid-day shortly after she awoke, I assumed, from her celebratory last night of Dartmouth socializing before she and her almost-sophomore friends left for the summer. The dorms officially closed at noon and everyone she knew, whether they had finished finals three days before or just recently, was staying until the bitter end, relishing every last moment of their first year Dartmouth experience.

"Mom, hi! How are you doing?"

"Great, sweetie, how was your last final?"

"Pretty good, better than expected I think," she said, " and I can't believe I'm done. I don't want to be a sophomore! I love it here...even though I want to come home, I really want to stay and be here with my friends...only without the studying part."

I let her know that I would much rather answer this sort of phone call instead of one in which she said she couldn't wait to come home, hated her school, and wanted to transfer.

"Yah, I guess you're right," she sighed, "...OK then, I'm packing and need to know if I should sell my books, donate them or keep them?" A twenty minute discussion ensued about whether Iraqi students (recipients of the donated books) would be better off reading "Public Policy: Politics, Analysis, and Alternatives" or if she'd be better off with ten cents on the dollar the books would fetch at the bookstore.

The second of her twelve calls came half an hour later. We discussed the books she wanted to bring home and whether I wanted to read them. She rattled off the names of thirty books for me to consider. How many suitcases should she ship home? Should True Value hardware pick up and store her boxes or should the boxes go into secure storage in the basement of her dorm? (In which case she would have to find a way to get them to next year's dorm across the Green instead of having True Value deliver them.) Should she lock her bike all summer in one of the campus bike racks? These and a myriad of other extremely important questions had to be answered before 3:30 p.m. when the dorm storage area would be locked up for the summer.

I was exhausted when our book club convened. After a few glasses of merlot, my fatigue dissipated and we selected our reads for the summer. The first was *River of Doubt*, about Teddy Roosevelt's search for the origins of an obscure river in the Amazon, and the other was *Eat, Pray, Love*, about a divorced woman's search for "everything" in Italy, India and Bali. These adventurers obviously weren't required to be around to accept phone calls from their college-aged offspring.

June 6

Kelly's flight was due to arrive late in the day, but John and I left early, demonstrating once again our excitement at seeing Kelly and having her home all summer. It also allowed us to drop my car off at Land Rover. The battery still insisted on dying every time we left it for two weeks, so the Service Manager, my new best friend, was going to attempt to solve the mystery. As I left the car he asked, "By the way, do you happen to leave the key in the ignition when you leave it?" *Does he think I am a complete automotive idiot?*

We drove to Denver, encountering road construction, high winds and a trip to the Design Center to drop off fabric samples from the Lakedale project, yet we still arrived at the airport early. Unfortunately, Kelly's flight was late. We waited at the top of the arrival escalators, cappuccinos in hand, finding it hard to fathom that Kelly's freshman year was over. And then she arrived, no doubt praying we wouldn't be waving a massive banner proclaiming "Welcome Home, Big Green Frosh of 2010!" ...a thought that had seriously crossed my mind.

She carried a backpack, a sleeping bag and a tennis racket case that bulged with electronic chargers and dirty laundry. Dark circles framed her large eyes, silent testimony to her last all-nighter as a freshman at Dartmouth. She hugged us with all the might of an exhausted first-grader home from her first sleepover, happy to be home, but sad that the adventure was over. Ambivalent. Not me. I grabbed her tennis racket case, squeezed her tightly, and didn't let her go for fifteen minutes. No tears messed up my mascara, but deep down, I knew that life had changed.

Kelly had weathered her first year well. She had survived the rigorous academics, learned how to navigate the sketchy basements of the frat houses, and forged friendships that were likely to last longer than careers or marriages. Her white t-shirts were still white, and I had received more emails and phone calls from her than I had ever anticipated. Despite all my misgivings- doubts- qualms- worries- uncertainties- fears- panic- attacks- reservations, I too had miraculously made it to the end of the year, a thought I had never thought possible in those first days of rattling around a house stripped of teenage laughter.

I would like to say I learned a lot about myself (all the self-help books will tell you this) in deeply tortured and psychologically liberating ways. But what I realized is that the whole experience was a process, like any other transition. Whether it was the five steps of grief, the twelve steps of AA, or the sixteen weeks of elimination rounds on Top Chef, it was a process that you had to get through…and come out OK on the other side.

Epilogue

A final recap of my goals for the previous nine months is probably in order, if only to reset my priorities for next year. I am taking the summer months off, as even the most dedicated goal-makers need time for retrospection and evaluation. Herewith my goals and their official results:

> Goal #1: High school was a long time ago, so I think I have to adjust to a new weight reality, that way the next time I set wildly irrational goals it won't be a huge disappointment if I don't actually achieve them. The other option would be to set the dial on the scale five pounds below the zero mark, then every morning I would wake up happy.
>
> Goal #2: I broke a sweat every day, primarily because my hormones were going crazy, and secondarily because of Matthew McConaughey's fine example.
>
> Goal #3: I downloaded eight CD's worth of photos.
>
> Goal #4: Redesign Lakedale. Done! Success! Our Canvas Cabins were featured on the cover of Sunset Magazine in May 2011, written about in Travel and Leisure magazine, and highlighted on the Today show.
>
> Goal #5: I researched some galleries in Seattle, but shockingly, wasn't offered representation, mainly because every gallery wanted me to have a website so they could view my artwork, and I had forgotten to make a goal to create a website. Next year.
>
> Goal #6: I made some art.
>
> Goal #7: Not one stitch sewn on the needlepoint wreath.
>
> Goal #8: The winner of the Clam Chowder contest...is unabashedly Shelley's Northwest Clam Chowder, followed closely by Chandler's, the Lime Kiln Café and Legal Seafood's.

Goal #9: The foot fungus is gone!

Goal #10: I cross-country skied, hiked on the snow or downhill skied almost every day.

And Kelly was gainfully employed at both Pelindaba Lavender Farm and San Juan Safari's Whale Watching tours for the summer. After graduating from Dartmouth, she spent nine months running a malnutrition clinic in Malawi, then completed a pre-medical post-baccalaureate program, and is now attending medical school in Seattle.

Made in the USA
San Bernardino, CA
07 February 2014